"This book is truly a treasure. For the past decade, Sandra Schneiders has been sharing her profound insights into the Gospel of John with disparate groups through various lectures and articles. Here she gathers this wisdom into one volume, providing an indispensable resource for preachers, teachers, scholars, and students of the Bible. She leads her readers to a profound understanding of the bodiliness of the resurrection and how Jesus continues to be present to his disciples, as depicted in John 20–21. She invites us into a transformative encounter with the Risen One who commissioned his disciples to continue his mission throughout time."

Barbara E. Reid, O.P.
Vice President and Academic Dean
Catholic Theological Union, Chicago

"Condensing and enriching a great range of scholarship, Sandra Schneiders' work belongs to a new wave of writing on the Resurrection. . . . In vigorous, clear language, this book serves to sharpen the focus of faith and spirituality on the event that shapes and sustains the hope of Christians. Further, by grounding Christian faith in the bodily character of the Risen One, these essays underscore the bodily dimension of our redemption and enlarge the meaning of spirituality itself. There is something for everyone in this book: no one working to defend, commend, and illuminate the meaning of faith in Christ can afford to miss it."

Anthony J. Kelly, CSsR
Professor of Theology
Australian Catholic University

"Sandra Schneiders' new book brings together a number of her essays on the Resurrection Narrative in John's gospel written since 2005, plus an earlier essay whose focus is more on the implications of the Resurrection for Christian living. These essays go beyond questions of 'what happened' to 'what does it mean for me today?' While Christian faith is rooted in the Resurrection, for many it remains simply a creedal statement or theological doctrine. Schneiders' essays offer the chance to critically and seriously engage with one gospel account of the Resurrection and also to be challenged to integrate this into a vibrant spirituality of 'presence.' The dynamic proclamation, 'He is risen,' can still resonate in Christian lives today."

Dr. Mary Coloe, PBVM
MCD University of Divinity
Melbourne, Australia

"Sandra Schneiders' reading of John 20 clarifies the importance of the bodily presence of the glorified Jesus for an understanding of the Christian Church as *Jesus Risen in Our Midst* [and] . . . reflects profoundly on the Johannine understanding of Jesus' death as taking away the sins of the world and the commissioning of the Spirit-filled Church to continue Jesus' mission by forgiving sin and by embracing those who have been forgiven. Again: to be *Jesus Risen in Our Midst*."

Francis J. Moloney, SDB, AM, FAHA
Senior Professorial Fellow
Australian Catholic University
Melbourne, Australia

"Sandra Schneiders' lifetime of work with the Gospel of John, intersecting her deep engagement with the field of hermeneutics, has produced a volume of insight into the challenges of the Resurrection of Jesus. These essays, gathered from the past few years, are freshly situated for the consideration of those interested in the crucial matter of the Resurrection of Jesus. Schneiders has anticipated the challenges of contemporaries and presented the issues to us in most provocative and helpful terms. This book is a must-read for any Christian seeking postmodern engagement with this most central mystery of Christianity."

Barbara Green, OP
Professor of Biblical Studies
Dominican School of Philosophy and Theology
at the Graduate Theological Union

"*Jesus Risen in Our Midst* is a feast of skilled exegesis and creative theological reflection. With the clarity and command that readers of Schneiders' work have come to expect, this collection of essays delivers consistently fresh perspectives on Jesus' Resurrection in the Gospel of John as it explores hermeneutics, embodiment, spirituality, and salvation throughout. Whether new to theology or a longtime student, this readable volume will challenge and delight."

Brian Robinette
Associate Professor of Theology
Boston College

Jesus Risen in Our Midst

Essays on the Resurrection of Jesus
in the Fourth Gospel

Sandra M. Schneiders

A Michael Glazier Book

LITURGICAL PRESS
Collegeville, Minnesota

www.litpress.org

A Michael Glazier Book published by Liturgical Press

Cover design by Jodi Hendrickson. *Resurrection of Christ and Women at the Tomb* by Fra Angelico. Fresco, 1440–41, Convent of San Marco, Florence. Image courtesy of Wikimedia Commons.

1   2   3   4   5   6   7   8   9

Library of Congress Cataloging-in-Publication Data

Schneiders, Sandra Marie.
    Jesus risen in our midst : the bodily resurrection of Jesus in the fourth Gospel / Sandra M. Schneiders.
      pages   cm
    "A Michael Glazier book."
    Includes index.
      ISBN 978-0-8146-8084-1 — ISBN 978-0-8146-8085-8 (ebook)
      1. Jesus Christ—Biblical teaching.   2. Bible. John XX, 19-23—Criticism, interpretation, etc.   I. Title.
    BS2615.6.R47S36   2013
    232'.5—dc23
                                                    2013019743

Contents

$$=== \textit{Part One} ===$$
The Bodily Resurrection of Jesus

$$=== \textit{Part Two} ===$$
John's Theology and Spirituality of Presence

Acknowledgments

No work is solely the product of its author and this volume is no exception. Besides my gratitude to the original publishers of the articles which are the chapters of this book, I want to express my special thanks to Amanda Kaminski, my able, efficient, and meticulous research assistant, who did virtually all the manuscript work on this book.

I also appreciate the care and efficiency with which Lauren L. Murphy, managing editor at Liturgical Press, has handled this manuscript. She has contributed much to its cogency, and it has been a joy to work with her.

My special thanks to Hans Christoffersen, my publisher at Liturgical Press, whose interest in this project and especially our intensely interesting conversations about the theology and spirituality of resurrection have been constant encouragement.

Acknowledgments

Introduction

The Relation of the Essays to One Another

This book is a collection of essays on the Resurrection of Jesus as it is presented in the Gospel of John. All of them, with the exception of the first chapter, which was published earlier, appeared between 2005 and 2011. Because they were published in academic journals or books, some outside the United States, they are not easily available to the nonspecialist reader. I have been asked on a number of occasions when I have been teaching or lecturing on this topic for copies of these articles or written access to their content, so I thought it would be worthwhile to bring them together in a single, easily accessible volume.

The first essay, a public lecture originally given to a mixed university and general audience at Trinity College, Dublin, and published in 1995, is an effort to articulate and respond to the situation of many contemporary believers when they confront the claim that Jesus of Nazareth, who really died at the hands of the Roman Empire in Palestine in the mid-first century of our era and was buried in a securely sealed tomb, rose bodily from the dead and is alive among us, the paradigm of the ultimate destiny of his followers. Borrowing a phrase from John Henry Newman, I have called the difficulty that this claim raises a problem of "imaginative implausibility." How is the believer, even one who sincerely professes faith in the Resurrection, to understand or conceptualize the extraordinary event proclaimed in the narratives of Jesus' bodily Resurrection from the dead that we find in the gospels? These narratives have no analogues in the rest of the New Testament, and their subject matter has no analogues in our ordinary historical experience. No other religion professes faith in the bodily resurrection (as opposed to resuscitation) of a historical (as distinct from a mythical) human being, much less bases itself on such faith, and promises its adherents that they will share in that experience. This first essay, therefore, attempts to provide a framework for the rest of the essays by situating the Christian profession of faith in the Resurrection of Jesus in the context of the challenge to contemporary faith of this *sui generis* Christian datum.

The other essays are all concerned with interpretation of the Resurrection as it is presented in chapter 20 of the Gospel according to John. As will be clear, this is not a haphazard choice among the available New Testament texts on resurrection. John 20 is not a collection of disconnected or interchangeable episodes but a single narrative, composed of a number of "scenes" or "acts," which together present a coherent and integrated interpretation of the Resurrection. Although these essays are not sequential in the sense of commenting on John 20 from the first verse to the last verse and there is no necessity to read the essays in the order they are presented here, they do offer, if read together, a comprehensive (although far from exhaustive) interpretation of John's theology and spirituality of the Resurrection.

Since each essay was originally presented as a freestanding lecture or article, each can be read on its own without reference to the others. This independence of the essays, however, results in some repetition. Certain themes and presuppositions occur in more than one essay, in some cases developed in detail and in others briefly summarized. I have not attempted to excise this repetition because the essays will probably be more useful if each remains independent of the others, able to be understood on its own terms. Teachers, for example, might want to use one essay in a class, and it is helpful to have all the material necessary for understanding that essay in the essay itself. Or a reader may be studying one topic or theme that is treated in one of the essays, and it will be more convenient not to have to refer to other essays for material intrinsic to the project in hand. Someone reading the whole book can easily skip material with which she or he is familiar from a previous essay or may find the repeated material more illuminating as it is seen in more than one context.

The material that appears in more than one essay can be summarized as follows:

1. It is presupposed that the Johannine Resurrection Narrative is *a single literary entity*, not a collection of separate or unrelated episodes. Each "scene" is integrated into the whole narrative the way acts are integrated into a play, and so understanding the structure of the whole

is important for understanding the parts and vice versa. Therefore, the appendix contains some diagrams of various ways of structuring chapter 20 as a whole, which should help illuminate the unity and diversity in the chapter.

2. The Resurrection Narrative is *integrated into the Fourth Gospel as a whole by means of two sets of texts*: (1) the "temple texts," namely, John 2:13-21 on the body of Jesus as the New Temple; John 7:37-39 on Jesus as the source of the living water as was the temple described in Ezekiel 47; and John 19:33-37 on the blood and water flowing from the pierced side of Jesus as the water flowed from the side of the temple; and (2) the "taking away of sin(s) texts" in John 1:29 and 20:19-23, which form an "inclusio" or literary "bookends" for the gospel as a whole.

3. The fundamental overall interpretation of the Resurrection in John's gospel as the *establishment of the New Covenant*, particularly as promised in Jeremiah 31:31-34 and Ezekiel 37:23-28, is in the background of each of the pericopes and in the foreground in the central pericope, John 20:19-23, the appearance to the disciples on Easter evening.

4. Basic to understanding what the Resurrection means in John is an understanding of *Semitic anthropology and sapiential eschatology*. In other words, the way the Evangelist understands the human person (anthropology) is essentially the way the Old Testament presents the human being, that is, as an indivisible whole in relation to God, rather than the way we moderns understand humans as composed of separable elements such as body and soul, flesh and blood, and able to be understood apart from any relation to the divine. Similarly, the way the Evangelist understands the "last things," or the final state of humanity and creation (eschatology), is more like the understanding of these matters that we find in the Wisdom literature of the Old Testament than the understanding that is more characteristic of the so-called historical books of the Bible and the prophetic books. John presents Jesus as operating more in terms of what biblical theologians call "realized eschatology" than the final eschatology characteristic of the Synoptic Gospels.

These two differences, in anthropology, or the understanding of the human being, and in eschatology, or the understanding of the end of history, both personal and universal, make John's gospel as a whole, and especially his interpretation of the Resurrection, quite different from that of the Synoptics (Matthew, Mark, and Luke). This difference is not a matter of contradiction but of mutually enriching complementarity. But if one tries to read John through Synoptic lenses or vice versa the result can be distorted and even erroneous interpretation.

5. A final point concerns *the distinction* that emerges in John (but not in the Synoptics) *between the Resurrection and the Glorification of Jesus*. What happened to Jesus on the cross is presented in John as his Glorification, or his return to God from whom he came forth into the world in the Incarnation. His return on Easter to his disciples from whom he had departed in death, a return that becomes the experience of all of his post-Easter disciples, is what John presents as Jesus' Resurrection. This is an important distinction because it emphasizes that there are two aspects to the mystery we normally refer to as the Resurrection, namely, what happened to *Jesus* at the end of his earthly life, which is the foundation of what is now true of his *disciples*. If Jesus himself is not glorified, there is no basis for the hope of his disciples to finally overcome death. But if Jesus, personally glorified in God, had not returned to his own, we would neither know nor be able to participate in Jesus' victory over death.

These basic theological themes are at least in the background, if not in the foreground, in virtually all the essays, each of which deals with one or more of the five "scenes" or "acts" in John's Resurrection Narrative, namely, the discovery of the empty tomb by Mary Magdalene and its examination by Simon Peter and the Beloved Disciple on Easter morning (John 20:1-10); the appearance in the garden of the glorified Jesus to Mary Magdalene on Easter morning (John 20:11-18); Jesus' appearance to the disciples in a closed room in Jerusalem on Easter night (John 20:19-23); the appearance of Jesus in the same place one week later in which Thomas, who was not present at the Easter evening appearance, is converted to Easter faith by Jesus (John 20:24-29); and the finale of the chapter in which the Evangelist includes in the mystery of the Resurrection all later disciples of the risen Jesus, those who have not seen and have believed (John 20:30-31).

The Approach to Scripture in These Essays

Operative in all the essays in this volume are certain presuppositions about the nature of the Bible as Christian Scripture and certain methodological, theological, and hermeneutical approaches to interpretation that flow from these presuppositions. Because these presuppositions influence the interpretations in a significant way and are not explained in detail in the essays as such, it might be useful to spell them out explicitly in advance.

The Canon of Scripture and Intertextuality

First, regardless of when or where or by whom or for what purpose different parts of the Bible were composed, they now form what Christians consider the "canon" of Scripture, that is, an authoritative theological whole rather than isolated literary pieces assembled extrinsically within the covers of a book. This canonicity generates the theological dimension of the literary feature of "intertextuality," or the mutual relationship of the parts to each other, the parts to the whole, and the whole to the parts. Regardless of how the texts were related to each other historically or in the minds of the biblical authors (which are both important), all the texts of the Bible are now related to each other in the light of faith in the messianic identity and mission of Jesus. This does not mean that the Jewish Scriptures do not have their own integrity that requires them to be treated on their own terms in relation to Jewish history and faith. But, for the Christian reader, the Jewish Bible is the Old (or First) Testament. It is a constant and active background and resource for the interpretation of the New (or Second) Testament, and the New Testament functions actively in the Christian interpretation of the Old Testament.

Sometimes in the New Testament there is explicit reference to, citation of, evocation of, or allusion to Old Testament persons, themes, actions, history, and so on. But often the influence of the Old Testament on the New is like the musical score of a film that is subtly educating the perceptions and emotions of the reader, making her or him sensitive to insights that may not become completely explicit but that influence interpretation. And, of course, intertextuality also works the other way around as the New Testament sheds a different light on the Old Testament that would not be seen by someone unfamiliar with the New. For example, only in the light of the Genesis creation account is Jesus seen as the "last Adam," but conversely, the Christian reads the story of Adam and Eve as the "fall" of the original ancestors because of the interpretation of the paschal mystery of Jesus as universal salvation.

This continual, sometimes explicit but very often implicit, influence of the Old Testament on John's gospel is one of the latter's most striking features. But, characteristic of John is that this influence is rarely explicit in the form of direct citations of the Old Testament such as we find very frequently in Matthew. The Old Testament is omnipresent in the Fourth Gospel but more in its "lighting" or its "sound effects," its characterizations, its resonances, its allusions, its evocations than in the form of explicit word-for-word quotations.

Much less characteristic of John's gospel is the kind of New Testament intertextuality one finds in Matthew, Mark, and Luke, which are clearly often citing one another or a shared source such as the hypothetical document scholars call "Q" (for the German *Quelle*, meaning "source," which is assumed to be common to the Synoptics). It is seldom a good idea to try to find a Synoptic source or parallel text in John. Even when there is some textual similarity between John and the Synoptics, John is often using his "borrowed" material in such entirely original ways that reading one in terms of the other leads to misinterpretation.

Presuppositions about Interpretation

Second, in the process of interpretation in these essays there are three types of presuppositions that are operative. The first is **methodological**. The essays in this volume are *basically literary-critical in approach* rather than historical-critical. The literary-critical approach is characterized primarily by its privileging of the final text in its actual form rather than the sources, prehistory, processes of composition, history of redaction, and so on. The literary critic works with the text as a unity, in the form in which we have it in the best available manuscripts. That does not preclude investigation of sources, theories of authorship, redaction criticism, and so on. But these are used in service of interpretation of the final product, the gospel as it stands, rather than for constructing a hypothesis about what the text means in terms of what its history of composition involved. Thus, questions of characterization, plot, narrative structure and other genres, language, themes, symbolism, and so on are more significant than investigations of historical facticity, processes of composition, or parallels with other sources. By way of example, for the literary critic, in contrast to a historical critic, the primary question about the scene of Jesus' death in John is not about whether his side was actually pierced with a lance (none of the Synoptics corroborates this detail) or whether such a wound would have produced a flow of blood and water given the physical condition of one who had died of suffocation caused by crucifixion. The primary approach to the meaning of the text involves attention to such features as the Old Testament text evoked by the Evangelist, the symbolism of blood and water as it has been developed throughout the gospel, the way in which this symbolic feature is integrated into the witness motif of the Mother of Jesus and the Beloved Disciple at the foot of the cross, the relation of this scene to the opening scene of Jesus' public life in John, namely, the wedding at Cana, and the like.

A second type of presupposition operative in the interpretation of John 20 in the essays in this volume is **theological**, namely, that the *locus* of revelation is not the historical events that the gospel text recounts, nor even the intention of the author, but the text itself. Our interest is not primarily in what John the Evangelist intended to say but in what the Gospel of John actually says. This gives rise to a type of interpretation that is very different from that with which many critical readers are familiar. The latter are looking for "what really happened" (to which the text, they believe, gives us access) as the revelatory basis of their faith. It is what Jesus actually said, or did, or suffered that constitutes revelation. This is why a group of researchers like the Jesus Seminar scholars are so concerned to establish whether the pre-Easter Jesus actually said such-and-such a sentence (that is, whether the sentence is "authentic") or whether the sentence reflects the understanding and interpretation of the community/evangelist that produced the text. The former is considered truly revelatory whereas the latter is later ("non-authentic") interpretation. When we have several versions of the same sentence, the challenge is to decide first whether Jesus actually said something like this and second, if he did, which of the available versions is closest to what Jesus actually said.

Anyone familiar with the Gospel of John will know that much of what is attributed to Jesus in John not only has no parallels in the Synoptics but could hardly have been said by a first-century Jewish prophet. But down through the centuries John's gospel has been considered supremely revelatory. From the earliest centuries (beginning with Clement of Alexandria in the second century, cited in Eusebius, *Ecclesiastical History* 6.14.7), John has been called "the spiritual Gospel," not despite its often "nonhistorical" (meaning nonfactual) character, but because of its deep salvific truthfulness. In other words, truth and fact are not the same thing, and we often do a better job of conveying the truth of something by bypassing the literally factual in favor of the metaphorical or symbolic or even by rearranging "facts" or supplying interpretations. But, in any case, the revelatory character of Scripture is a property of Scripture as *text*, not of the text as factual record. This is not at all to deny that Jesus was a real, historical human being who actually lived, acted, spoke, etc., nor that the gospels give us reliable access to this human being and his life. But we do not have a tape recording, a court stenographer's notes, or a camcorder video of the life of Jesus. We have a profound interpretation of the meaning of Jesus as the ultimate revelation of God, which we access not primarily by archaeological excavations but by theological interpretation.

My position (and that of many contemporary, especially literarily oriented, scholars), therefore, is that the locus of revelation is the text itself, what the inspired biblical authors wrote for the sake of our salvation. In other words, our faith is normed by the inspired text of Holy Scripture, not by historical facts, many of which we cannot establish with absolute accuracy but which, even if we could establish their facticity absolutely, would not in themselves be revelatory. Many of Jesus' contemporaries knew exactly what he did and said because they saw and heard him. But they did not believe. On the contrary, many who never saw or heard the pre-Easter Jesus, came to believe in him because of the word of those bearing witness. Our faith rests on the word, the text, of the apostolic witnesses through which we encounter Jesus in the New Testament.

The third presupposition is **hermeneutical**. If the locus of revelation is the text, the *event* of revelation takes place in the interaction between text and reader, that is, in the reading (or hearing) by which one interprets the text. This interaction or encounter between reader and text gives rise to meaning, to understanding. And it is understanding that is transformative.

Transformation is the purpose of our encounter with God through the word of God mediated by the biblical text. The reader will note that none of the essays in this book is a purely or exclusively academic project. My purpose in writing them was not to critically analyze the text for its own sake or to unravel historical conundrums or mediate disagreements between texts or scholars. My purpose was to facilitate the transformative encounter with the word of God in the interaction between the reader and the text.

Wilfred Cantwell Smith, the erudite scholar of comparative religions who died in 2000, in his influential book *What Is Scripture?* suggests that Scripture is less a noun (denoting a book or its contents) than a verb (a way of acting), that is, less a thing than a process. In his wide-ranging study of how the sacred texts of each of the world's great religions function in their respective believing community, he demonstrates that, in attempting to engage the major issues and crises of its concrete historical existence, the community uses its sacred texts to find sustaining cultural meaning. The texts the community considers sacred, revealed, and normative supply the reservoir of language, symbols, narratives, personal models, rituals, and so on by which the community negotiates its engagement with matters of ultimate concern. The texts are not dogmatic "answer books" or moral "manuals" but treasuries of experience with the Ultimate, the Transcendent, which model and mediate ongoing cultural engagement with ultimate concerns in the changing circumstances of historical existence. Thus, ongoing interpretation rather than definitive fixation of meaning is the sign of the life of the texts in the community. This process of "scripturing," rather than a fixed body of immutable truths enshrined in a document, is what characterizes Scripture as revelatory rather than a text as repository of information. Although this living relationship with the text, and through the text with Ultimate Reality, is realized in very different ways in different traditions, the sacred texts remain Scripture only to the extent that they function interactively within the community rather than becoming objects, however revered. In Christian terms we might say that only as long as the Bible resists our temptation to turn it into a relic or talisman does it remain Scripture. When our engagement with the text becomes a matter of "What does the Bible say?"—meaning "What is the (one and only correct) answer to this question or position on this topic?"—we have ceased "to scripture," and the biblical text has become an idol.

The essays in this book are not an attempt to present the correct information about the Resurrection of Jesus but to facilitate the reader's living engagement with the all-important question of what the Resurrection means in the life of believers. As Paul says, if Christ is not raised, your faith is in vain and you are still in your sins (see 1 Cor 15:14). But he was not attempting to prove to them that the Resurrection is a fact, much less to threaten them into an orthodox profession required for either Church membership or eternal salvation. He was trying to engage them in the adventure of faith in Jesus who is not a figure of the past, someone who died and is available to his disciples only as a memory, but alive and present to and among and in them. That is the same project that, I hope, engages the reader of these essays, whom I am inviting to read the Resurrection Narrative of the Fourth Gospel with the same lively faith that energized the first disciples of the risen Jesus and whose testimony constitutes the biblical text we read today and invites all subsequent believers to enter into this mystery, to surrender to it, to live ever more deeply into it.

Overview of the Content

The essays in this volume fall rather naturally into two parts: the first concerned with the bodiliness of the Resurrection of Jesus and how he is present to his disciples throughout time; the second concerned with the central pericope of John 20, namely, the establishment of the New Covenant (John 20:19-23) and the commissioning of the disciples to continue the mission of Jesus, to take away the sin that prevents people from participating in that covenant.

Part 1: The Bodily Resurrection of Jesus

Chapter 1: The Bodily Resurrection of Jesus and Christian Spirituality. As mentioned above, this chapter provides a framework for Christian reflection on the Resurrection of Jesus by identifying the real issue, namely, the actual presence and action of Jesus in the life of his post-paschal disciples, which depends on Jesus' personal Resurrection. Unless Jesus is actually risen in the full integrity of his humanity, his presence to his post-paschal disciples is reduced to a memory of One who, in fact, has died and is no longer personally present. Because bodiliness is integral to humanity, Jesus' real Resurrection and presence to his disciples requires bodily resurrection. This essay is concerned with the meaning of body, ways of understanding bodiliness that are compatible with both the gospel data on the Resurrection and contemporary rationality, and the implications for faith, spirituality, and discipleship of the real presence of the risen Jesus to and in and among his disciples of all time.

Chapter 2: Touching the Risen Jesus: Mary Magdalene and Thomas the Twin in John 20. This essay is focused on the issue of the bodiliness of the risen Jesus as it is presented in the first and the fourth pericopes of John 20, the encounter between Mary Magdalene and Jesus in the Garden of the Tomb and the encounter between Thomas the Twin and Jesus in the place where the disciples were gathered on the evening of the first Sunday after Easter. Both pericopes are concerned with the issue of "touching Jesus": Mary Magdalene restrained from touching him, and Thomas invited to touch him. The issue for the contemporary believer is "Where is Jesus?" and "How can he be encountered?" These two pericopes, which flank the central pericope of the establishment of the New Covenant, narratively explore the answer to these two questions. In effect, Jesus is present to his post-paschal disciples in the community of believers but only to those who, in fact, believe. Mary Magdalene must move from the dispensation of the pre-paschal Jesus-in-the-flesh whose corpse she was seeking on Easter morning into the post-paschal dispensation in which the living Jesus is present in the community to which she bears witness; Thomas must move from his fixation on the type of experience of Jesus that characterized his historical career into the acceptance of the ecclesial presence of Jesus in and through the witness of the disciples. In both cases, the obsession with the historical-physical must give way to faith in the ecclesial-bodily presence of Jesus. Touch, the most intimate of the senses, is not abolished but transformed, as is the believer's experience of the risen Jesus.

Chapter 3: The Resurrection of the Body in the Fourth Gospel: Key to Johannine Spirituality. This essay is the most comprehensive and synthetic of the collection. It deals with the whole of John 20, including the introduction and conclusion and the central pericope on the establishment of the New Covenant. It deals with the issue of the bodiliness of the risen Jesus in terms of Semitic anthropology and sapiential eschatology in the attempt to develop a theory/theology of the body in the dispensation of the Resurrection. The essay pulls together all the issues of part 1 in relation to the spirituality of the contemporary believer.

Part 2: John's Theology and Spirituality of Presence

Chapter 4: The Raising of the New Temple: John 20:19-23 and Johannine Ecclesiology. This chapter deals in detail with the central pericope of John 20, the raising up in the midst of the disciples of the New Temple, that is, the bodily risen Jesus, and his establishment of the New Covenant between the community of his disciples who are now the new People of God and the One who is now the God and Father not only of Jesus but also of his disciples. In this pericope the Johannine "great commission" is given to Jesus' new corporate Body, the Church. Empowered by Jesus' Spirit whom he breathes into them, the disciples will continue the work Jesus was empowered and sent to accomplish, namely, the taking away of the sin of the world.

Jesus, in his Glorification on the cross, took away the "sin" (singular) of the world, the refusal of God's love. He definitively broke the power of Satan over humanity. But dealing with the "fallout" of Satan's work, the "sins" (plural) of humans down through the ages, will be the task of the Church until the time when all humanity will share in the Resurrection of the Son. This is the "greater works" that Jesus promised his disciples they would do after his departure.

Part of the task of this chapter is to try to distinguish the Johannine "great commission" from the Matthean notion of "binding and loosing," or granting and refusing absolution of particular sins, which is not a Johannine concept or theological motif and is hardly sufficiently global or transcendent to constitute a description of the Church's mission until the end of time.

Chapter 5: "Whose Sins You Shall Forgive . . .": The Holy Spirit and the Forgiveness of Sin(s) in the Fourth Gospel. This chapter deals with the same pericope, the appearance of Jesus to the disciples on Easter night, and the Johannine "great commission." But the focus in this essay is an analysis of the theology of sin, which is deeply enmeshed with the violence that undermines the community Jesus came to found and its defeat through the forgiveness Jesus mediates rather than on the sealing of the New Covenant with the New People of God that was the focus of the preceding chapter. In particular, this chapter is concerned with the role of the Holy Spirit in the overcoming of sin. The Holy Spirit who descended on Jesus at the beginning of his public life is given by Jesus to his disciples to enable them to be his presence in the world and to carry on his work of defeating the power of the Prince of this World and drawing all people to Jesus in the community that is his body.

Chapter 6: The Lamb of God and the Forgiveness of Sin(s) in the Fourth Gospel. This essay, the most recent, published in 2010, is the culmination of the work on the Johannine "great commission." Its context is the contemporary situation of sinfulness, namely, the worldwide escalation of violence. The theories of two contemporary thinkers, René Girard on scapegoating violence and Eugen Drewermann on the psychological problem of the refusal of creaturehood, are used to analyze the problem of violence: Where does it come from? Why is it so universal, endemic, and seemingly ineradicable? Why are humans so totally incapable of dealing with it? How does the salvific work of Jesus offer its solution? How are his post-Easter disciples called to participate in that work?

The particular focus of the article in relation to the Fourth Gospel is on the unique Johannine title for Jesus, "the Lamb of God" who takes away the sin of the world. An investigation of the Old Testament background of this title in the Abraham and Isaac narrative, the Suffering Servant figure in Isaiah, and the symbol of the Paschal Lamb helps unfold the nature of the foundational sin, namely, the refusal of creaturehood, and the character of the only remedy for it, namely, the undergoing of scapegoating violence by Jesus whose salvific suffering takes away the sin of the world. Jesus accepted the creaturehood that humans have refused and by doing so broke the hold of Satan on the world that God so loved.

The interpretation of Jesus' salvific work opens up the meaning of the participation of his disciples in that work that is communicated to them by the risen Jesus in the gift of the Spirit on Easter night.

Conclusion

Although these essays do not constitute either a full commentary on or interpretation of the Johannine Resurrection Narrative or a complete theology of the Resurrection of Jesus or its significance for believers, I hope the collection will function to introduce readers in a new way into the theological problematic of the Resurrection in the New Testament and show how wrestling with the biblical material on this theme can move beyond endless arguments about unavailable facts or pointless apologetic that can never produce or augment faith. By seriously engaging the biblical text on the Resurrection of Jesus, not as a trove of facts about the first century, but as a privileged mediation of the paschal mystery, readers can find their way into the world of eternal life Jesus opened for us in his victory over death. If those who read these essays emerge from the experience more sensitized to the spirituality of the Fourth Gospel, better readers of the biblical text, and more committed participants in the life of the One risen in our midst, it will have more than achieved its purpose.

Abbreviations

FE	Fourth Evangelist
FG	Fourth Gospel
LXX	Septuagint
NT	New Testament
OT	Old Testament

Part One

The Bodily Resurrection of Jesus

Chapter 1

The Bodily Resurrection of Jesus and Christian Spirituality

I. Introduction

The primary concern in this essay on the Resurrection of Jesus is not purely exegetical or abstractly theological but arises from the realization I have come to through privileged involvement in the spirituality of many contemporary Catholic Christians that the active presence of Jesus in their lives presents a very real problem. Jesus Christ is, theologically speaking, at the heart of Christian faith and spirituality. His effective disappearance from the horizon of reality for many people, especially the more educated, is not a peripheral matter but a threat to the integrity and specificity of their Christian faith.

A number of factors have converged in recent decades to undermine the once self-evident conviction about the reality and activity of a living Jesus in the daily life and experience of the Christian. Among these factors is the encounter of Christianity with the great world religions. As thoughtful Christians have come to know the nobility and purity of life, the courageous social commitment, and the theological and philosophical sophistication of the pilgrims on these ancient spiritual paths, they have developed serious hesitations about the absolute and exclusivist claims of the Church for Jesus' uniqueness as the sole savior and only way of

Originally published as "The Resurrection of Jesus and Christian Spirituality," in *Christian Resources of Hope*, ed. Maureen Junker-Kenny (Dublin: Columba Press, 1995), 81–114.

salvation for all peoples, claims that are intimately connected to belief in Jesus' divinity and Resurrection.[1] The avatars and spokespersons of the divine in these other religions seem to play the same role in the lives of their devotees that Jesus does in the Christian scheme of things, but none of these other religions makes claims about resurrection from the dead and subsequent indwelling presence. Although this challenge to some of the central affirmations of classical Christology is not the subject of this essay, the reflections that follow may have some relevance to that discussion.

A second factor contributing to the erosion of Christian faith in the real presence of the living Jesus in the life of the believer comes from contemporary science and especially from cosmology influenced by post-Newtonian physics. If the real Jesus is, in some sense, bodily then, if he is alive and active, he would seem to require a "place" in which to exist. Since the idea of a geographical, extraterrestrial place is no longer plausible to the contemporary mind, the lack of a "where" for Jesus (to say nothing of Mary and the saints) raises a serious question about the "what" of the claim that he is alive and active in the real world.

A third source of conceptual difficulty for the contemporary believer comes from modern depth psychology and cultural anthropology. These disciplines raise unavoidable questions about personal, individual, and *a fortiori* bodily survival beyond death for anybody, including Jesus, as well as serious questions about how, and therefore if, personal indwelling of one bodily person in another is possible. The spiritualization of these questions is actually an avoidance of them because the issue is not whether there can be, or is, a divine (or at least supra-human) spiritual influence in human life (which is a widespread, if not virtually universal, conviction among religious people)[2] but whether Jesus, risen from the dead, is still active in the world and specifically in the life of the believer.

---

[1] Serious discussions of and a variety of possible responses to the problem posed by the encounter of traditional Christology with the world religions can be found in Paul F. Knitter, *No Other Name? A Critical Survey of Christian Attitudes toward the World Religions* (Maryknoll, NY: Orbis, 1986); Elizabeth A. Johnson, *Consider Jesus: Waves of Renewal in Christology* (New York: Crossroad, 1990), esp. chap. 9; Thomas N. Hart, *To Know and Follow Jesus: Contemporary Christology* (New York/Ramsey, NJ: Paulist Press, 1984), esp. chap. 10; Monika K. Hellwig, *Jesus, the Compassion of God: New Perspectives on the Tradition of Christianity* (Wilmington, DE: Michael Glazier, 1983), esp. part 3.

[2] This is what Huston Smith refers to as "the primordial tradition," certainly more widespread among humans than the purely materialistic or atheistic alternatives. See Huston Smith, *Forgotten Truth: The Primordial Tradition* (New York: Harper and Row,

The cumulative effect of these (and probably other) factors on the religious imagination of many contemporary believers is that it has become very difficult to conceive of Jesus, who really died on the cross in the first century, as personally alive and active in the present. As Newman once observed, what we believe must be imaginatively plausible, that is, credible to the imagination.[3] The inability of a reasonably sophisticated modern person to imagine Jesus as personally alive and present, active in the world and indwelling his disciples, is handled in various ways in the spirituality of different people.

Some have, not without deep regret and sadness, consigned Jesus to history. He is for them a supreme moral model because of the way he lived, what he taught, and how he died. His memory challenges and motivates them. If there is any way, however mysterious, in which those who have died are present to us, e.g., through memory or affection or within the energy of the cosmos in which we participate, Jesus certainly shares that type of presence. But essentially he is a figure of history, not of the present.

Other people have subsumed Jesus into the Spirit understood as a cosmic, perhaps personal but probably impersonal, life force that holds the universe together and gives support and direction to all things. This cosmic spirit is, at least for Christians, the Spirit of Jesus in that it keeps alive the project Jesus initiated. But again, Jesus himself must be recognized as part of the past, present in remembrance and even in the power of the Spirit, but not personally available to the contemporary believer.

A more conventional and perhaps less spiritually stressful approach is that of the fideist who simply professes the faith of the Church, whatever that entails, without attempting to make sense of such creedal affirmations as "I believe that Jesus Christ sits at the right hand of God and will come again in glory to judge the living and the dead," not to mention "I believe that Jesus died, was buried, and rose again on the

---

1976), and his reply to the challenge of Steven Katz, "Is There a Perennial Philosophy?," *Journal of American Academy of Religion* 55 (Fall 1987): 553–66. See also James Burnell Robinson, "The History of Religions and the Primordial Tradition," in *Fragments of Infinity: Essays in Religion and Philosophy,* Festschrift in Honour of Professor Huston Smith, ed. Arvind Sharma (Dorset: Prism, 1991), 217–33, which relates Smith's theory to the current "dialogue of the world religions."

[3] Gerald O'Collins, in *Jesus Risen: An Historical, Fundamental and Systematic Examination of Christ's Resurrection* (New York: Paulist Press, 1987), 131, discusses the role of logical, practical, and creative reason in faith in the Resurrection and places this insight of Newman under the third category.

third day," or "Those who love me will keep my word. . . . [I] will come to them and make [my] home with them" (John 14:23).[4]

II. The Crux of the Problem: Resurrection

The theological crux of the problem in spirituality around the real presence and personal activity of Jesus in the life of the believer is the Resurrection. It is virtually certain, historically, that a Jewish peasant, Jesus of Nazareth, lived in first-century Palestine and that he really died by Roman execution with the collusion of the hierarchy of his own people. The faith of the Church holds, however, that this is not the end of the story. Jesus, it asserts, rose from the dead on the third day and is still with us. It is precisely this affirmation of the personal, bodily Resurrection of Jesus and his continued presence and activity in the world that poses a stumbling block for the religious imagination of some contemporary believers. Unless something that is intellectually coherent within the horizon generated by modern science, cosmology, psychology, anthropology, and history can be said about resurrection, the real presence of Jesus in the spirituality of the contemporary Christian, however deeply desired, can remain imaginatively implausible.

A very brief sketch of the career of the Resurrection in the faith experience, that is, in the spirituality (as distinct from official theology),[5] of the Church will help locate the contemporary problem. The Church was born, somehow, in the experience of the Resurrection or, more exactly, in the experience of the risen Jesus by some of his historical companions. These people—e.g., Mary Magdalene, Simon Peter, the assembled disciples, the two Emmaus disciples, and eventually Saul of Tarsus (who was not a companion of the historical Jesus but was his contemporary)— witnessed to their personal experience of having seen and interacted with the living Jesus, the numerically identical person whom they (with the exception of Paul) had known during his earthly life, sometime shortly after his death and burial. Faith in the personal, indeed bodily, Resurrection of Jesus, including its significance as divine vindication of

---

[4] The text is in the plural because the promise is that Jesus and the Father will come to the disciple. I put it in the singular to emphasize that the promise involves the presence of Jesus and not simply of God. All citations from the Bible, unless otherwise noted, are from the New Revised Standard Version.

[5] For a good historical synopsis of the theology of the Resurrection, see O'Collins, *Jesus Risen*, 7–98.

Jesus' life and mission and its implication of eternal life for his followers, was the central tenet of early Christianity, that which essentially differentiated it on the one hand from the Judaism within which it arose and on the other hand from the religions of its Hellenistic surroundings. Faith in the Resurrection of Jesus made martyrdom possible because it assured those who shared in the sufferings and death of Jesus that they would also rise with him. The early Christians were Easter people and "alleluia" was their song. To a much greater extent than in the West, the Eastern Church has preserved this paschal religious culture.

In the Middle Ages the Christian faith underwent a pervasive reformulation in the categories of neo-Aristotelian philosophy. Questions about resurrection, both that of Jesus and that of Christians, were reexamined and perhaps overly determined by the preoccupations and the possibilities of the new philosophy. Questions centered on issues such as the physical requirements for resurrection (e.g., whether all the bodily parts of the deceased had to be available if he or she was to be raised) and the qualities of glorified bodies (such as subtlety, which enabled them to pass through solid substances).[6] While these concerns had some implications for the religious imagination and popular piety of medieval Christians and some effect on Church practice (e.g., the prohibition of any form of disposal of the dead that would make bodily reassembly at the general resurrection impossible), they probably contributed little to the substantial enrichment of faith.

For the four centuries after the Council of Trent (1545–63) the Resurrection of Jesus was, in terms of spirituality, a quiet little doctrine that was dutifully professed once a week at the end of the Creed and was dramatically celebrated once a year at Easter. During the Easter season, it was solemnly proclaimed as the heart of the faith and then remanded to the liturgical and spiritual sidelines as the Church returned to "ordinary time," that is, to spiritual business as usual in which the historical life and teaching of Jesus, his exemplary Passion and saving death, and the life and virtues of Mary and the saints supplied the content for the devotional life of believers. (I am always intrigued by the fact that, even

---

[6] For the classical medieval synthesis on the conditions (e.g., age, sex, etc.) and qualities (i.e., impassibility, subtlety, agility, clarity) of the resurrection body, see Thomas Aquinas, *Summa Theologica* Supplement QQ 79–85. Margaret Miles, "The Revelatory Body: Signorelli's 'Resurrection of the Flesh' at Orvieto," *Harvard Divinity Bulletin* 22 (1992): 10–13, is a fascinating study of the late medieval problematic concerning the resurrection of the body as it is reflected in the arguments over the depiction of nudity in religious art.

today, many retreat directors, spiritual guides, and preachers seem to run out of steam in the face of the mystery of the Resurrection. What can be said about it that is morally motivating or spiritually functional in the life of believers? Like Milton's Hell, which is so much more interesting and convincing than his Heaven, the life of struggle and the self-giving death of Jesus are much easier to sink one's spiritual teeth into than his glorious Resurrection, which no one witnessed and no one has, as yet, emulated.)

There is no question that those who carried the Christian and especially the Catholic faith to the new world in the post-Reformation era were much more effective in communicating the reality of the Passion than that of the Resurrection to the peoples they encountered. Outside the Easter season, the Resurrection functioned in the post-Tridentine Church mainly as the *pièce de résistance* in its apologetic armory. It was the ultimate miracle that "proved" that Jesus was God and Christianity the one true religion.

In the 1950s the liturgical renewal that was maturing in the wake of the biblical renewal blessed by Pius XII in 1943 in his encyclical on the study of Scripture, *Divino Afflante Spiritu*,[7] reasserted the centrality of Easter in the liturgical year and of the paschal sacraments—baptism, confirmation, and Eucharist—in the Christian life. This rediscovery of the biblical, liturgical, and therefore spiritual significance of the Resurrection[8] was corroborated in the 1960s and 1970s by the theological renaissance connected with Vatican II, which unleashed a sudden resurgence, even an explosion, of speculative interest in the Resurrection. Literally thousands of books, monographs, dissertations, articles, and symposia proceedings on the subject were published. Even today the Resurrection is a virtual theological cottage industry. A Portuguese scholar recently published an article nearly three hundred pages long

---

[7] The text of the encyclical *Divino Afflante Spiritu* is available in English in James J. Megivern, ed., *Official Catholic Teachings: Biblical Interpretation* (Wilmington, NC: McGrath, 1978), 316–42.

[8] Books that crossed the boundaries of biblical study, liturgy, theology, and spirituality, such as Francis X. Durrwell, *The Resurrection: A Biblical Study* (New York: Sheed and Ward, 1960); Anscar Vonier, *The Glorification of Christ and the Eucharist* (Bristol: Burleigh, 1938; reprinted from *Buckfast Abbey Chronical* [July 1938]); and Columba Marmion, *Christ in His Mysteries*, trans. Mother M. St. Thomas, 7th ed. (St. Louis: Herder, 1940), signaled the reemergence of the Resurrection as a significant feature of immediate pre- and postconciliar spirituality.

with more than five hundred bibliographical references surveying recent research on the Resurrection.[9]

Although my concern in this essay is precisely the Resurrection of Jesus as the crux of the problem of Jesus in contemporary spirituality, I am not going to plunge into the current multifaceted discussion of such issues as the facticity and character of the Easter appearances, the historical reliability of the accounts of the empty tomb, the character of the Easter witness, the properties of the risen body, the content of the Easter kerygma, and so on. All of these questions have been exhaustively, and in some cases excellently, treated in recent biblical and theological litera-ture on the subject.[10] I am interested in the point of intersection between the biblical-theological issue of the Resurrection of Jesus and the problem in spirituality of the presence and role of Jesus in the faith life of the believer. For both substantive and strategic reasons, I think (or at least hope) that I can get at this problem by addressing a single facet of the resurrection problematic (which also has some relevance for the ques-tions alluded to above) and one that is not often dealt with directly by either New Testament scholars or theologians, namely, the issue of the *body*, and specifically the body of the risen Jesus.

I may be wrong, but in my ministerial experience with people dealing with issues in their own spirituality, e.g., Eucharist, personal prayer, and ministry, the problem about Jesus centers on the imaginative noncred-ibility of Jesus' post-death bodiliness and therefore of his personal con-tinuance and real presence today. In other words, to be very precise from the standpoint of spirituality, it is not the *historicity* as such of the Easter appearances or the empty tomb that constitutes the stumbling block for faith. The problem is the *conditions of possibility* of appearances or an empty tomb. The question is usually asked in terms of historicity, i.e., *did* these things happen, but the real concern is *could* these things happen. Unless a real, living body can be ascribed to Jesus after his death, any

[9] M. Isidro Alves, "Ressurreição e Fé Pascal," *Didaskalia* 29 (1989): 277–541.

[10] See, for example, Gerald O'Collins, *The Easter Jesus*, new ed. (London: Darton, Longman and Todd, 1980); *Interpreting the Resurrection: Examining the Major Problems in the Stories of Jesus' Resurrection* (Garden City, NY: Doubleday, 1984); *Jesus Risen* (see note 3 above) for theological discussion of the state of the question; Reginald H. Fuller, *The Formation of the Resurrection Narratives* (New York: Macmillan, 1971), and Pheme Perkins, *Resurrection: New Testament Witness and Contemporary Reflection* (Garden City, NY: Doubleday, 1984) for New Testament scholarship on the subject; Raymond E. Brown, *The Virginal Conception and Bodily Resurrection of Jesus* (New York: Paulist Press, 1973) for a biblical theology treatment.

talk of actual personal resurrection, his or ours, belongs in the realm of mythology, that is, of likely stories about otherworldly reality.

In what follows I want to propose an understanding of, or an approach to, body in relation to the risen Jesus that is, quite frankly, a hypothesis. I venture to propose it because it seems to me to offer some possibilities for dealing with some conundrums about the Resurrection of Jesus and our own resurrection that, to my knowledge, have not been dealt with to the satisfaction of many people. My hope is not to establish unarguable biblical proof or theological evidence but simply to open a path of reflection for committed Christians who want to be able to believe in the real presence of Jesus in their lives but who can only do so if what they believe is compatible with what they know.

By way of proleptic summary, then, I want to propose a way of thinking about *body* that will allow us to take seriously (not literally) what the New Testament says about the Resurrection of Jesus, that is, about the appearances and the empty tomb and the response of the first disciples, as well as the faith experience of the Church down through the ages, especially that of the mystics, and therefore to imagine the *living presence of Jesus in our lives* without having to suspend or bracket our modern consciousness as it is shaped by history, anthropology, psychology, and post-Newtonian science. Specifically, I want to explore the possibility that thinking in a new way about body will allow us to affirm the personal bodily Resurrection of Jesus in a way that can be meaningful for a twenty-first-century person.

III. New Testament Data

In order to pose properly the relevant questions about body, specifically as they pertain to the body of the glorified Jesus,[11] we must briefly examine the New Testament data on the subject. This data can be divided conveniently into material about the appearances of the glorified Jesus

---

[11] I prefer the term "the glorified Jesus" to "the risen Jesus" because the former does not prejudice the discussion of resurrection. To say that Jesus is "glorified" is to claim that he is alive in a way that transcends historical, earthly life. To say that he is "risen" is to make some claims about how glorification takes place, i.e., by a transformation of the body. The latter is precisely the point at issue in this discussion. In other words, I want eventually to conclude to the Resurrection as a way of understanding the Glorification of Jesus that, in itself, could be affirmed without taking any particular position on the possibility or reality of Jesus' relation through the body with intra-worldly subjects at the present time.

and material about the empty tomb. I am going to try, eventually, to establish, contrary to the contention of some biblical scholars and some theologians, that these two sets of data are intrinsically and necessarily related to each other precisely because they are both concerned with the body of the risen Jesus, specifically where and how it *was* and where and how it *was not*.

Our first concern is with the appearances of the risen Jesus. These events or occurrences (whether historical, delusional, imaginary, real, or fabricated) are presented in the New Testament in two forms: kerygmatically or as proclamation, and narratively or as story. The major kerygmatic presentations occur in 1 Corinthians 15:3-8, probably the oldest formulation we have, and in the Petrine sermons in Acts 2 and 3. In the first, Paul announces that Jesus died, was buried, and was raised and that he appeared after his death to two series of witnesses: Cephas (Peter), the Twelve, and more than five hundred disciples together and, in quasi-parallel form, James (the leader of the Jerusalem Church as Peter is of the "great Church"), all the apostles (a group larger than the Twelve but associated with them in the foundational ministry of the Church), and Paul himself (who, like the five hundred, belongs to the post–public life community). In Acts, Peter testifies to the fact that Jesus whom the Jews had killed was raised up by God and lives now at God's right hand. In these kerygmatic accounts the Resurrection of Jesus is asserted on the basis of his having appeared to some of his followers who became, in virtue of their experience, witnesses to the reality of the Resurrection and Jesus' continuing life among them.

In each of the four gospels we find narrative accounts of the post-death appearances of the risen Jesus. In Matthew 28 we have the story of Jesus appearing first to Mary Magdalene and the other Mary (vv. 9-10) and then to the Eleven in Galilee (vv. 16-20). In Luke 24 we have the elaborate narrative of the encounter with Jesus of two disciples, Cleopas and another (perhaps the wife of Clopas who is known to the tradition as a follower of the earthly Jesus [see John 19:25]), on their way from Jerusalem to Emmaus (vv. 13-31); a brief reference to an appearance to Simon (v. 34); and the story of the appearance to the Eleven and their companions (vv. 36-53). In John 20 we have the narratives of Jesus' appearance first to Mary Magdalene (vv. 14-17), then to a group of disciples that seems to have included but not been limited to the Twelve in Jerusalem on Easter evening (vv. 19-23), and finally to Thomas in the (same?) group of disciples a week later (vv. 26-29). In chapter 21 of John, regarded by many scholars as an appendix added by someone other than the Evangelist, we have one of the most dramatic narrations of a resurrection appearance, Jesus' breakfast with the Seven (not all of whom are members of the Twelve) on the shore of the Lake of Galilee and his conversation with the chastened Peter. And finally, in the appendix to Mark's gospel, chapter 16:9-20, we have abbreviated stories of the risen Jesus appearing first to Mary Magdalene (v. 9), then to two disciples walking in the country (v. 12), and finally to the Eleven at table (v. 14). Although this section of Mark is probably a conflation of stories from the other gospels (the first a parallel of Matthew and John; the second of Luke; the third of Luke and John), it does offer a corroboration of the most important narratives of Easter appearances: that to Mary Magdalene and to the group of disciples (including, no doubt, Peter, although it is interesting that Mark, like Matthew and John, gives no account of an individual appearance to Peter).

If the proclamation and the narrative material is combined, we find that the New Testament testifies to Jesus' appearance to individuals (Mary Magdalene, Simon Peter, and Thomas), to small groups (the women at the tomb, the Emmaus disciples), to symbolic groups (the Eleven or Twelve, the Seven), to large groups (the Eleven and their companions, the community of disciples gathered together without and then with Thomas, a group of more than five hundred), and finally to Paul who is the "last" not only chronologically but theologically.[12] In other words, the data about the appearances is extensive and diverse and suggests by its quantitative and qualitative variety that we are not dealing with a single or private experience that was multiplied by psychological "contagion" or literary replication. We are dealing with something that "happened," whatever that was or means.

What is significant for our purposes in this essay is what is asserted by the New Testament accounts and what conclusions about the glorified Jesus as risen are implied by these assertions. In the simplest terms, the New Testament accounts, both kerygmatic and narrative, concur in asserting that Jesus *manifested himself,* i.e., revealed himself or made himself visible, and that he *was seen* by those to whom he manifested himself. The purpose of these self-manifestations or self-revelations was to confirm the faith of his disciples and to commission them to share that faith with the whole world.

Two important conclusions about the risen Jesus, and specifically about his body, can be derived from the appearance accounts. First, the ap-

[12] See Daniel Kendall and Gerald O'Collins, "The Uniqueness of the Easter Appearances," *The Catholic Biblical Quarterly* 54 (1992): 287–307, esp. 295–97.

pearances were *not available to "neutral" observers*. Jesus, although present, could not be seen unless he manifested himself and could only be seen by those to whom he manifested himself.[13] Furthermore, even these "seers" could not recognize him unless he identified himself to them. In other words, we are not dealing with a natural, physical body such as Jesus had before his death, which was visible to anyone who was present where Jesus was present and who was recognizable by his physiognomy as any other mortal is. There is nothing naïve (however artless they may seem) about the accounts of the appearances. Those who saw the risen Jesus knew that whatever "seeing" meant it was not a purely biological, optical event in the natural order, i.e., within the arena of historical cause and effect and governed by the coordinates of space and time.

Second, the appearances, however extraordinary and nonphysical in the natural sense of the term, were *objective* in the sense that they were not self-induced on the one hand or hallucinatory on the other. They were real, and their cause was independent of the experiencing subject. The narratives testify to this "objectivity" in a number of subtle but convincing ways. The recipients, we are told, did not expect to see Jesus alive. Mary Magdalene, the disciples on the way to Emmaus, the gathered disciples in Luke were lost in grief and despair and were totally astonished, even to the point of disbelief, by the appearances. Furthermore, the recipients were manifestly incapable of inducing the appearances. Mary Magdalene searches for the body, questions the angels and Jesus himself; the disciples on the way to Emmaus admit to Jesus their despair. Had they been able to "conjure up" his presence, these stories would have been unnecessary and pointless. It is also important to note that the appearances are not "visions of the night" like Joseph's or the Magi's dreams in Matthew's infancy narrative (see Matt 1:20-23; 2:12, 19-20) or ecstatic experiences like Paul's rapture to the third heaven (2 Cor 12:2) or Peter's vision at Joppa (Acts 11:5-10) or the apocalyptic vision of the Seer on Patmos (Rev 1:9ff).[14] The Easter appearances happened in "broad daylight" while their subjects were fully awake and going about their ordinary, historical business such as meeting, eating,

---

[13] This is the conclusion of Fuller, *The Formation of the Resurrection Narratives*, 48, and has been widely accepted by scholars.

[14] For a fuller discussion of the differences between the Easter appearances and other visionary or ecstatic experiences in the New Testament, see O'Collins, *The Easter Jesus*, 20–22. In particular, he points out that the Easter appearances do not happen in sleep or even at night, do not take place while the recipient is in ecstasy, have no apocalyptic features, are never described as "visions," and are never silent.

traveling, and fishing in the very real world of houses, gardens, cities, roads, and boats. Finally, the Easter appearances were unique, limited to the time just after the death of Jesus, and they came to a definitive end after the appearance ("as to one untimely born" [1 Cor 15:8]) to Paul on the road to Damascus.[15] Although the history of spirituality is replete with accounts of visionary encounters of the mystics with Jesus, e.g., those of Julian of Norwich, Teresa of Avila, or Catherine of Siena, the Church has never suggested that these visions were identical in kind or comparable in significance with the Easter appearances. The faith of the Church does not rest upon these experiences even though it is greatly enriched by them.

From the foregoing observations it is clear (if, of course, one accepts the biblical witness to the appearances of the risen Jesus) that the New Testament accounts intend to assert that in the appearances we are dealing with some bodily reality, i.e., something that can be perceived, about which it is appropriate to say, "I saw." The risen Jesus does not, however, always "look" the same, i.e., he is not physically recognizable either in relation to his pre-death appearance or in terms of other Easter appearances. In short, there is a bodily reality that is not an ordinary, natural, physical body. But it is also not an invisible spirit or a group consciousness of some kind. The glorified Jesus, as he appears to his disciples, is a singular, personal, and perceptible agent who is numerically identical with the One who died on the cross on Good Friday and who interacts with his disciples who are still in this world and subject to the conditions of historical existence. We are dealing with historical experience (that of the disciples) of nonhistorical reality (the glorified Jesus) somehow mediated by body (which is what we mean by the risen Jesus).

Let us turn now to the empty tomb, remaining clear about our objective. It is not historical curiosity or apologetic potential that focuses our exploration but what the empty tomb offers to our reflection about the body of the risen Jesus. I will raise four questions about the tomb, two of which must be answered at this point if we are to proceed with the argument, and two of which will be held in suspension until the end of our considerations about the nature of body.

First, in view of questions that have been raised repeatedly by modern biblical and theological scholarship, we must ask whether, in fact, the tomb of Jesus was empty on Easter morning. Scholars who wish either

---

[15] See Kendall and O'Collins, "The Uniqueness of the Easter Appearances."

to deny that it was empty or to assert the irrelevance of the question and/or the insignificance of the answer are concerned to protect faith in the Resurrection from the vicissitudes of historical research on the one hand and from physicalist or resuscitationist interpretations of Resurrection on the other. Both concerns are legitimate, but in this case the price (denial of the fact of the empty tomb) is too high, both in terms of scholarship and in terms of the meaning of resurrection; furthermore, it is unnecessary. The empty tomb has never been proposed, either in the New Testament itself or by the Church, as "proof" of the Resurrection.[16] The tomb is empty, according to the normative text ascribed to the angel in Mark 16:6, *because* Jesus is risen. No one concludes that Jesus is risen because the tomb is empty. There could have been any number of explanations for such a fact, some of which—e.g., theft of the body—were apparently proposed even during the New Testament era (as suggested by Matt 28:11-15).

There are a number of very good reasons to accept the accounts of the empty tomb as witness to the reality of the situation. First, the earliest testimony in Jerusalem to the Resurrection, testimony that was enormously troubling to the civil and religious authorities, could have been discredited easily by anyone producing the body from the tomb. If Jewish or Roman authorities could have done so, they surely would have. Whether or not the former circulated stories of theft of the body and paid off tomb guards to corroborate it, they obviously agreed that the body, for whatever reason, was not in the tomb.

Second, the contention of some scholars[17] that no one knew where the body of Jesus was buried since it was probably thrown into a common grave for criminals seems ill-founded. The early community took pains to obviate such a hypothesis. Joseph of Arimathea is a character who appears nowhere in the accounts of the life of the historical Jesus, but he suddenly appears in all four gospels to take the body of Jesus from the cross and bury it. Furthermore, in all four accounts he is not alone (which would have made it possible to claim that he had been invented solely for the apologetic purpose of establishing the location of the grave) but accompanied or viewed by others in his activity. In Matthew 27:57-61

---

[16] This is not to say that some scholars have not attempted to use the empty tomb as some kind of proof. See, e.g., the article by Francesco Spadafora, "Prova fisica della resurrezione de Gesù N.S.," *Divus Thomas* 55 (1952): 64–66.

[17] See, for example, John Dominic Crossan, *Jesus: A Revolutionary Biography* (San Francisco: Harper, 1994), 155–60.

Joseph is observed by Mary Magdalene. In Mark 15:42-47 he is observed by Mary Magdalene and Mary the mother of Joses. In Luke 23:50-55 he is observed by the women who had accompanied Jesus from Galilee who, according to Luke 8:2-3, are Mary Magdalene, Joanna, and Susanna. And in John 19:38-42 Joseph is assisted by Nicodemus, and in the following episode Mary Magdalene knows exactly where to go to look for the body.

A third telling argument for the historicity of the empty tomb is the fact that only women are associated with the story of its discovery. If the early Church had invented the story in order to "prove" the Resurrection, they would surely have established its facticity by the testimony of legal witnesses, i.e., males. In fact, the male disciples do not believe the testimony of the women in Luke or, perhaps, in John. In both cases, male disciples go to the tomb in response to the witness of the women and find things as the women have said, that is, they find the tomb empty of Jesus' body. But the discovery of the empty tomb and the original witness to the fact was ascribed to the women, which suggests that it was not invented and was not regarded as apologetically important or used in order to establish the fact of the Resurrection.[18] Furthermore, Paul, in writing to converts who lived far from Jerusalem and would be unlikely ever to visit the site, does not mention the empty tomb. He apparently does not consider it integral to his witness to the Resurrection. In other words, there is no real motive in terms of apologetics for inventing the empty tomb story. It is probably recounted because it happened. The women went to the tomb on the morning after the Sabbath and found it open and empty of Jesus' body.[19]

Finally, as Gerald O'Collins says, any argument against the empty tomb has to be constructed in spite of, indeed in contradiction of, the unanimous literary evidence, which is a tricky proposition if one wants to maintain the validity of the testimony to the Easter event itself that is delivered in the same documents by the same witnesses.

The second question is perhaps more important than the first: does it matter whether or not the tomb was empty since its being empty proves nothing about the Resurrection? For several reasons I would maintain that it matters a great deal whether the tomb was empty, but not because

[18] O'Collins, *Jesus Risen*, 126, also considers this argument persuasive.

[19] In some cases there is "something" in or at the tomb: angels, men in white, grave clothes (seen by the two disciples in John and referred to in the account of the visit of the male disciples in Luke). The point is that what was not in the tomb was the body of Jesus.

this constitutes a proof of bodily resurrection. First, the tomb with its sealing stone was, for the Jews of Jesus' time, the ultimate sign of being cut off from life. The fact that the tomb was found open and empty, in conjunction with the appearances, was a most important sign that Jesus was not in the power of death but alive with God. This is exactly the point of Peter's long disquisition in Acts 2:24-36 contrasting David who "both died and was buried, and his tomb is with us to this day" (v. 29) with Jesus whom God would not allow to experience the corruption of death but whose liberation from the tomb was foretold by David who could not have been speaking of himself when he said "you will not abandon my soul to Hades, or let your Holy One experience corruption" (v. 27, citing Ps 16:8-11). This is also the point of the first Easter episode in John in which the Beloved Disciple sees the face veil lying rolled up in a separate place and believes (John 20:7-8) even though neither the Beloved Disciple nor Simon Peter yet understands that Jesus is risen from the dead (John 20:9). What he believes is that Jesus is glorified, i.e., that he is no longer in the power of death but alive with God.[20] Understanding that the *glorified* Jesus (i.e., Jesus living after his death) is *risen* (i.e., again in interaction with his disciples) arises not from viewing the empty tomb but from the commissioned witness of the one who receives the foundational Easter appearance and comes "announcing" or proclaiming it (*aggelousa* [John 20:18]), Mary Magdalene.

Second, if, as some scholars have suggested, Jesus is alive with God, that is, resurrected in the theologically significant sense of that word,[21] even though his body decayed in the grave, then there is essentially no difference between the Resurrection of Jesus and whatever is true of any just person who has died in God's favor. Again, the point of Peter's contention about David, whom Peter believes to be safe with God but whose "tomb is with us to this day" with the bones of David inside it, is that the Resurrection of Jesus is unique, unprecedented, *sui generis*. A major facet of resurrection hope is that Jesus is the firstfruits of the new creation, that something original and unprecedented has occurred in

---

[20] See my article, "Seeing and Believing in the Glorified Jesus (John 20:1-10)," in *Written That You May Believe: Encountering Jesus in the Fourth Gospel*, rev. and exp. ed. (New York: Crossroad, 2003), 202–10, for a more complete substantiation of this point.

[21] One reason I distinguish between "Glorification" and "Resurrection" is to obviate the confusion implied in this position. One could maintain that Jesus was glorified, i.e., alive with God, even if he were not risen, i.e., bodily interactive with his own. But the point of the resurrection stories, esp. in John, is that Jesus is not only glorified but also risen.

him that is the foundation of a hope for all who follow him, a hope that exceeds any that was possible before him (see esp. Col 1:15-18).

Finally, refusal or denial of the empty tomb tradition reveals a hidden Docetic or at least platonically dualistic presupposition. It involves asserting that Jesus is not his body but a separable, solely spiritual "person" who can leave his body behind as a disguise or a shell and still be fully and completely who he is, that is, the glorified Lord risen from the dead.

The significance of maintaining *that* the tomb was really empty on Easter morning and that this fact, although not a proof of bodily resurrection, is nonetheless *theologically important* can appear only in response to the final two questions about the empty tomb, which I will raise at this point by way of anticipation but put off answering until after we have explored more carefully the notion of body. The third question is "Why was the tomb empty?" and the fourth, very closely related to it, is "What happened to the body of Jesus that was buried?" In other words, these questions really mean to inquire into the relationship between the crucified body of the earthly (pre-Easter) Jesus buried in the tomb and the risen body of the glorified (post-Easter) Jesus encountered in the appearances.[22] Hopefully, a nuanced understanding of that relationship will supply some resources for contemplating the possibility of Jesus being really, i.e., bodily or humanly, present and active in the world today.

IV. Thinking about Body

In recent decades Christian theologians, and indeed educated believers in general, have moved beyond the dualistic theories of the relation of

---

[22] My own tendency to distinguish among the earthly Jesus, the glorified Jesus, and the risen Jesus is confirmed by the distinction Marcus Borg makes between the pre-Easter and the post-Easter Jesus. In *Jesus in Contemporary Scholarship* (Valley Forge, PA: Trinity Press International, 1994), 195, Borg says, "I would like to replace the phrases 'the Jesus of history' and 'the Christ of faith' with 'the pre-Easter Jesus' and 'the post-Easter Jesus.' By 'the pre-Easter Jesus,' I mean of course the historical Jesus; by 'the post-Easter Jesus,' I mean the Jesus of Christian experience and tradition in the years and centuries after the death of the pre-Easter Jesus." I think his concern is similar to mine, namely, that what we are talking about by terms such as "the risen Jesus" and "the post-Easter Jesus" is not a pure construction of faith but Jesus who lived on earth, lives with God, and is interactively present to his disciples throughout Christian history.

body to soul in the human subject that characterized post-Tridentine thinking. The platonic conception of the body as "prison" of the soul that must dominate the body in this life and that escapes from the body in death, as well as the bipolar understandings of physical versus spiritual, body versus soul, or matter versus spirit, have been largely supplanted by understandings of the human subject as "embodied spirit" or as "inspirited body." The human is a single subject with two dimensions or aspects, each of which characterizes the subject as a whole, each of which is equally although differently essential to who we are and determinative of our identity, action, relationships, value, and so on. The body is not a servant to be used and/or abused (*pace* St. Francis on "brother ass"), nor is it a dispensable casing of the spirit (*pace* Plato).

As the medieval historian Carolyn Walker Bynum in a typically brilliant and fascinating study[23] points out, however, it is not nearly as easy to shed our dualism as we might think. Bynum did a detailed investigation of the seemingly absurd and even repulsive (to modern sensibilities) medieval disputations about the material continuity of the human body in resurrection. The medievals discussed such things as whether bits of one's body, like fingernails and hair, would have to be found and reassembled for the general resurrection at the end of the world, or whether the body of a person who had been digested by a cannibal would be resurrected as part of the eater or the eaten. The point of her investigation is that these disputations were not frivolous arguments among underemployed academics but serious engagements, by way of "cases," with the issue of the role of the body in personal identity.

As Bynum points out, we have our own versions of these very arguments. We also are concerned about whether, if enough parts or certain parts of a person are replaced, the person remains him- or herself. In films and stories we have speculated about whether the murderer who receives the heart of the saint (or vice versa) might begin to act like the donor. And we continue to question whether it is ethical to replace a defective human heart with an animal organ or to experiment with the body or organs of a person who has died. Until very recently the Church did not permit cremation and the scattering of the ashes of the deceased but insisted that the entire body be interred in a single place. The underlying question is the integrity of the person in relation to the body, and

---

[23] Carolyn Walker Bynum, "Material Continuity, Personal Survival, and the Resurrection of the Body: A Scholastic Discussion in Its Medieval and Modern Contexts," *History of Religions* 30 (August 1990): 51–85; see esp. 52–57.

there seems to be an ambiguity if not contradiction in maintaining that the person *is* his or her body and yet that the body, at least in part, can be separated from the person or even interchanged with body parts from another person or an animal without intrinsically affecting the identity of the person.

The medievals actually had available a solution to the dilemma posed by the belief that unless every scrap of the material body of the deceased could be "found" by God and reassembled the person would not be her- or himself at the general resurrection. The potential solution lay in Thomas Aquinas's application of Aristotelian hylomorphic theory to the human person. If, as Aquinas posited, the soul is the substantial form of the body, then the human being is not two separate complete substances, a subsistent body and a subsistent soul, each able to exist on its own. Rather, the person is a single substance proceeding from the interaction of two principles, matter and form, which must be united for the person to exist. Whatever matter the soul informed, whether or not it was the identical second matter of that person's earthly life, would be the actual body of that person. But, as Bynum points out, even Thomas was not really faithful to his own theory when it came to the issue of the resurrection of the body of human beings. And he was probably right, she concludes, because the theory that the soul could inform any matter tends to reduce the body to a mere actualization of prime matter, and our experience is that the body is, in the history of the person, "personalized" and therefore constitutive of the person in a highly specific and irreplaceable way. Aquinas was more in line with this personalistic understanding of the self in his insistence that the just person, in the period between personal death and the general resurrection, was in a somewhat incomplete condition, the incompleteness being specific in relation to the person's own body and not materiality in general, and that in the resurrection souls will be reunited with their own bodies.[24]

I would like to try to get out of this impasse by posing the question in another way. Rather than asking whether or not the specific body is essential to the person or, more graphically, how much of oneself one can lose or have replaced before one ceases to be oneself, let us ask, "What is the significance of body? What does body mean?" In other words, to escape the dilemma that faces us if we start by an examination of the

---

[24] See *Summa Theologica* Supp. Q. 78, art. 3; Q. 79, art. 1.

body either physically or philosophically, we will inquire into the nature of the *body as symbol of the self*.

It would seem that body signifies at least four things. First, body grounds and manifests *identity through change*. It is striking that, although the body in all its parts is completely reconstituted physically appoximately every seven years through the replacement of every cell within it, the person remains numerically identical. Photos of a person at ages five, twenty, and fifty will reveal that the person is the same individual. Those who know the person can attest to that identity. At no point in the process does the person experience sloughing off his or her body or becoming someone else. The body, although physically completely different, is the principle of identity, the locus of recognizability. The body registers and expresses both the change and the identity at one and the same time.

Second, the body is the principle of *personal consistence*. It is the body that makes the person one in herself and distinct from all others.[25] In the terms of medieval philosophy, matter is the principle of individuation. The body marks the person off, inwardly in relation to the self and outwardly in relation to everything and everyone else. No matter how widely one extends oneself into the world through action and interaction, the bodily self remains distinct and consistent. The embodied self is "bounded" by body. There is a qualitative difference between an attack on one's ideas or projects and an attack on oneself. No matter how close one is to another physically, even in sexual union, the two are never actually one.

Third, and in complementarity with the existential solitude just described, the body provides the condition of possibility and the ground of *interaction with others*. Because one is located in space by one's body, one can be found by others, recognized, and engaged by them. The body allows one to be present, to speak and hear, to touch and be touched, in short, to interact physically and spiritually with others. The most poignant

---

[25] An interesting corroboration of this point from studies in cultural anthropology and Jungian psychology is the recognition that the "virgin archetype" as it is realized in the virgin goddesses of ancient mythology (Artemis, Athena, and Hestia) signifies the "one-in-herself" character of the one who "belongs to no man" and especially who does not act out of the desire to please, to be approved, or even to control. She "does what she does . . . because what she does is true," as Jean Shinoda Bolen puts it in *Goddesses in Everywoman: A New Psychology of Women* (New York: Harper, 1984), 36; see the whole of chap. 3. This cultural and psychological significance of virginity closely connects what I am calling personal consistence with body.

verification of this feature of bodiliness is the devastating experience of the absence of a loved one who has died. Faith in the communion of saints, in the presence and effective intercession of those who have gone before, does nothing to alleviate the total interactive nonavailability of those who have died. The popular film *Ghost* presented this feature very well as the absolute inability of the deceased main character to effect any material change in the historical world despite his very real presence, knowledge, love, and fierce desire. He required temporary embodiment in a medium in order to interact with his bereaved friend, and he eventually acknowledged the inevitability of his final bodily disappearance from her life.

Finally, body allows the individual to constitute the node of a *network of relations among others*. All of the people related to a single individual are somehow related to each other through that person. This relationship may or may not be rendered explicit, as when a person introduces to each other two or more of his or her friends. But whether or not the relations are made explicit, the fact that each is related to the subject relates them to each other.

Examination of the New Testament material on the Resurrection of Jesus reveals that what is being affirmed about him is not the physicality of the risen body, about which the texts are extremely discreet and even ambiguous, but the fact and the significance of Jesus' mode of presence among his disciples, a mode of presence that can only be affirmed in terms of body.

First, the risen Jesus was recognized as identically the same person whom his disciples had known in his earthly, i.e., pre-Easter, life, who had really died on the cross and had been buried. The One they encountered after the crucifixion was Jesus, not some shade or ghost or trace or representation of him. This seems to be a major point of the accounts of Jesus' encounters with Mary Magdalene, the disciples on the way to Emmaus, Thomas, and the disciples in Jerusalem.

Second, the risen Jesus whom his disciples encountered in the appearances was a distinct person. They do not describe an experience of cosmic energy or a generalized experience of light or beauty[26] or being caught up in a force field or absorbed in an experience of mystical union or

---

[26] In Acts 9:3-7 Saul sees a light and hears the voice of Jesus; his companions heard the voice but saw no one, perhaps not even the light. The voice of Jesus asking Saul why Saul was persecuting him and identifying himself as "Jesus whom you are persecuting" makes clear the personal identity of the one whom Saul encountered.

simply inwardly enlivened by the Spirit. They experienced Jesus as a person distinct from themselves and from everything else, someone who became really present (visible) to them and then ceased to be present (vanished from their sight) and whose presence and absence they did not control. The Emmaus account is particularly graphic on this point.

Third, while Jesus was present to them the disciples could interact with him. They could see him, talk to him, hear him speaking to them, even touch him. Jesus interacted with them, ate with them, conversed with them. They did not simply imagine him present, imagine what he would do if he were present. They experienced him actually doing things they could not have predicted, such as appearing in a room whose doors were barred, making breakfast for them, questioning them about things they had said when he was not perceptibly with them.

Finally, Jesus' disciples experienced themselves as having in common their relationship with him in the present and not merely a shared memory of his having been with them in the past. They recounted to each other their experiences with the risen Jesus and they knew they were talking about the same person. When the Emmaus disciples returned and recounted their experience on the road, the others affirmed that Jesus was indeed risen because he had also appeared to Simon (see Luke 24:33-34). But perhaps the most striking manifestation of this particular feature of the risen Jesus was Jesus' response to Saul when the latter asked, "Who are you?" and Jesus replied, "I am Jesus whom you are persecuting." Not only is Jesus the center of the network of relationships among his disciples but he is so identified with them that their relationships with each other are their relationship with him.

V. Rethinking Materiality in Terms of Symbol

Most of the challenges to faith in the bodily Resurrection of Jesus center on the issue of materiality. What kind of body did the risen Jesus have? Where could it be now? How could Jesus appear and disappear bodily and apparently be bodily in more than one place at a time? Could the risen Jesus really be touched? Could he eat fish and, if he did, what became of the food? How could Jesus enter a sealed room? What happened to the body in the tomb? Although most theologians would not formulate the questions this way, or indeed at all, these are often the questions lurking just below the surface of sophisticated linguistic gambits (e.g., casting theological doubts on the historicity of the empty tomb) designed to keep such questions from arising.[27] Theologians are much more comfortable talking about the *glorified* body than about the glorified *body*. Paul was dealing with exactly these questions with his Corinthian correspondents: "But someone will ask, 'How are the dead raised? With what kind of body do they come?'" (1 Cor 15:35).

The source of the problem would seem to be our coterminous equation of bodiliness, materiality, and physicality, an equation that is verified in all the instances of our actual experience of bodily beings in this world but that, I would like to suggest, is not philosophically absolutely necessary. It may be possible to think of body as implying materiality but not necessarily physicality with the further implication that materiality is not necessarily physical. Paul seems to have been implying something like this when he spoke of "heavenly" (*epouránia*) and "earthly" (*epígeia*) bodies (1 Cor 15:40), or "physical" or "natural" (*psychikón*) and "spiritual" (*pneumatikón*) bodies (1 Cor 15:44-49).

Perhaps we can limber up our imaginations by recalling that matter has at least three states, solid, liquid, and gaseous, and that the same matter can be transformed from one to the other. Furthermore, energy can function as particles or as waves, and matter and energy can be transformed into one another. In other words, materiality is not as static a concept as we spontaneously imagine when we hear the word. Although we naturally think of "material" as implying a freestanding "chunk of stuff" (i.e., physicality), the concept is actually more malleable.

Second, while we ordinarily use the word "body" to mean matter in its solid state, we also use it metaphorically to refer to very immaterial things such as a "body of evidence" or the "body of an argument." In other words, body has as much to do with unity and consistency as it does with physical solidity.

Third, physicality in the strict sense of the term has to do with materiality understood as extension in space and time through the positioning of parts outside of parts with the "decomposability" that is inherent to such composition. But extension in space and time, which is the essence of materiality, is not necessarily identical with having parts outside of parts. Thoughts, for example, or influence can be extended through space and time, as can intentions and projects.

If we combine these ideas, we can readily see that all real bodies in our experience are composed of matter, and all the matter we know of is in some sense physical. Body can, however, be thought of nonmateri-

---

[27] This is the point of O'Collins in *The Easter Jesus*, 90–97.

ally (at least metaphorically), suggesting that bodiliness is not primarily materiality but unity and consistence, and *a fortiori* bodiliness is not necessarily physical. Furthermore, materiality itself is primarily constituted by extension in the world of space and time, and extension is not necessarily or exclusively physical. In other words, it is possible, at least conceptually, to distinguish body from materiality and physicality, and materiality from physicality. If this type of distinction can be achieved conceptually, perhaps it could be verified in reality.

Using these presuppositions I would like to suggest that by substituting a theory of body as symbol[28] of the self for a theory of body as second matter in relation to form it would be possible to construct a coherent theory of Jesus' bodily but nonphysical Resurrection that could account for the experience of the disciples after the crucifixion as well as ground the experience of the real presence of Jesus in the life of subsequent disciples.

The primary role of body in the constitution of the human being is not as a physical "house" for the spiritual soul or even as matter in relation to the soul as substantial form. Rather, body is the symbol, or symbolic presence, of the self. It is the perceptible material through which the person is one-in-himself/herself, distinct from others, intersubjectively available, and able to be interpersonally involved with a plurality of other selves who are related to each other because of their relation with the one symbolized. This symbolic material, the body, can and does undergo all kinds of change and transformation in order to symbolize adequately, to "body forth," the self in its various states such as child or adult, ill or well, and so on. Because the body is a symbol of the self and not an arbitrary sign of something other than itself, however, it remains recognizably identical throughout the processes of change, even very dramatic and radical ones such as the loss of limbs, bodily functions, major organs, or even consciousness.

The point at which the body as symbol ceases to be identical with the person is the moment of death. At that point the body is no longer, properly speaking, the body (the symbolic presence) of the person; it is a corpse. In other words, while continuing to exist materially, it has been transsymbolized. It is now the presence of an absence; it is the trace in

---

[28] I am making use of a theory of symbol rooted in the thought of Paul Tillich as developed by Paul Ricoeur. I have explained it at length in my book *The Revelatory Text: Interpreting the New Testament as Sacred Scripture*, 2nd ed. (Collegeville, MN: Liturgical Press, 1999), 33–36.

this world of a presence that has ended. That is why the corpse is so awe-inspiring, so reverence-evoking, even so terrifying. This is especially true for those most closely related to the deceased person because what is no longer present is a personal organizing center of meaning and relationship. The disappearance of this presence requires, indeed causes, a radical restructuring of life and relationships among those who remain behind. The corpse, no longer symbolic of the self of the person, is now the symbol or perceptible presence of the absence of the person. It makes clear to us that the person is no longer available, no longer interactively present to us, no longer recognizable or reachable by us. The network of relationships that centered in this person must be renegotiated. This is probably the reason why it is more difficult, for example, for a family to have a member simply "missing in action" for decades than to know the person has been killed and to be able to bury the corpse. Not having the corpse, the symbol of the definitive end of the person's intra-worldly presence, means that the family's relationships remain in a state of suspended animation. The person is neither present nor absent, and the network of relationships cannot be renegotiated or stabilized.

Symbol, in short, is not something imaginary or fictive, nor is it a mere "sign," that is, something that stands for something other than itself. It is the way of being present of something, such as person, that cannot be encountered except in and through its symbolization. Perceptibility is necessary for symbolic presence precisely because it is the essence of a symbol to make perceptible what in and of itself is not perceptible. For example, the kiss expresses love; rape embodies hatred; the Gospel makes divine self-gift revelatory; the body makes the person available. Perceptibility (and therefore materiality) of some kind is intrinsic to symbolization, but what is essential to the notion of symbol is that it renders present and available that which it symbolizes. Consequently, the risen Jesus requires materiality of some sort, that is, perceptibility, in order to be encountered by his historical disciples. The body of the risen Jesus functions symbolically just as his earthly body did, but the difference lies in the character, not the fact, of his bodiliness. In other words, what changes through Resurrection is not the reality but the mode of the bodily or symbolic presence of Jesus among his disciples. The major difference between our earthly (material/physical) bodies and the glorified (nonphysical) body of Jesus as symbolic is that the physical materiality of our bodies entails space-time limitations and the intrinsic decomposability of physicality that no longer apply to Jesus' body since he is no longer within history. "Death no longer has dominion over him" (Rom 6:9), and neither do the conditions of intra-historical existence.

I am suggesting that what we mean by saying that Jesus is risen is neither that he was physically resuscitated as an ordinary participant in intra-worldly history nor that he became a nonbodily spirit. Rather, he was transformed in God in such a way that he could symbolize himself in ways that transcend our ordinary experience or capability (or his while he was on earth). He could now "body forth," that is, materialize and therefore symbolize, his presence at will without being subject to the limitations of physicality that we spontaneously associate with materiality, namely, subjection to the limitations of causality, space and time, and the inevitability of death through physical decomposition. In other words, the glorified Jesus realizes in himself the essential meaning of corporality, bodiliness (including a transcendent relationship to materiality), without the limitations of physicality precisely because he is no longer a participant in intra-worldly history, in the space-time continuum of cause and effect to which physicality responds. The glorified Jesus has absolute control of his self-symbolization in a way that mortals (including the pre-Easter Jesus) do not. For the glorified Jesus, to be "bodily" is to be personally and identically (i.e., numerically) himself in the full integrity of his humanity and able to be present and active in relation to us in whatever ways are appropriate or necessary for us. This implies that he can "materialize" himself in any way, in any place, in any time that responds to his purposes. The relationship between bodiliness and materiality that obtains in the historical individual is reversed in the glorified Jesus. For the former, materiality determines bodiliness, and this is probably the best definition of physicality. For the latter, the glorified Jesus, bodiliness (that is, the capacity for self-symbolization) determines materiality, and this is what we mean by the glorified body or what Paul called the spiritual body, materiality completely instrumental to person.

VI. Implications of the Theory of Body as Symbol for Questions about the Resurrection of Jesus

In what follows I would like to revisit some of the thorny questions about the Resurrection of Jesus to see if a symbolic rather than hylomorphic theory of body can make possible more coherent responses. If so, the real presence of the glorified Jesus not only to his earthly disciples during the immediate post-Easter period but to later disciples throughout history may be more imaginatively plausible and therefore able to function in living faith rather than by way of willed suspension of disbelief.

What happened to the body of Jesus in the tomb?

If the body, as I have suggested, is the symbol of the person, then Jesus, if he is alive, could not leave behind a corpse. The corpse is the sign of the absence of the person, the departure of the person from interactive presence with others; it is a trace within history of a person who is no longer present and active in history. If Jesus is truly risen he is not dead; he is not absent; he is, on the contrary, alive, present, and active and, when he chooses to be so, active within history or in relation to people within history. A corpse of the living Jesus would be a counter-symbol. It makes no more sense to ask where the corpse of Jesus "went" than to ask where my five-year-old body is now that I am an adult. The answer is that the child body, the symbol of my five-year-old self, is not because my five-year-old self no longer exists. Or better still, it is subsumed in the present symbol of myself, the body that I am today. The body of the pre-Easter Jesus is not resuscitated, nor did it decay. It is not. Or better still, it is subsumed into the symbolic capacity of his glorified self. I suspect that this is why Jesus, although able to prevent his disciples from immediately recognizing him, was truly *recognized* by them when their eyes were opened. His bodily continuity is the locus of his recognizability.

Was the body of the glorified Jesus who appeared to his disciples "solid"? Could he eat, be touched, and so on? In other words, was it a real body or just an appearance of one?

As symbolic mode of presence, Jesus' body is real. How its relation to materiality is actualized in any given situation depends on how Jesus chooses to be present. If the appropriate mode of presence requires a quasi-physicality in order to express, to symbolize or "body forth," his identity, his consistency, his interactive presence, there is no reason why it cannot assume the qualities of physicality such as the ability to be touched or to eat. This type of self-symbolization was characteristic of the post-Easter appearances in a way it has not been in even the most "bodily" of mystical experiences of later Christians, and this is probably one feature of what Daniel Kendall and Gerald O'Collins refer to as the "uniqueness" of these foundational appearances.[29] For example, St. Teresa of Avila testifies that, after her experience of transforming union became virtually habitual, Jesus was almost always perceptibly present at her

---

[29] Kendall and O'Collins, "The Uniqueness of the Easter Appearances," 299.

side.[30] Julian of Norwich speaks of seeing Jesus suffering on the cross.[31] Catherine of Siena received a wedding ring from Jesus during an experience of mystical espousal.[32] Despite the bodiliness of these experiences, they do not involve the quasi-physicality of the post-Easter accounts. All of these mystics refer to their experiences as "visions," Teresa specifying that they are "intellectual" as opposed to imaginative visions. Although these questions about the nature of mystical experiences are immensely complicated and not the subject of this essay, I mention them because a symbolic theory of the bodiliness of the glorified Jesus does seem to offer some resources for a theoretical understanding of the Jesus-mysticism of some Christian mystics, an issue that has been highly problematic in cross-traditional studies of mysticism and even in Christian theology precisely because Jesus-mysticism requires that Jesus, and not just the Holy Mystery that is God, exist and be active in the present. To speak of Jesus requires reference to his integral humanity and thus to his bodiliness.

What can be said about Jesus' personal identity? Does he exist today; does he live? Or is he simply the "Christ of faith," "risen in the community," a "cause that goes on"?

The glorified Jesus is all of these but not reducible to any of them or to all of them taken together. The primary ongoing symbolization of the glorified Jesus in this world is his present historical body, which is all the baptized who are corporately one as the Body of Christ through the power of his indwelling Spirit. The earthly or pre-Easter Jesus, whose life is the model and whose teaching is the inspiration of these believers, is, for them, the Christ of faith, i.e., the One who is mediated to them in Scripture and the other sacraments and received in faith. They can literally claim with Paul, "It is no longer I who live, but it is Christ who lives in me" (Gal 2:20). And the cause of Jesus does go on, precisely because they are, corporately, his body in this world furthering his project. But

---

[30] See Teresa of Avila, "Interior Castle," in *Teresa of Avila: The Interior Castle*, trans. and ed. Kieran Kavanaugh and Otilio Rodriguez (New York: Paulist Press, 1979), 150–55. This description occurs in Sixth Dwelling Places, chap. 8, 150–55.

[31] See Julian of Norwich, "Showings," in *Julian of Norwich: Showings*, trans. and ed. Edmund Colledge and James Walsh (New York: Paulist Press, 1978), e.g., 136, 141, 193, 207.

[32] This extraordinary experience is recounted in Catherine's biography by Raimondo da Capua, [*Legenda major*] *S. Caterina da Siena*, trans. Giuseppe Tinagli (Siena: Cantagalli, 1934), book 1, chap. 12, 165–70.

this mystery in its entirety is only possible if the real Jesus himself exists, lives, acts. If Jesus is dead and buried, a figure of history available only in and as a memory, all of this becomes playacting. In other words, the glorified Jesus *is* the Christ of faith, *is* the principle of his Body the Church, *is* the One whose cause continues in and through his disciples down through history.

VII. Implications for Spirituality

The question that stimulated this reflection on the Resurrection of Jesus arose from the concern within contemporary spirituality with the role of Jesus in the faith life of the believer. Therefore, it is now time to draw out the implications of this reflection for Christian faith and especially for Christian hope.

Let me begin by attempting to state in relatively non-mythological language[33] what I mean by the Resurrection of Jesus. It should be clear at this point that I want to distance myself from those theological positions that would define the Resurrection of Jesus as the definitive disappearance of the personal Jesus and his replacement by a community that continues his vision and work; a purely subjective, although highly motivating, experience of Jesus' ongoing significance on the part of his disciples; an absorption of Jesus, without remainder, into the cosmic mystery that some people call God, and so on. *By the Resurrection I mean that Jesus, who really lived in first-century Palestine and really died on the cross, is alive with God in the full integrity of his humanity, that is, as a body-person, and is interactively present in and among us now and forever.* What then are some of the implications for Christian spirituality of such an understanding of the Resurrection?

First, this understanding of the Resurrection implies that prayer to Jesus (not just prayer to God through Jesus or in the Spirit of Jesus), both kataphatic and apophatic, is grounded in reality. Kataphatic or dialogical prayer to Jesus is an address to a person who is truly alive and available to the baptized believer. Apophatically experienced personal union, or

---

[33] All human language about "heavenly," that is, transhistorical, reality is necessarily mythological because we have to use our earthly categories to describe and talk about what transpires in another sphere of reality. We are using mythological language when, for example, we speak of Jesus "ascending" into heaven or "sitting at the right hand of God."

what is sometimes called Jesus-mysticism, is neither hallucination nor a case of essentially nonthematic universal mysticism mediated through Christian symbols. It is experience of the glorified Jesus who is able to effect a union between himself and his disciples so intimate and immediate that Paul's claim that Christ lives in him (Gal 2:20) or John's presentation of Jesus' claim to be in us and we in him (e.g., John 14:20) are to be taken with absolute seriousness.

Second, it is the living Jesus who is really identified with his disciples. The baptized act "in persona Christi," not in virtue of ordination, or by permission or delegation, or only when doing sacred actions. The indwelling of Jesus is quite real, and he is more intimate to us than we are to ourselves. It is quite possible for us to be oblivious of this fact and even effectively to nullify its potential for good by our actions. But the reality remains that those who have been laid hold of by Christ are actually changed by his real presence in their being and life. Furthermore, when we relate to our neighbor, either to do good or to do ill, we are not imagining that we are relating to Jesus, imaginatively substituting his face for theirs so that we can "act as if." The glorified Jesus' words to Saul who was persecuting the Christians, "I am Jesus, whom you are persecuting" (Acts 9:5), or Matthew's presentation of Jesus' words at the last judgment, "As you did it to one of the least of these my brothers and sisters, you did it to me" (25:40), are not the pious hyperbole of the early Church. When Jesus said to Catherine of Siena, in vision, that she could really serve him by serving her neighbor[34] he was not offering a temporary palliative to her fervor until she could encounter him in glory but reminding her of the truth of the Gospel claim. To speak of the "whole Christ" is not metaphorical language but a recognition of the corporate reality of which the risen Jesus is the unifying principle.

Third, Jesus, now glorified, is no longer limited, either personally or as principle of his corporate members, by gender, ethnicity, race, age, chronological setting, or any other characteristic that is a function of physicality. However we might imagine Jesus in prayer (and most people probably imagine him as a young man with Semitic features), Jesus' real continuity with his historical self is no longer personally limiting. His bodiliness is not physical. When some of the medieval mystics spoke of Jesus as "mother" they were not distorting his reality but attending to something in Jesus that he himself affirmed but that was "muted" in his

---

[34] Raimondo da Capua, *S. Caterina da Siena*, book 2, chap. 1, 171–81.

earthly life by the fact of his physical maleness, namely, his maternal or nurturing character in relation to his disciples. Jesus, although he died in his early thirties, is no less identified with the elderly in their aging than he is with young people. Jesus is no more Jewish than Gentile, male than female, straight than gay, white than black, well than sick, European than Asian or Hispanic. Jesus is fully identified with his body, which is individually each of his members and corporately the Church.

Fourth, Jesus exists as a person in the Holy Mystery we call God. He is not diffused in some cosmic ether or energy field or absorbed into some overarching universal process. It is precisely because of this that we can profess, "I believe in the resurrection of the body," which is not a confession of belief in personal immortality of the disembodied spirit and even less in the absorption of the subject into an impersonal cosmic process. The early Church's faith that Jesus is the "firstfruits" of those who have fallen asleep (see 1 Cor 15:20) and the assurance that what is true of Jesus now will be true of all of his disciples is a profession of faith in personal, bodily resurrection. My contention is that the contemporary believer can only make this profession with intellectual integrity if we can achieve some kind of understanding of body that is compatible with what we know of the cosmos and anthropology.

VIII. Conclusions

What the New Testament says about the Resurrection of Jesus marks it off from anything we know or experience to have been the case with anyone else who has died, even Mary, the Mother of Jesus, whose "assumption" has been defined although its biblical basis and specific content are anything but clear. The decay of corpses other than Jesus' and the appearances of Jesus to his disciples during a specified and limited amount of time signifies that the eschaton (which is probably not a cosmic event marked by astrological phenomena) has begun in Jesus but that it is still to come in regard to those who have died in Christ and thus who truly live even now (see John 11:25-26). As John's account of the resuscitation of Lazarus in contrast to the Resurrection of Jesus makes clear, there is a real difference between what happened to Jesus after his death and what has so far been verified in his disciples.[35] But the object

---

[35] See my article, "The Community of Eternal Life (John 11:1-53)," in *Written That You May Believe*, 171–83.

of Christian faith and hope is precisely that the difference is not definitive, that those who have fallen asleep await the resurrection that is already achieved in Jesus (see Rom 8:23).

We do not know in detail what awaits us, but some affirmations are perhaps well grounded in what we can know of Jesus' Resurrection. First, we are destined for personal, bodily (in the sense of "body" that has been the subject of this essay, namely, personal identity and interpersonal relationship) life in God with Jesus through the Spirit. Second, because death is not the end, because death is not a descent into nothingness, a disappearance of body into undifferentiated matter and of spirit into impersonal energy signaling the end of personal integrity and interpersonal relationship, what we do in this life really matters. The relationships that we forge with Jesus, in Jesus with God, and with our sisters and brothers in Christ have a future. Our spiritual lives and ministerial commitments are worth the candle. Our efforts at world transformation make sense, even when we do not perceive the results in our own earthly careers. We are not howling against the night that will ultimately end it all or killing time here waiting for a completely other existence that has no continuity with this one. We are building the City of God into which we and our world will be transformed although the manner of this transformation is beyond our imagination.

As Paul said long ago, if Christ is not risen, our hope is in vain and we are, of all people, the most deluded (see 1 Cor 15:12-14). The one thing the Church has always gotten right is the proclamation, "Jesus Christ is truly risen, Alleluia!"

Chapter 2

Touching the Risen Jesus:
Mary Magdalene and Thomas the Twin
in John 20

I. Introduction

In the last analysis, anything theology says about the resurrection of the body of those who have died in Christ stands or falls in terms of what we say about the bodily Resurrection of Jesus himself. And our only access to the Resurrection of Jesus, whether bodily, physical, spiritual, or none of these, is the New Testament. Although there is a great deal of material in the New Testament about the Resurrection, only three passages focus directly on the bodiliness of the Risen One. The first is 1 Corinthians 15, in which Paul argues with members of the Corinthian community who, for philosophical reasons, regarded the material in general and the body in particular as worthless. Paul argues for the possibility, actuality, and significance of bodily resurrection as such, whether of Jesus or of believers.[1] The second is Luke 24:36-43, the narrative of

Originally published as "Touching the Risen Jesus: Mary Magdalene and Thomas the Twin in John 20," in *The Resurrection of Jesus in the Gospel of John*, ed. Craig R. Koester and Reimund Bieringer (Tübingen: Mohr Siebeck, 2008), 153–76.

[1] For references on the probable ideological *Sitz-im-Leben* of the Corinthian correspondence, see Jerome Murphy-O'Connor, "The First Letter to the Corinthians," in *The New Jerome Biblical Commentary*, ed. Raymond E. Brown, Joseph A. Fitzmyer, and Roland E. Murphy (Englewood Cliffs, NJ: Prentice Hall,1990), 812. For a very good, brief treatment of Paul's position in contrast to the Corinthian position, see Peter Lampe, "Paul's Concept of a Spiritual Body," in *Resurrection: Theological and Scientific*

Jesus' appearance to the startled and terrified disciples who think they are seeing a ghost. The Risen One invites them to tactilely verify the solidity of his body, that he has "flesh and bones," in order to convince them that he is indeed the Jesus who was crucified and not a ghostly apparition.[2] Both the Pauline and Lukan texts were addressed to predominantly Hellenistic audiences whose dualistic anthropology made bodily resurrection *a priori* impossible or meaningless or both.

Interesting as these polemics are, and not unrelated to contemporary issues about the possibility of an afterlife, neither text addresses the primary concerns of this essay, namely, the question of what role the bodiliness of the risen Jesus plays, and how it does so, in the relationship between Jesus and his disciples after the Resurrection. Does the body of Jesus that mediated his pre-Easter relationship with his disciples continue to play that role for his post-Easter disciples, including us?[3] If "bodily" is synonymous with "physical," then we are caught between two equally unacceptable positions. Either, on the one hand, Jesus is simply resuscitated, i.e., physically revived, which leaves him and us still subject to the conditions of space, time, and causality, and vulnerable to death, or, on the other hand, his Resurrection is purely spiritual, and we are outside the Christian community's faith in the "resurrection of the body." By way of prolepsis, I am going to propose that Jesus' Resurrection is *not* physical but *is* bodily and therefore that his body continues to mediate his relationship with his disciples but in a way that is both continuous and discontinuous with the way it did in his pre-Easter career.

I will argue this on the basis of the third New Testament text that focuses on the body of the risen Jesus, namely, the Johannine Resurrection

---

Assessments, ed. Ted Peters, Robert John Russell, Michael Welker (Grand Rapids, MI: Eerdmans, 2002), 103–14.

[2] Hans-Joachim Eckstein, "Bodily Resurrection in Luke," in *Resurrection: Theological and Scientific Assessments*, 115–23, discusses both the polemic in Luke against the anthropological dualism of his predominantly Gentile community and Luke's subtle alternative to that position.

[3] Following Marcus Borg in *Meeting Jesus again for the First Time: The Historical Jesus and the Heart of Contemporary Faith* (San Francisco: HarperSanFrancisco, 1994), 15–17, I prefer to use the terms "pre-Easter" and "post-Easter" to designate Jesus' life before the Resurrection and his life after the Resurrection, respectively. The traditional term "earthly Jesus" can set up a theologically problematic dichotomy between the "Jesus of history" and the "Christ of faith" and implicitly deny the ongoing presence of the risen Jesus in the historical experience of his contemporary earthly disciples.

Narrative, John 20, and specifically verses 11-18 (the Mary Magdalene episode) and 24-29 (the Thomas the Twin episode). In the first passage the risen Jesus prohibits Mary Magdalene from touching him, and in the second he invites, even commands, Thomas the Twin to touch him. Our question is, what does John 20 say about the body of the risen Jesus and its role in his relationship with his disciples?

II. Presuppositions about the Theology of John

Before turning to the texts in question, we have to lay a certain amount of biblical groundwork, first about the theology of the Fourth Gospel relative to resurrection and second about the structure and dynamics of the Johannine Resurrection Narrative as a whole. In the first section we need to look briefly at the eschatology and anthropology of the Fourth Gospel, which together govern John's approach to the Resurrection of Jesus. In the second section we will look at the theological progression within the Johannine Resurrection Narrative and at the development within it of the dialectic between seeing, hearing, touching, i.e., sense experience, and believing.

John's Eschatology[4]

As is commonly recognized, the eschatology of the Fourth Gospel differs strikingly from that of the Synoptic Gospels. This difference is often expressed as the contrast between realized (i.e., present) and delayed (i.e., future) judgment. These two eschatologies involve much more, however, than a temporal difference. Each is a theological approach to life, death, judgment, and afterlife.

In the Fourth Gospel Jesus' death is not presented, as it is in the Synoptics, as a *kenosis*, the nadir of his earthly life, a human condemnation from which God vindicated him through resurrection. In John, Jesus' death itself is the apotheosis, the victorious culmination of his life. In

---

[4] Following convention among Johannine scholars I will use the term "John" to refer to the Fourth Evangelist (FE) or to the gospel itself. This implies no position on the much-debated issues of Johannine authorship and the identity of the Evangelist. My position on these questions is available in *Written That You May Believe: Encountering Jesus in the Fourth Gospel*, rev. ed. (New York: Crossroad, 2003), 233–54.

and by his death, Jesus is glorified by God and exalted to God's presence.[5] He is proclaimed as king and reigns gloriously from the cross (John 19:19). Consequently, Rudolf Bultmann observed in the mid-twentieth century:

> If Jesus' death on the cross is already his exaltation and glorification, *his resurrection* cannot be an event of special significance. No resurrection is needed to destroy the triumph which death might be supposed to have gained in the crucifixion.[6]

Bultmann and others have suggested that John's gospel really ends with the crucifixion in chapter 19 and the Johannine Resurrection Narrative is merely a concession to the tradition that was normative by the time this gospel was written at the end of the first century. While this is hardly a satisfactory conclusion, it raises pointedly the question of what role the Resurrection Narrative does play in John's gospel. It clearly does not play the vindicatory role it does in the Synoptics, but, I would argue, it is crucial to John's theological purposes.

The two strands or types of eschatology we find in the New Testament are the descendants of two types of eschatological reflection that developed in the latest Old Testament and the intertestamental writings.[7] The first type, which we might call "resurrection eschatology," was futuristic and apocalyptic. It developed in the context of the Syrian persecutions and the Hasidean-Hasmonean controversies in Palestine in the second to first centuries BCE. Faithful Jews, like the mother and seven brothers in 2 Maccabees 7, were being persecuted and even martyred for their fidelity to Torah, but they were strengthened by the hope that they would be vindicated by God after death. The clearest Old Testament expression of this eschatology is found in Daniel 12:1-3, predicting the awakening

---

[5] Ὑψόω, "exalt" or "lift up," is used several times in John to speak of Jesus' lifting up on the cross as his exaltation (e.g., 3:14; 8:28; 12:32), and δοξάζω, "glorify," is used to speak of the effect on Jesus of his "lifting up" in crucifixion (e.g., 7:39; 12:16; 12:23; 13:31-32), namely, that he is glorified by God and glorifies God by his death.

[6] Rudolf Bultmann, *Theology of the New Testament*, vol. 2, trans. Kendrick Grobel (New York: Charles Scribner's Sons, 1955), 56.

[7] Although both the category "intertestamental" itself and the dates for the period and its literature are debated, for my purposes it designates the overlapping of Old Testament and New Testament experience and the writings reflective of that experience, extending roughly from 200 BCE to about 100 CE. My thanks to my Old Testament colleague, John Endres, for help with this issue.

of "many . . . who sleep in the dust," and 2 Maccabees 7, both of which are influenced by the Suffering Servant image from Deutero-Isaiah.[8] The martyrs are assured that they will be restored even in their bodies, that Israel will be reconstituted, and that the unjust will be finally punished.

This type of eschatology, characteristic of the Synoptic Gospels, was that of the Pharisees of Jesus' time. Matthew 25:31-46 portrays such a final vindicatory event, a last judgment, conceived as a sudden cosmic cataclysm (see Matt 24:15-44; Mark 13; Luke 17:22-37), when all will be raised to appear before the glorified Christ who will assign them to eternal reward or punishment on the basis of their comportment in this life. The role of bodily, even physical, resurrection in this eschatology is essentially functional. It renders the just and the unjust present for final judgment in which divine justice will be fully manifest. And it ensures the participation of the whole person in the final sentence.

John's gospel, unlike the Synoptics, operates within the other strand of late pre-Christian Jewish eschatology, which I will label "immortality eschatology." This eschatology is realized and sapiential rather than future and apocalyptic. It developed in the Hellenistic context of Diaspora Judaism, probably in the late second to first century BCE. Jews who had remained faithful to Torah even though living in a Hellenistic context were being persecuted and even killed, not only by pagans, but also by their religiously and culturally assimilated fellow Jews.[9] Once again, there is appeal to a post-death solution to the problem of the intra-historical victory of the unjust. The clearest (deutero)canonical expression of this eschatology occurs in Wisdom of Solomon 1–6.

The Wisdom Hero in this story, who epitomizes the faithful Jews, is persecuted unto death by the disciples of Folly who mock his fidelity to the Law, repudiate his claim to be God's son, and are infuriated by his accusation that they are unfaithful to their training and tradition (cf. Wis

---

[8] For a detailed comparison of texts showing the influence of Isa 26:20; 26:19; and 66:24 on Dan 12:1-3, see Sandra M. Schneiders, *The Johannine Resurrection Narrative: An Exegetical and Theological Study of John 20 as a Synthesis of Johannine Spirituality*, vol. 1 (Ann Arbor, MI: University Microfilms, 1983), 85–86.

[9] An excellent and provocatively suggestive treatment of the Wisdom of Solomon, its eschatology in relation to its *Sitz-im-Leben*, and its possible relation to the New Testament is Barbara Green's "The Wisdom of Solomon and the Solomon of Wisdom: Tradition's Transpositions and Human Transformation," *Horizons* 30 (Spring 2003): 41–66.

2:10-20).[10] The Septuagint (LXX) version of the fourth Suffering Servant Song (Isa 52:13–53:12) and of the Daniel 7 figure of the Son of Man surely influenced the portrait of the martyred hero in Wisdom of Solomon,[11] which was also influenced by Hellenistic notions of immortality. Unlike the future apocalyptic resurrection eschatology of 2 Maccabees, this sapiential eschatology presents the death of the righteous as an exaltation for judgment on his enemies and an immediate entrance into an intimate relationship with God in a nonterrestrial, post-death realm. The text tells us that, even though the hero is physically killed, "the souls of the just are in the hand of God. . . . They seemed, in the view of the foolish, to be dead . . . but they are in peace. . . . God took them to himself" (Wis 3:1-6).

Bodily, much less physical, resurrection such as we see in resurrection eschatology does not figure explicitly in this sapiential understanding of the destiny of the just and unjust because the judgment of the ungodly takes place in their very choice of evil by which they "summon death" (cf. Wis 1:16), and the just are exalted by and assumed to God in their very destruction by the unjust. The exaltation of the just, however, is not simply immortality of the soul in the Greek philosophical sense, that is, the natural indestructibility of a spiritual substance. Their immortality is *life* in the Jewish sense, i.e., a gift from God, who alone possesses it by nature[12] and who freely bestows it on those who are loyal to the covenant. Furthermore, life, even after death, in which the body did not participate in some way would have been inconceivable to the Jewish imagination. So, while it says nothing explicit about bodily resurrection,

---

[10] For the development of the extrabiblical literary genre of "wisdom tale" within which we meet "wisdom heroes" in noncanonical dress who resemble Joseph, Daniel, and Susanna, see G. W. Nicholsburg, *Resurrection, Immortality, and Eternal Life in Intertestamental Judaism*, Harvard Theological Studies 26 (Cambridge, MA: Harvard University Press, 1972), 49–55. The distinctiveness of the biblical wisdom heroes is that their wisdom consists in fidelity to Torah rather than in secular *savoir faire* or philosophically based ethics.

[11] See Schneiders, *The Johannine Resurrection Narrative*, 98–101, for the textual evidence for this position.

[12] This was explained well by Joseph Moignt, "Immortalité de l'âme et/ou résurrection," *Lumière et Vie* 21 (1972): 65–78, who takes essentially the same position as Oscar Cullmann in his classic text, "Immortality of the Soul or Resurrection of the Dead: The Witness of the New Testament," The Ingersoll Lecture, 1955, *Harvard Divinity School Bulletin* 21 (1955–56): 5–36.

sapiential eschatology is fundamentally susceptible to it[13] and even in a way requires it.

This sapiential eschatology is easily discerned in the Fourth Gospel and is operative in John's presentation of the death of Jesus as the Wisdom Hero. His death is his exaltation in and by which his persecutors are judged and he is glorified (cf. John 16:8-11). This leads to two conclusions about the role of the Resurrection Narrative in John's gospel.

First, because bodily resurrection is compatible with, perhaps even implicit in, even though not explicitly affirmed by sapiential eschatology, bodily resurrection *could easily become explicit* in this eschatology if the right pressures were brought to bear upon it (e.g., by the Easter experience of the first followers of Jesus).

Second, if bodily resurrection *did* become explicit (as I believe it did) within sapiential immortality eschatology, it would not have the same meaning it has in apocalyptic resurrection eschatology. It would not be seen as vindication of the persecuted since this vindication takes place in the very death/exaltation of the Just One. Nor would resurrection appear as a victory over death because death never has any real power over the one who is a child of God. Resurrection would be essentially a manifestation of the meaning for the whole bodyperson of life in God now lived in all its fullness. And, in the case of Jesus, as we will see, it would be a condition of possibility for his post-Easter personal presence to his disciples and his continuing action in the world.

I would suggest that the bodily Resurrection of Jesus in John is presented precisely in terms of sapiential eschatology. The Johannine Resurrection Narrative in John 20 is, therefore, not a concession to the constraints of early Christian tradition. It is a narrative-theological exploration of the Easter experience of the first disciples and the implications of that experience for the spirituality of the Johannine community and later disciples. In other words, the two dimensions of Jesus' paschal mystery, his *Glorification* on the cross (i.e., his passage out of this world to his Father)

---

[13] It is important, however, but beyond the scope of this essay, to note that Jewish anthropology was influenced by Hellenistic philosophy in the immediate pre-Christian period. This is evident in the use of terms such as "incorruption" (ἀφθαρσία) in Wis 2:23 and "immortality" (ἀθανασία) in Wis 3:4. On the other hand, the characteristically biblical approach appears in Wisdom of Solomon in the notion that death is not intended by God but entered the world through the envy of the devil (cf. Wis 2:23-24) in contrast to the notion of death as a natural passage into nonexistence that the enemies of the Wisdom Hero enunciate in Wis 2:1-22.

and his *Resurrection* (i.e., his promised return to his own), though related, are not strictly identical in John. The Glorification is the condition of possibility of the Resurrection. Consequently, the appearances in John are not primarily about *Jesus'* post-death experience but about his *disciples'* experience of his return to them.

John's Anthropology

Closely related to the eschatology of the Fourth Gospel is its anthropology. Much discussion about bodily resurrection is subverted from the start by the fact that modern Westerners tend to read the gospel texts through the lens of a basically dualistic and substantialist philosophical anthropology. John's anthropology, although expressed with Greek vocabulary that has clearly influenced his understanding of the person, is thoroughly rooted in the Hebrew language and sensibility.[14] The pertinent Greek terms, ψυχή (usually translated as "soul"), ζωή ("life"), θάνατος ("death"), σάρξ ("flesh"), αἷμα ("blood"), πνεῦμα ("spirit"), and σῶμα ("body"), constitute a complex semantic field in which all the terms are interrelated and mutually qualifying. Although in English these terms each denote a *component or state* of the human being, in biblical usage they each denote the *whole person* from some perspective or under some aspect. Ignoring this difference can result in serious misunderstanding, such as the tendency of many moderns to hear cannibalistic overtones in Jesus' invitation to eat his flesh and drink his blood in John 6:52-58. It is crucial to understand what these anthropological terms meant in the context of John's first-century Judaism in order to understand how

---

[14] A good introduction to Semitic anthropology is Hans Walter Wolff, *Anthropology of the Old Testament* (Mifflintown, PA: Sigler, 1996; originally published by SCM in 1974). As we have seen with respect to his eschatology, the Gospel of John is not devoid of Hellenistic influences coming probably through Old Testament sapiential materials, esp. Wisdom of Solomon. This influence is controlled, however, by Hebrew understandings of God, the human, and the end of human life. A thorough study of Johannine anthropology, which is completely beyond the scope of this chapter, would proceed by tracing the path from the concrete and stereometric (to use Wolff's term) Hebrew usage through the changes rung on the terms in the Greek of the LXX into the Fourth Gospel. I suspect that the most original development is precisely John's exploitation of the distinction, not possible in Hebrew, but possible in Greek, between σάρξ and σῶμα.

they function in the Fourth Gospel as a whole, but especially in the account of Jesus' Glorification and Resurrection.

Time constraints prevent examining each of these terms, but two of them are critical to our purposes here: σάρξ in relation to αἷμα, that is, flesh and blood, and σῶμα. For moderns σάρξ and αἷμα denote two separable components of the human being, one solid and one liquid. Flesh in John's anthropology is not, however, a part of the human, distinct from bones and blood, but the whole person as natural and mortal.[15] To say that in Jesus the Word of God (λόγος τοῦ θεοῦ) became flesh (σάρξ) is to say that the Word became fully human (i.e., mortal).[16] In the psalms especially we see "flesh" used to speak of humanity in its weakness and mortality: "God remembered that they were flesh, a passing breath that returns not" (Ps 145:21; see also 56:5; 65:3; and elsewhere). In John 6:51 Jesus says that he *is* the living bread come down from heaven and that the bread he will *give* for the life of the world "is [his] flesh." Jesus is not talking about a physical part of himself. He is saying that in giving himself totally in death, which is only possible because he is flesh (i.e., mortal), he gives life to the world as bread gives life to one who eats it.

The most important term in this anthropological semantic field in relation to the Resurrection of Jesus, and the one that John uses in a subtle way that marries Semitic and Hellenistic understandings of the human, is σῶμα, "body."[17] Because moderns tend to think of the body as a distinct substance in the human composite, the physical component as distinguished from the spiritual, they tend to equate it with flesh, itself misunderstood as the soft, solid component in distinction from blood and bones. In other words, body tends to be understood as a physical substance that is integral to but only a part of the person.[18]

---

[15] "Flesh" is a good translation of σάρξ, which is a more differentiated term than the Hebrew *bāśār*, which denotes the human in his or her infirmity or weakness (Wolff, *Anthropology*, 26–31). But the Hebrew term covers the meaning of "body" virtually completely whereas Greek distinguishes σάρξ from σῶμα, a crucial distinction for John's theology of resurrection.

[16] For a very rich treatment of the meaning of flesh in John, see Dorothy Lee, *Flesh and Glory: Symbol, Gender, and Theology in the Gospel of John* (New York: Crossroad, 2002), 29–64.

[17] Here I disagree with Lee, *Flesh and Glory*, 45–46, who suggests that there is no significant difference between σάρξ and σῶμα. I will argue that there is a critically important difference. Jesus rises not as "flesh" (σάρξ) but as "body" (σῶμα).

[18] It is interesting that psychosomatic medicine is discovering in various ways how completely the whole human is "body," not in the reductive sense of being nothing

For John, body is the person in symbolic self-presentation. The person may be living or dead,[19] but it is the whole self, the bodyself, who is living or dead. In Semitic thought, once the body of the dead person begins to decay, to fall apart, the person is no longer a person. Whatever trace of the individual may survive in Sheol, it is not a human being because it does not enjoy subjectivity, community, or union with God.[20] The body is quintessentially the person as self-symbolizing (i.e., as numerically distinct, self-consistent and continuous), a subject who can interact with other subjects and who is present and active in the world.[21] A corpse, in John's vocabulary, is also called a body (John 19:31, 38, 40; 20:12) precisely because it symbolizes the whole person, the bodyself, in its transition from being to nonbeing or from presence to absence. The corpse is the symbolic (i.e., perceptively real) person in the process of becoming absent, and when the person is finally and fully absent, when the corpse has decomposed (which, importantly, does not happen in the

---

but physical matter, but in the sense of being, as a whole, a "bodyperson." This understanding is closer to the biblical understanding than the reductionistic anthropology spawned by the Scientific Revolution and the Enlightenment. Nevertheless, contemporary understandings of the human are still quite dichotomous, as is evidenced by the often mechanistic approaches to medical procedures.

[19] The Hellenistic influence on John's thought as well as the exploitation of the possibilities of the Greek language are clear here. *Bāśār* is used to speak not of a corpse (although *nepeš* occasionally is) but only of living creatures whereas John does not use σάρξ (which the LXX uses for *bāśār*) but σῶμα to speak of the corpses on the cross (19:31) and specifically of the dead body of Jesus (19:38, 40; 20:12) and of his risen body (2:21-22).

[20] I have never seen a better definition of Sheol than that of John L. McKenzie who says in *Dictionary of the Bible*, s.v."Sheol," that Sheol "is less a positive conception of survival than a picturesque denial of all that is meant by life and activity."

[21] I have dealt at length with the concept of symbol, especially as it functions in John's gospel, in *Written That You May Believe*, 63–77. See also, Lee, *Flesh and Glory*, 9–28. A still very important work on symbol in theology and especially on the body as the primary symbol by which a person is present to him- or herself as well as to others is Karl Rahner, "The Theology of the Symbol," *Theological Investigations*, vol. 4: *More Recent Writings*, trans. Kevin Smyth (Baltimore: Helicon Press, 1966), 221–52, esp. 245–52 on the body. Joseph A. Bracken, in "The Body of Christ—An Intersubjective Interpretation," *Horizons* 31 (Spring 2004): 7–21, dialogues with Rahner's position from the standpoint of neo-Whiteheadian metaphysics. It is especially interesting that the term "body" does not seem to play a distinct enough role in Semitic thought to merit a term of its own in distinction from "flesh." The only bodies known to human experience were fleshly ones, either the potential human, the "earth creature" (*hāādām*) of Gen 2:7, or the living person, *nepeš* or *bāśār*.

case of Jesus), it is no longer considered a body. In short, if the pre-Easter Jesus as *flesh*, that is, as mortal human being, was the symbolic presence of God's glory in this world (cf. John 1:14), Jesus as *body* is his own symbolic presence to his contemporaries. Prior to his death, the two, flesh and body (i.e., the mortal human person called Jesus), are coterminous as they are in all humans in this life. The issue of "body" as distinct from "flesh" only arises when Jesus dies and the two are no longer coterminous.[22]

The issue of Jesus' real presence in and after his passage through death dominates the last supper in John (chaps. 13–17) as well as the Resurrection Narrative (chap. 20). Where is the Lord? Has he gone where his disciples cannot follow? Are they orphans, deprived of the glory of God that had been present in the flesh of Jesus? Are future believers condemned to a faith based on hearsay about events in which they did not and do not participate? Unless Jesus is bodily risen, unless he is alive in the full integrity of his humanity (i.e., symbolized bodily), he is not present, either as the presence of humanity in God or as God's divinely human presence to us.

The crucial anthropological-theological issue for the topic of resurrection is then the relation of flesh to body, i.e., of the pre-Easter person of Jesus as mortal human being to the post-Easter person of Jesus as glorified Son of Man. By way of anticipatory summary, I will propose that the relation of flesh to body is precisely what is altered by Jesus' Glorification. In his pre-Easter existence as flesh, the body of Jesus (i.e., his personal symbolic presence) was conditioned by his mortality. He was subject to death and to the limitations of space, time, and causality that natural human life entails. In his Glorification Jesus goes to the Father as a human bodyself, and in his Resurrection he returns to his own in the full integrity of his humanity. His body is real, both continuous and discontinuous with his pre-paschal body. To say that the glorified and

---

[22] I find very suggestive the point made by Mary Coloe in "Like Father, Like Son: The Role of Abraham in Tabernacles—John 8:31-59," *Pacifica* 12 (February 1999): 1–11: "In speaking of Jesus as both Temple and Tabernacle there is no dichotomy as the two are intrinsically related as the flesh (1:14) is related to the body (2:21). The Tabernacle and the Temple serve the same symbolic function even though they recall different historical eras" (p. 4, n. 6). I think that, in fact, flesh and body denote different and subsequent modes (analogous to historical eras) of the presence of Jesus to his disciples. Flesh indicates his career as a mortal and body his glorified life. But the two terms denote the same person and the same presence of the glory of God among humans in that person.

risen Jesus is a bodyperson is to affirm that he is numerically distinct, a personal subject who can be intersubjectively present and active,[23] but he is no longer flesh. And he will be present as this same bodyself throughout post-Easter time in the range of symbols through which his personal presence will be manifest.

III. The Structure and Dynamics of the Johannine Resurrection Narrative

Increasingly, Johannine scholars recognize that the Resurrection Narrative of the Fourth Gospel is not a random collection of interchangeable episodes but an organic literary/theological unity and that the clue to its meaning lies in its structure.[24] There, however, the consensus ends. Scholars have proposed a surprising number of very plausible structures for John 20, including chronological and geographical, numerological and verbal, narrative and dramatic, theological and spiritual ones, many of which are complementary rather than contradictory, even though they lead to different interpretations.[25] Obviously, we cannot review them

---

[23] A fascinating article on the body of Jesus in its displacements, transformations, and resignifications that brings a confirming postmodern light to bear on this topic is Graham Ward, "Bodies: The Displaced Body of Jesus Christ," in *Radical Orthodoxy: A New Theology*, ed. John Milbank, Catherine Pickstock, and Graham Ward (London/ New York: Routledge, 1999): 163–81, esp. 168 on the point here. See also his article, "Transcorporeality: The Ontological Scandal," *Bulletin of the John Rylands University Library of Manchester* 80 (August 1998): 235–52.

[24] Dorothy A. Lee, "Partnership in Easter Faith: The Role of Mary Magdalene and Thomas in John 20," *Journal for the Study of the New Testament* 58 (1995): 37–49. Although she regards the structure as an important indication of meaning, she does not consider the first scene, the Beloved Disciple and Simon Peter at the tomb, to be truly integral to the meaning of the Johannine Resurrection Narrative (pp. 38–40). She considers the pericope a minor prolepsis preparing for chap. 21. I disagree with this position, although I find her treatment of Mary Magdalene and Thomas as "narrative partners" in Easter faith encircling the central episode of the appearance to the disciples enlightening.

[25] Recently, Robert Crotty in "The Two Magdalene Reports on the Risen Jesus in John 20," *Pacifica* 12 (June 1999): 156–68, summarized and criticized a number of the major attempts to decipher the structure of John 20: Francis Moloney, *The Gospel of John*, Sacra Pagina, vol. 4 (Collegeville, MN: Liturgical Press, 1998), 516; Dorothy A. Lee, "Partnership in Easter Faith"; Brendan J. Byrne, "The Faith of the Beloved Disciple and the Community in John 20," *Journal for the Study of the New Testament* 23 (1985): 83–97; Ignace de la Potterie, "Genèse de la foi pascale d'après Jn 20," *New*

here but I will propose two complementary structures, one theological and one spiritual, without implying agreement or disagreement with other theories. My proposal is in service of the purpose of this particular essay, namely, responding to the question of how the body of the glorified Jesus functions in the relationship between Jesus and his post-Easter disciples.

The Theological Structure of John 20

In verses 1-2 the narrative is introduced. Mary Magdalene comes to the tomb in darkness (always negatively symbolic in John), finds the *stone* taken out of the tomb, and reports to Simon Peter and the Beloved Disciple that "they have taken the *Lord* out of the tomb and we do *not know where* they have laid him" (20:2). The "we," even though Mary was alone at the tomb, marks the problem as not merely personal but communal.[26] The programmatic question that drives the first half of the Johannine Resurrection Narrative, verses 3-18, is announced: "Where is the Lord?" after his death. It also suggests one possible answer: Jesus is a corpse. He is truly gone.

In the next episode, verses 3-10, Simon Peter and the Beloved Disciple run to the tomb. The evangelist carefully structures this story so that Peter enters the tomb first and sees its contents: the grave clothes and the face veil, the σουδάριον, of Jesus lying not with the clothes but carefully wrapped up and definitively put aside (20:7).[27] The Beloved Disciple

---

Testament Studies 30 (1984): 26–49; Donatian Mollat, "La foi pascale selon le chapître 20 de l'évangile de saint Jean (Essai de théologie biblique)," in *Resurrexit: Actes du symposium internationale sur la résurrection de Jésus*, ed. E. Dhanis (Rome: Libreria Editrice Vaticana, 1974), 316–34; L. Dupont, C. Lash, G. Levesque, "Recherche sur la structure de Jean 20," *Biblica* 54 (1973): 482–98; Raymond E. Brown, *The Gospel according to John*, Anchor Bible 29A (Garden City, NY: Doubleday, 1970), 965. This list is by no means exhaustive. Crotty, of course, offers his own structuration of the chapter.

[26] Crotty in "The Two Magdalene Reports," 159, follows many commentators in seeing the "we" as an "aporia," a trace of a source text that originally included other women (as we find in all three Synoptic Resurrection Narratives) who accompanied Mary Magdalene to the tomb. Unlike many, however, he suggests that John uses the "we" to make Mary Magdalene a representative of the community versus the "they" who have taken the Lord (164). I prefer this position to the attribution of redactional clumsiness to a writer of John's skill. I also think it carries ecclesiological freight.

[27] ἐντετυλιγμένον is in the perfect tense, denoting a punctual action whose effects are permanent or enduring in effect.

enters second and sees what he did not see from the outside when he first peered in. From outside he had seen only the grave clothes (20:5). Inside, he sees also the face veil, and we are told that he "saw and believed," an expression John uses for the appropriate faith response to a sign (e.g., 2:23; 6:30; 11:40).

This sign, the face cloth now laid aside, is both continuous and discontinuous with the signs done by Jesus in his public ministry. One characteristic of signs in both dispensations is that they are symbolic and therefore intrinsically ambiguous. Everyone present saw the healed Man Born Blind in chapter 9 and the raised Lazarus in chapter 11. Some saw and believed. Others saw and did not believe. In this episode both Simon Peter and the Beloved Disciple see the face cloth. The Beloved Disciple believes; Peter does not.

But this sign is also different from those worked by the pre-Easter Jesus. Jesus himself is not visibly present doing a work. In this episode the disciples are offered as sign an object that must be interpreted as revelatory, probably in terms of the face veil of Moses, which he wore to shield the Israelites from the glory of his face but removed when he dealt "face to face" with God (cf. Exod 34:29-35).[28]

The finale of the scene (v. 9), however, has often defied exegetes: "for as yet they did not understand the scripture, that he must rise from the dead." So, if not the Resurrection, what did the Beloved Disciple believe? I would suggest that he believed what Jesus had repeatedly said of his death (e.g., 13:1; 16:28; 17:1; 17:24), namely, that by it he would be glorified. The Beloved Disciple believed that on the cross, though he truly died, Jesus was exalted into the presence of God. The face cloth of his flesh (i.e., his mortality in which his glory had been veiled during his pre-Easter career) is now definitively laid aside. Jesus, the New Moses, has gone up the mountain to seal the New Covenant between God and the New Israel.

The reader now has the beginning of the answer to the question, "Where is the Lord?" He is with God. He is glorified. But there is more, something the disciples do not yet understand, namely, that Jesus is not only glorified but risen from the dead.

In the next episode, verses 11-18, Mary Magdalene is again at the tomb. This scene is redolent with allusions to the garden of the first creation

---

[28] For the linguistic argument for this Old Testament background for John's use of σουδάριον, see Schneiders, *Written That You May Believe*, 207–8.

and especially the place of trysting of the Song of Solomon, the wedding song of the covenant between Yahweh and Israel. In the tomb Mary sees not grave clothes and face veil but two angels sitting, one at the head and one at the feet of the place where the body (σῶμα) of Jesus had lain. This verbal picture, and even the words, recall the golden throne, the "mercy seat," of the ark of the covenant (cf. Exod 37:6-9 and the LXX version, Exod 38:5-8), which was guarded by two cherubim, one at either end of "the meeting place of God and humans."[29] Mary Magdalene is weeping in desolation at the absence of Jesus, whom she clearly equates with a corpse that has been taken away. When Jesus, the Good Shepherd, calls her by name, she turns: she is converted from her despair to recognition of him as indeed the "teacher" she had known in his pre-paschal life. There is infinitely more in this rich scene, but for our present purpose, it provides the second dimension of the answer to the question, "Where is the Lord?" He has returned to his own. When Mary comes proclaiming (ἀγγέλλουσα) the Easter Gospel to those who are now the "brothers and sisters" of Jesus, she says explicitly, "I have seen the Lord" (20:18). The Beloved Disciple saw and believed through a sign that Jesus was glorified, alive with God. Mary Magdalene has experienced him risen, returned to his own.

With the proclamation of the Easter Gospel, that Jesus is both glorified and risen, the narrative enters its second phase, verses 19-29, which takes place not at the dawn of the new era in the garden of the tomb to the first apostle but in the evening of the first day of that new era, in Jerusalem "where the disciples were gathered" as a community. The question "Where is the Lord?" now gives way to the question that dominates the second half of the Johannine Resurrection Narrative, "How can the risen Lord be experienced?" This first scene of this second part, verses 19-23, Jesus' coming to the community, is the centerpiece of the Johannine Resurrection Narrative. Despite locked doors, Jesus rises up in the midst of the community. Behind the Greek (ἔστη εἰς τὸ μέσον, literally, Jesus "stood into the midst" of the community) stands the Aramaic verb for "rise up," which can refer either to standing up physically or rising from the dead. As he had promised in his first public act in the temple of Jerusalem, Jesus, on the third day, raises up the new temple of his body

---

[29] Richard J. Clifford, "Exodus," in *New Jerome Biblical Commentary*, ed. Raymond E. Brown, Joseph A. Fitzmyer, and Roland E. Murphy (Englewood, NJ: Prentice-Hall, 1990), 3:49, 56.

in the midst of the community. In the temple Jesus' opponents had challenged him:

> What sign can you show us. . . . Jesus answered them, "Destroy this temple, and in three days I will raise it up." . . . But he was speaking of the temple of his body [σῶμα]. When, therefore, he was raised from the dead, his disciples remembered that he had said this; and they believed the scripture and the word that Jesus had spoken. (John 2:18-22)

The scene then unfolds in two actions, both inaugurated by Jesus' "Peace to you," fulfilling his promise to give them, upon his return, a peace the world cannot give (cf. 14:27; 16:33). The character of the first action is signaled by the verb δείκνυμι ("show" or "manifest"), a Johannine term denoting revelation. Jesus shows them his hands and his side (i.e., he reveals to them the meaning for them of his Glorification), and they rejoice at this revelation that the Lord himself is indeed in their midst, glorified but still marked with the signs of his paschal mystery. His bodyself is both continuous and discontinuous with the One they had known who had promised that his going away would constitute a new coming to them (14:28).[30]

The second action, following the repeated gift of peace, is a commissioning of this New People as God had commissioned Jesus. He breathes on them and says "Receive the Holy Spirit." The verb "breathe" (ἐμφύσαω) is a *hapax legomenon*, occurring only here in the whole New Testament. It occurs only twice[31] in the Old Testament: in Genesis 2:7 when God, at the first creation, breathes life into the earth-creature and it becomes the first living human being and in Ezekiel 37:9-10 when the prophet in

---

[30] Both verbs in this text are in the present. One would expect "after I have gone away I will come back to you," but instead we have, literally, "I go away and I come to you." It might be paraphrased, "My going away is my coming to you," i.e., my departure from you in the flesh is my coming to you in the Spirit. In fact, this is why it is expedient or necessary for the disciples that Jesus depart (cf. John 16:7). As flesh, he would be unable to establish the kind of mutual interiority with his disciples that he can in the Spirit who will be with them and in them (cf. John 14:16-17).

[31] Actually, the verb appears four times in the LXX, the two instances adduced here, plus Wis 15:11, which recalls the enlivening of Adam and thus is not an independent third instance, and 1 Kgs 17:21, recounting the prophet Elijah's reanimation of the son of the widow of Zarephath. The LXX inaccurately (but perhaps deliberately) translates the Hebrew for "stretched" or "measured" as "breathed," perhaps alluding to the creation narrative.

God's name breathes life into the dry bones to re-create, to raise from the dead, the people Israel. In this Easter scene it occurs for the third time when Jesus breathes the promised Spirit of the New Covenant into the community of disciples, creating them as the New Israel.

The structure of this scene is that of the Sinai covenant experience, in which the great theophany on the mount was followed by the giving of the Law, which made Israel the People of God. Through the prophet Ezekiel God had promised a New Covenant:

> I will make a covenant of peace with them; it shall be an everlasting covenant with them; and I will bless them and multiply them, and will set my sanctuary in the midst of them for evermore. My dwelling place shall be with them; and I will be their God and they shall be my people. The nations will know that I the Lord sanctify Israel, when my sanctuary is in the midst of them for evermore. (Ezek 37:26-28; cf. 34:25 and Isa 54:10)

God now appears not in thunder and lightning but in the person of Jesus glorified and risen. And as promised in Ezekiel 36:27-28 ("I will put my spirit within you, and make you follow my statutes"), the Holy Spirit, the New Law, is poured forth in their hearts. Jesus, as God had promised, here establishes the New Covenant with the New Israel raising up in its midst the New Temple of his body. Thus is the Church founded, commissioned to continue Jesus' mission of taking away the sin of the world and holding fast all those whom God had given him. It is important to note that the Evangelist does not tell us that Jesus, having completed his work, leaves or departs. Jesus has definitively returned to his own. He will come and come again, but he never leaves. That he is present and knows what transpires in his community is clear from what follows.

The final scene in the Johannine Resurrection Narrative, verses 24-29, concluding with 30-31, the Thomas episode and its conclusion, at first seems out of place.[32] Nothing in the preceding scene suggested that

---

[32] Although I cannot deal with it here, there is a hypothesis that seems to have some merit to the effect that this episode might have had anti-Gnostic purposes. Mary Magdalene and Thomas are important figures in the Gnostic literature, and they play very significant roles in John's gospel that they do not play in the Synoptic resurrection accounts. See April D. DeConick, "'Blessed Are Those Who Have Not Seen' (John 20:29): Johannine Dramatization of an Early Christian Discourse," in *Nag Hammadi Library after Fifty Years* (Leiden: Brill, 1997), 381–98, who proposes that the Thomas episode was composed to refute the Thomasine Christians in Syria whose character-

anyone was missing when Jesus appeared on Easter night. Thomas is identified as "the twin."[33] His double identity is immediately specified: he is both "one of the Twelve" and thus was a companion of the pre-Easter Jesus and participant in the pre-Easter signs, and he was "not with" the gathered disciples on Easter night when Jesus appeared and thus is one of those who will know the Resurrection not through an Easter experience but through the testimony of the Church, "We have seen the Lord."

Thomas refuses this new structure of faith, refuses to enter this new dispensation. He insists that he will believe only if he can touch the very wounds of Jesus, only if he can return to the dispensation of pre-Easter faith, only if he can continue to relate to Jesus in the flesh. Note that Thomas is not spontaneously mistaking the glorified Jesus for the pre-paschal Jesus, as had Mary Magdalene. He is demanding that Jesus be for him as he had been prior to the Glorification. And note further that Thomas does not "doubt," as is so often averred. He refuses: "I will not believe." In John's gospel believing and refusing to believe are always a matter of free choice, not the natural response to irrefutable evidence or the lack thereof.

Jesus comes again, a week later, on Sunday night, the time of the early Church's eucharistic celebrations. Again he "rises up in the midst of them," greets them with peace, but this time, though the doors are shut marking the boundaries of the Church community, there is no mention of fear of the authorities. Jesus' initial gift of peace has cast out fear. We are in post-paschal time. But Jesus directly addresses Thomas whose inner thoughts and outer words he knows perfectly. "I know mine and mine know me" (John 10:14).

He invites Thomas not to do what Thomas had demanded, to physically probe the wounds in his hands and side in order to verify his physical resuscitation, but to a different but just as real experience of his

---

istic soteriology appears in the Gospel of Thomas. She proposes that the Gospel of Thomas may date from 70 to 80 CE and thus might have been available to the Fourth Evangelist.

[33] M. de Jonge, "Signs and Works in the Fourth Gospel," in *Miscellanea Neotesta-mentica* 2, Supplements to Novum Testamentum 48 (Leiden: Brill, 1978), 119, calls Thomas "a borderline case" because he is the last of those who see signs and the first of those who must believe on the word of witness. I agree that he stands on the border between the Easter experience and later experience of the risen Jesus, but I do not think that signs are replaced by the word of witness. Rather, one kind of sign gives way to a new kind of sign.

true identity. He says, "Bring here your finger and see my hands." One does not "see" with one's finger. The imperative, ἴδε, "Behold!" or "See!" as M. de Goedt pointed out many years ago, functions in the Fourth Gospel as part of a revelation formula.[34] The invitation is not to see physically but to grasp what cannot be seen with the eyes of flesh (e.g., that Nathanael is a true Israelite without guile or that the Beloved Disciple on Calvary is now the true son of the Mother of Jesus). The wounds of Jesus are not a proof of physical reality but the source of a true understanding of the meaning of Jesus' revelatory death.

Then the invitation reaches deeper. Jesus commands Thomas to put his hand into his open side from which had issued the life-giving blood and water, symbol of the gift of the Spirit in baptism and the Eucharist that Jesus had handed over in his death and had focused in the gift to the community a week earlier when Thomas was absent. This is followed immediately by the imperative μὴ γίνου ἄπιστος ἀλλὰ πιστίς. Note that Jesus does not say, "Do not doubt." Ἄπιστος means to refuse to believe, to be unfaithful, to be treacherous. Thomas's immediate response, not an attempt to touch Jesus physically but an acknowledgment of what he can grasp only by faith, makes clear his conversion from unfaithful to faithful, his transition from his stubborn absorption with the flesh of Jesus, "Unless I touch physically I will not believe," to his self-gift to the Risen One, "My Lord and my God." In other words, Jesus says to Thomas not what the Lukan Jesus says to his disciples who disbelieve their eyes through startled joy: "Feel me and see that I have flesh and bones, that I am not a ghost," but rather "Thomas, grasp in faith what my saving death means and appropriate in faith the fruits of that death, the Spirit poured forth from my open side." He is saying in effect what he said to Simon Peter at the Last Supper, "Unless you enter by faith into the new dispensation inaugurated by my Glorification you can have no part with me."

Jesus welcomes Thomas's conversion unreservedly and confirms his Easter faith by one of the only two macarisms in the Fourth Gospel. Jesus equates the two kinds of believing. Faith based on seeing pre-paschal signs, which was appropriate to the first dispensation, is supplanted by post-paschal faith that will be based on a new kind of sign, like the folded-up face veil, the apostolic testimony of Mary Magdalene and the

---

[34] Michel de Goedt, "Un schème de révélation dans le quatrième évangile," *New Testament Studies* 8 (January 1962): 142–50.

rest of the disciples, the words of Scripture, which will now be mediated by the Church. "Blessed are those [now including Thomas] not seeing and believing." It is not later disciples who are assimilated to Thomas but Thomas who is assimilated to the later believers. The pre-paschal era is over, even for those who participated in it.

The Evangelist then concludes the gospel by directly addressing the disciples of the post-Easter dispensation. The pre-Easter Jesus, says the Evangelist, did many visible signs, only some of which are written in the gospel. But the written gospel has exactly the same function in the faith of later disciples that the signs Jesus performed in Palestine had for the apostolic generation.[35] Through believing, these later disciples will have life in Jesus' name just as did his pre-Easter companions. Contrary to what some exegetes, who insert an adversative conjunction between the two parts of verse 29, would suggest, namely, that Jesus derogates Thomas's faith based on seeing and exalts the faith of those who have not seen signs and yet have believed, Jesus does not assign superiority to either the first generation's experience or that of later disciples. As Dorothy Lee has said well, the faith of future believers is dependent on the witness of the apostolic community but in no way limited by that dependence: "Thomas's confession is a narrative bridge between Easter Sunday and the life of the believing community."[36] The point is neither that faith in response to signs is defective nor that sense experience, seeing and hearing and touching, will have no further role in faith. The mode, not the fact, of seeing must change because the mode, not the fact, of Jesus' bodily presence to his disciples has changed.

The Dialectic of Sense Experience and Believing

We turn now, very briefly, to make explicit the dialectic between sense experience and believing that emerges as the spiritual structure of the Johannine Resurrection Narrative before drawing conclusions about the

---

[35] Peter Judge, "A Note on Jn 20,29," in *Festschrift Frans Neirynck*, ed. F. Van Segbroeck, C. M. Tuckett, G. Van Belle, J. Verheyden, vol. 3 (Leuven: University Press, 1992), 2183–92, cites U. Schnelle and D. A. Carson as scholars who, like himself, take the position that the Thomas incident itself is a sign and the gospel will function in the same way for later believers.

[36] Lee, "Partnership in Easter Faith," 48.

body of the risen Jesus from the Mary Magdalene and Thomas incidents specifically. (See fig. 3 in the appendix.)

After the introductory verses in which the question "Where is the Lord?" is introduced we have a scene in which Jesus does not appear visibly. The Beloved Disciple comes to faith in the Glorification of Jesus upon encountering a sign, the folded face veil. At the other end of the Johannine Resurrection Narrative is the Evangelist's conclusion assuring later disciples that in Scripture, in which Jesus also does not appear visibly, Jesus is really and salvifically encountered. In other words, at the beginning and the end of the Resurrection Narrative is an encounter with Jesus through signs, through sensible material realities, in which Jesus does not appear in visible form. Both of these scenes recount experiences that are historically realistic, the kinds of experiences believers have in "ordinary time," if you will, as they taste bread and wine, hear words, feel water.

Moving inward we have three scenes that take place in "extraordinary time," that are clearly a theological narratizing of spiritual experience, real but not physical, rather than the recounting of ordinary human events taking place in ordinary time. In the very middle is the scene of the establishment of the covenant community that will be in the world the ordinary mode of the glorified Jesus' presence and action (i.e., will be his body). Assured of his identity and presence and enlivened by his Spirit, the community will forgive sins and hold fast in communion all those whom God will entrust to it as Jesus took away the sin of the world (cf. 1:29) and held fast all those the Father had given him (cf. 6:37; 6:39; 10:27-29; 17:12; 18:9).

Flanking this historicized narration of the founding of the Church as the fully realized bodily but nonphysical and definitive presence of Jesus in the world are two episodes that occur in an "in-between" time/place, what we might call "Easter time," when Jesus is both present and absent. Their purpose is to narratively unfold the intrinsic relationship between Jesus himself, as a distinct bodyperson, and the ecclesial community that is his body in the world. In other words, they are about the relationship of Jesus to Christ, mediated by the category "body," the body of the risen Jesus, which is the principle of the ecclesial Body of Christ. The two are identical, though not reductively so—distinct but inseparable. It is time, then, to examine these two scenes in terms of Jesus' seemingly contradictory commands to Mary Magdalene not to touch him and to Thomas the Twin to touch him.

IV. Conclusions on Touching the Risen Jesus

Both Mary Magdalene and Thomas the Twin undergo conversions that consist in turning away from a mode of experience that is no longer possible and turning toward a new, unfamiliar, but equally real mode of experiencing Jesus. Both, in response to a negative imperative of Jesus (what they must not do: do not touch, do not be faithless) followed by a positive imperative (what they are now called to: find me in the community, recognize me in believing), must pass over from the pre- to the post-Easter dispensation. But the emphasis in each episode is different. The two actors are in different positions in the story, Mary Magdalene bridging the pre-Easter with the Easter time; Thomas the Twin is bridging the Easter with the post-Easter time. And their experiences respond to the two presiding questions: Where is the Lord encountered? How is the Lord encountered?

Mary Magdalene is the first pre-Easter disciple to encounter the risen Lord. She erroneously thinks that the past dispensation has been reinstated. Things will be as they had always been. Literal misunderstanding in John's gospel is a literary technique to describe growth in faith. Mary reaches out to touch Jesus, to relate to him as she had in the past, using a form of address suitable to that time, "Rabbouni," but Jesus forestalls her attempt: "Do not touch me."

There is no textual basis for the often expressed opinion that Mary was clinging hysterically to Jesus or trying to hold him back from ascending.[37] The verb is ἅπτω, "touch," not κρατέω, "grasp" or "hold on to." (The verb κρατέω is in John's vocabulary, and he uses it in its normal sense in the very next scene, in 20:23.) Jesus' response is μή μου ἅπτου. The imperative verb is in the imperfect tense, reflecting an ongoing or continuous activity, and the negative particle is in the emphatic position. The point is that physical "touching"—which is an apt metonomy for the physically mediated historical experience of two people relating "in the flesh," that is, as mortal human beings—has come to an end. Jesus says: "Go to my brothers and sisters." The place where Mary will now encounter Jesus as he really is, glorified and risen, is the community. Mary must pass over from the pre-Easter to the Easter dispensation. Her

---

[37] See Lee, "Partnership in Easter Faith," 42, against this interpretation, which, however, Frank J. Matera, in "John 20:1-18," *Interpretation* 43 (1989): 405, and Teresa Okure, "The Significance Today of Jesus' Commission to Mary Magdalene," *International Review of Mission* 81 (April 1992): 180, both defend.

proclamation to the other disciples makes clear that she has indeed made that transition. She no longer speaks of "Rabbouni." As first apostle of the Resurrection, she proclaims "I have seen the Lord."[38] In the Thomas episode things are quite different. The Easter experience has taken place. The ecclesial community, constituted by the New Covenant mediated by Jesus on Easter night, proclaims to Thomas, "We have seen the Lord." Mary was the first of the Easter community of apostolic witnesses. Thomas is the first of the post-Easter generation who must respond in faith to their witness.

Thomas does not, like Mary, simply misunderstand his experience; he categorically refuses to believe the testimony of the community. He says, in effect, "You may have seen the Lord, but I haven't, and until I do see physically I will not believe." Thomas does not deny their experience. He simply says he will not substitute their experience for his. What he misunderstands is that it is not their experience that he must accept in place of his own but their witness upon which his own experience must be grounded. It is the problem of all believers down through the centuries who must somehow grasp that faith is not accepting something as true on the basis of external authority. It is allowing the testimony of the Church to initiate one into personal experience through the Spirit of the living God present in Jesus.

It is important to note that Thomas's attitude would have been just as problematic during the time of the pre-Easter Jesus as it was after Easter.

---

[38] Although discussing this point is beyond the scope of this essay I want to note the growing consensus among biblical scholars and theologians that Mary Magdalene is, by every criterion available in the New Testament, an apostle. Pheme Perkins, in "'I Have Seen the Lord' (John 20:18): Women Witnesses to the Resurrection," *Interpretation* 46 (1992): 31–41, says that the Johannine Mary Magdalene episode at least establishes a woman as an independent witness to the Resurrection. Teresa Okure in "The Significance Today of Jesus' Commission to Mary Magdalene," 184–85, correctly makes the point that Mary Magdalene is not simply "the apostle to the apostles," as if her mission ended once theirs began. She is the apostle commissioned to announce the Resurrection to the Church. Her role is not limited, however, to announcing the Resurrection (like the Emmaus disciples), but she is commissioned (like Paul) to proclaim the Good News, i.e., the new status of believers as children of God. Lee in "Partnership in Easter Faith," 46–47, says that she is the first apostle, the first disciple of the Risen Lord, and the representative of the community of faith. A major exegetical/theological study of all the New Testament material on Mary Magdalene, and which comes to virtually the same conclusion, is Gerald O'Collins and Daniel Kendall, "Mary Magdalene as Major Witness to Jesus' Resurrection," *Theological Studies* 48, no. 4 (December 1987): 631–46. The growing consensus about Mary Magdalene's apostolic identity appeals primarily to the Johannine text.

Sense experience plays an important role in faith but not as physical proof of the "facts." One could eat the bread at the Sea of Tiberias and, precisely as Jesus says to the crowds who sought him afterward, not see the sign of Jesus as the bread of life (cf. 6:26) but be seeking a reliable guarantee of material food. The Pharisees in chapter 9 saw the blind man healed and the Jews in chapter 11 saw Lazarus called forth from the tomb after four days. So one could probe the wounds of the risen Jesus and not see the sign of his real presence. Similarly, in post-paschal time, Jesus is available, whether in Eucharist or Scripture or mystical experience, only to faith.

Jesus, who is already "there" because he knows what Thomas has said, appears in the community from which Thomas had been separated not only physically but spiritually. And Jesus' being there, his real presence, is precisely what the community mediates to Thomas by its testimony. The community is not reporting a past event that Thomas accidentally missed and now has to accept on someone else's word. It is witnessing, pointing to, a present reality available to him in faith as it is to them in faith. Jesus' command to Thomas is: "Be not unbelieving, but believing." The invitation to touch, as we have seen, is not an invitation to physical verification that cannot cause or ground faith but to sacramental experience, to seeing what the crucifixion really means, to appropriating what the open side really offers.

Sacramental experience is not disembodied. It is an experience of the spiritual precisely in the material. Jesus invites all of his post-Easter disciples to an experience that is in continuity with but different from the faith based on the signs performed in the pre-Easter dispensation. The continuity consists in the material mediation, the actual sensible experience of seeing, hearing, tasting, touching. The mediating material, however, is no longer perishable bread at the Sea of Tiberias but the eucharistic meal flowing from the open side of the glorified Jesus, no longer physical eyesight restored in the waters of Siloam but the baptismal opening of the eyes of faith in the water pouring from that same source. Thomas signifies his conversion in his exclamation, "My Lord and my God," which is a response not to flesh probed but to what Thomas could not see physically but only in faith. He and all later disciples come to faith through an experience of signs, material mediations of spiritual reality. But the signs in the new dispensation are not the visible flesh of the pre-Easter Jesus but the sacramental body of the Lord that is, and is mediated by, the Church.

The whole second half of the Johannine Resurrection Narrative is an unfolding of the new dispensation of signs that will supplant the signs of the pre-Easter dispensation. The fundamental sign, the ur-sacrament, of the really present Jesus is the ecclesial community itself, which is now the Body of Christ, the New Temple raised up in the world. The community witnesses in the word of proclamation rooted in Scripture, through the celebration of the sacraments, through its ministry of reconciliation, through its community of mutual love that washes feet and lays down life, and through the mutual indwelling of its members in Jesus in contemplative prayer. The response to that witness, from the first disciples and down through the ages, is the recognition of Jesus as Lord and God to which Jesus replies, "Blessed are you . . . because you believe."

The purpose of these two episodes of "touching" is to help the reader make the same transitions that Mary Magdalene and Thomas the Twin had to make, from a romantic fantasy of contemporaneity with the pre-Easter Jesus through the paschal experience of death and new life to faith in the glorified and risen Lord. But in making this transition two extremes must be avoided. One is to see the Church not as a mediation of the risen Jesus himself but as an exhaustive substitute for a Jesus who no longer exists. The other is a gnostic attempt to relate to Jesus in a purely spiritual Jesus-and-I spirituality that rejects the sacramental structure of the ecclesial body of the Lord as a merely human organization that plays no necessary or essential role in our encounter with Jesus. Mary Magdalene had to realize that the Church is the *Body of Christ* (Jesus is not a corpse), and Thomas had to realize that the *Church* is the Body of Christ (not an unsatisfactory substitute for him).

The ecclesial community, doing in the world the works that Jesus did (cf. 14:12), is truly the Body of Christ, the corporate person who is the organ of Jesus' salvific action in the world. But this can only be the case if Jesus himself, the principle of that ecclesial body, is actually alive in the full integrity of his personal humanity. This is the significance of maintaining that Jesus is bodily risen from the dead (i.e., that which body signifies, namely, numerical identity, personal subjectivity grounding interpersonal presence and effective action in the world) and is verified in him after his death on the cross. Jesus is no longer in the flesh (i.e., he is no longer mortal). He is no longer subject to the conditions of time, space, causality. The description of the tomb as empty of his corpse, his being not recognizable to Mary Magdalene, his being able to appear in the midst of his disciples despite locked doors, his knowing what Thomas thought and said in his absence are narrative devices for insisting on both the real bodiliness and the non-fleshliness of the risen Jesus.

If Jesus is not a real, distinct, personal subject, a real bodyperson, there is no ontological foundation for the Jesus mysticism that has been a constant feature of the Church's spirituality, at least from the stoning of Stephen who saw Jesus standing at the right hand of God and Paul who learned that it was Jesus whom he was persecuting, down to our own day. But if Jesus is merely physically resuscitated, if he is still in the flesh, then he cannot be mediated by a community from which he would be not only distinct but separate.

In summary, John's Resurrection Narrative is not about Jesus' vindication after his shameful death. It is about where and how his disciples, the first generation symbolized by Mary Magdalene and all those who were not with them when Jesus came symbolized by Thomas the Twin, will encounter Jesus as their Lord and God.

In the gospel itself believing is presented as a response to seeing the works of Jesus and hearing his revelatory discourse. Johannine scholars continue to argue over whether John's gospel was written to delegitimate faith based on seeing signs in favor of faith based solely on hearing or to present seeing and hearing as indispensable mediators of revelation.[39] I believe that the very nature of the Incarnation as the symbolization of the Wisdom/Word of God in sensible form indicates the latter position. The Word of God became flesh; we have seen his glory; our hands have handled the Word of Life. And he is still with us.

Precisely because Jesus appeared in the flesh (i.e., as a mortal human being), however, his human career as flesh had to come to an end. But if, as I believe to be the case, the dynamic of sensible experience mediating faith is a permanent feature of the revelatory economy of salvation, it must somehow continue after the departure of the pre-Easter Jesus through death. Chapter 20 of John's gospel, enlightened by the Last Discourses in which Jesus explains his "going away" through death as a new mode of "coming to" his disciples in the Spirit, is an attempt to elucidate how the sense-experience-mediating-faith dynamic is realized in a new mode after the Resurrection. The Mary Magdalene and Thomas the Twin episodes explore the personal appropriation by disciples of the

---

[39] For a good overview of this dispute ranging from those who regard John's gospel as a critique and/or rejection of faith based on signs through those who see signs as playing a critical role in faith only during the career of the pre-Easter Jesus to those seeing signs as permanently important in faith even though the kind of sign is different after the Resurrection, see Judge, "A Note on Jn 20,29." My position belongs in the last category.

new location and the new mode of experience of Jesus, risen bodily and now acting through his ecclesial body. The category of body, no longer equated with flesh, body that is material in the sense of being a principle of individuation but not in the sense of being a principle of physicality, is used by the Evangelist to assure the reader that it is Jesus himself who is not only glorified in God's presence but has returned to us and that we will see him and hear him and touch him, experience his real presence in our lives and in our world, through our participation in the life of the ecclesial community. But we are also assured that we are, and are challenged to be, individually and communally, his real presence, his body in the world. Jesus says that "in that day," namely, our own post-Easter day, "you will know that I am in the Father and you in me and I in you" (John 14:20) and that "the works that I do you also will do, and greater than these will you do" (John 14:12).

Chapter 3

The Resurrection of the Body in the Fourth Gospel: Key to Johannine Spirituality

I. Introduction

I last saw Raymond Brown a few weeks before he died. By strange coincidence our conversation on that day turned to death, its inevitability, its meaning for us personally and for our work, and what lay beyond that mysterious frontier. Ray told me he had been asked if, following the publication of his massive *Death of the Messiah*, he planned to write a work on the Resurrection. He had replied, "I prefer to research that topic face to face." It was such a quintessentially Raymond Brown remark, deep spirituality buried in a self-effacing *bon mot*. Little could either of us have guessed how soon that research would begin. I venture as fool where his wisdom forbade him to tread. I hope he will accept this essay on the Resurrection as a tribute to his enormous contribution to scholarship, his even greater gift to the Church, his wise mentorship, and our friendship.

Originally published as "The Resurrection (of the Body) in the Fourth Gospel: A Key to Johannine Spirituality," in *Life in Abundance: Studies of John's Gospel in Tribute to Raymond E. Brown*, ed. John R. Donahue (Collegeville, MN: Liturgical Press, 2005), 168–98.

My purpose in this lecture is to explore the contribution of the Fourth Gospel (henceforth FG, which I will also refer to as John)[1] to our understanding of the meaning of the Resurrection of Jesus, which is the foundation and the distinguishing feature of Christian faith. As such, it is, or should be, at the center of Christian spirituality, that is, of the lived experience of the faith. I am going to propose that bodiliness is the linchpin of resurrection faith. The Church professes belief in the resurrection of the body. The bodiliness of the risen Jesus, however, is often discreetly circumvented in both scholarly treatments of and preaching on the subject of resurrection. I suspect that the reason for this reticence is that, for the post-Enlightenment critical mind, bodily resurrection is imaginatively implausible and thus intellectually unassimilable.[2] On this topic, faith seeking understanding runs into an imaginative impasse. The Gospel of John might offer the critical mind some resources for negotiating that impasse.

I will proceed in five unequal steps. First, I will lay out some methodological presuppositions for my reading of the text of John 20, the Resurrection Narrative. Second, I will briefly sketch the contours of Johannine anthropology and, third, offer a brief synopsis of Johannine eschatology, particularly as it differs from that of the Synoptics. Fourth, I will look at the texts in John that form the context for the interpretation of 20:19-23, the raising of the body of Jesus as the New Temple.[3] Finally, I will interpret John 20:19-23, within the context of the chapter as a whole, as the

---

[1] For convenience I will refer to the Fourth Gospel and to the evangelist as "John" without thereby implying any particular position on the identity or gender of this individual. I basically accept the reigning consensus of scholars that the Fourth Gospel was written, sometime between 80 and 110 (probably around 90) CE, by an anonymous, second-generation Christian who was part of a "school" within the Johannine cluster of communities. See Maarten J. J. Menken, "Envoys of God's Envoy: On the Johannine Communities," *Proceedings of the Irish Biblical Association* 23 (2000): 45–60, for a good summary of the results of scholarship concerning the matrix out of which this gospel emerged.

[2] I have dealt with this issue at some length in chapter 1 of this book, "The Bodily Resurrection of Jesus and Christian Spirituality."

[3] Throughout this chapter, I am indebted to the excellent work of Mary Coloe, *God Dwells with Us: Temple Symbolism in the Fourth Gospel* (Collegeville, MN: Liturgical Press, 2001). Her treatment of Jesus' action in the temple in John 2 is the best interpretation I have read, largely because it places this mysterious episode within the theological context of the gospel as a whole rather than reading it as a Johannine version of the Synoptic accounts, which have somewhat different functions within their respective passion narratives.

textual expression of Johannine faith in the personal Glorification of the human Jesus, his bodily Resurrection, and the spirituality that expresses that faith.

II. Presuppositions

The enormous volume of scholarship on the Resurrection in general and John in particular[4] requires me to focus my approach in this chapter clearly. My basic presupposition is that the text itself, i.e., the literary work that is the FG as it now stands, and specifically that text as a narrative, both mediates theological claims and intends to transform its readers through their engagement with it.[5] As the Evangelist states explicitly in the first conclusion of the gospel, "these things have been written that you may believe that Jesus is the Christ, the Son of God, and that believing you may have life in his name" (John 20:31). In other words, I am using literary criticism to access the theology and spirituality of the gospel rather than historical criticism to establish the facts.[6] I am

---

[4] Giovanni Ghiberti published two exhaustive bibliographies on the Resurrection covering material up to 1974: "Bibliografia sull'esegesi dei racconti pasquali e sul problema della risurrezione di Gesù (1957–68)," *La Scuola Cattolica* 97, Supplemento bibliografica 2 (1969): 68–84, and "Bibliografia sulla Risurrezione di Gesù (1920–73), in *Resurrexit* (Città del Vaticano: Vaticana, 1974), 643–764. A Portuguese bibliography on the Resurrection including more than five hundred items was published in 1989: M. Isidro Alves, "Ressurreição e Fé Pascal," *Didiskalia* 29 (1989): 277–541. Three recent international symposia on resurrection that supply bibliography are the following: *The Resurrection: An Interdisciplinary Symposium on the Resurrection of Jesus*, ed. Stephen T. Davis, Daniel Kendall, and Gerald O'Collins (Oxford: University Press, 1996); *Resurrection* (papers from the conference on resurrection on February 21, 1998, in Roehampton, England), ed. Stanley E. Porter, Michael A. Hayes, and David Tombs, Journal for the Study of the New Testament Supplement Series 186, Roehampton Institute London Papers 5 (Sheffield: Sheffield Academic Press, 1999); *Auferstehung— Resurrection: Fourth Durham-Tübingen Research Symposium; Resurrection, Transfiguration and Exaltation in Old Testament, Ancient Judaism and Early Christianity*, Tübingen, September 1999, ed. Friedrich Avemarie and Hermann Lichtenberger (Tübingen: J. C. B. Mohr, 2001). Recent bibliography on the Resurrection in John can be found in John Paul Heil, "Blood and Water: The Death and Resurrection of Jesus in John 18–21," *The Catholic Biblical Quarterly* 27 (1995): 172–80.

[5] See Gail R. O'Day, *Revelation in the Fourth Gospel: Narrative Mode and Theological Claim* (Philadelphia: Fortress Press, 1986), for an excellent treatment of this subject.

[6] See the very helpful excursus by Francis J. Moloney, "Excursus: Narrative Approaches to the Fourth Gospel," in *An Introduction to the Gospel of John*, ABRL (New

not asking about the history of the text, either its sources or its redaction, although I will pay attention to historical-critical issues when appropriate.[7] Nor am I concerned with the historicity of the events recounted, i.e., "what really happened" after Jesus' death. My research has convinced me that Jesus' dead body was buried and the location of his tomb was known to certain of his disciples, that he actually rose from death to new life, and that he really appeared to his disciples during a certain period of time. In other words, I am assuming that the resurrection account in the gospel is true and has a historical basis even though the meaning of "history" differs in relation to different aspects of "the hour." My concern, however, is with the resurrection account in the Johannine text as we now have it. Consequently, I subscribe to the basic *methodological* presupposition of literary criticism in general, namely, the narrative unity of the final text.[8]

This methodological choice rests on the *theological* presupposition that the mediator of biblical revelation is the text itself rather than the historical events to which the text witnesses. In other words, the locus of revelation is not behind the text but in the text.[9] Of course, unless something had happened on the first Easter there would be no story to tell. But finally, our only access to the meaning of what happened is the story itself. Engaging an ancient text in such a way that it mediates meaning in the present requires exegesis, i.e., the attempt to understand what the text in its own context says. But finally only interpretation, which goes

---

York: Doubleday, 2003), 31–39. Moloney supplies excellent bibliography on literary approaches and their necessary relation to historical approaches to the biblical text.

[7] A renewed interest in the historical and literary processes that produced the Fourth Gospel as well as the sources the Evangelist might have used is reflected in the collection *Jesus in Johannine Tradition*, ed. Robert T. Fortna and Tom Thatcher (Louisville, KY: Westminster John Knox Press, 2001).

[8] Jean Zumstein, "Lecture narratologique du cycle pascal du quatrième évangile," *Études Théologique et Religieuses* 76, no. 1 (2001): 1–15, gives a very good explanation of how the "incoherencies" that historical critical work discovers are often products of the method itself and that, if the text is dealt with as a narrative, many of these apparent "seams," "aporias," "doublets," and inconsistencies cease to be such.

[9] O'Day, *Revelation in the Fourth Gospel*, makes this point with full argumentation. She concludes, "*Revelation lies in the Gospel narrative and the world created by the words of that narrative*" (94, emphasis in the text). I would nuance this somewhat by saying that revelation occurs in *interaction with the text* in order to avoid the implication that revelation is somehow quasi-propositional.

beyond exegesis, allows the text to exercise its transformative power on the reader.[10]

Consequently, my final presupposition is *hermeneutical*. The purpose of this study is to engage the text as a mediation of meaning. Although I assume that there is continuity between the intention of the real author, i.e., the Fourth Evangelist (henceforth, FE), and the meaning of the text as it stands, it is the text that gives us access to new possibilities of Christian being in the world. What is finally important is not what the historical agent we call "John" intended to say but what the text we call John actually does say. The reader's interaction with the text gives rise to meaning that transforms the reader into the believer who has life in Jesus' name.[11]

III. Johannine Anthropology

Much discussion about bodily resurrection is subverted from the start by the fact that modern Westerners tend to read the gospel texts through the lens of a basically Greek philosophical anthropology in which the human being is understood very differently from the way it is understood in the Semitic anthropology of the biblical writers, including the evangelists. John's anthropology, although expressed with Greek vocabulary that has clearly influenced his understanding of the person, is thoroughly rooted in the Hebrew language and sensibility.[12] The pertinent Greek terms, ψυχή (usually translated as "soul"), ζωή (translated as "life"),

---

[10] See the conclusion, "Reading for Transformation," of Dorothy Lee, *Flesh and Glory: Symbol, Gender, and Theology in the Gospel of John* (New York: Crossroad, 2002), 233–37.

[11] See Paul Ricoeur, *Interpretation Theory: Discourse and the Surplus of Meaning* (Fort Worth: Texas Christian University Press, 1976), esp. pp. 91–95 on "appropriation."

[12] A good introduction to Semitic anthropology is Hans Walter Wolff, *Anthropology of the Old Testament* (1974; reprint, Mifflintown, PA: Sigler, 1996). The Gospel of John, as we will see in dealing with his eschatology, is not devoid of Hellenistic influences coming probably through OT sapiential materials, esp. Wisdom of Solomon. This influence is controlled, however, by Hebrew understandings of God, the human, and the end of human life. A thorough study of Johannine anthropology, which is completely beyond the scope of this paper, would proceed by tracing the path from the concrete and stereometric (to use Wolff's term) Hebrew usage through the changes rung on the terms in the Greek of the LXX into the FG. I suspect that the most original development is precisely John's exploitation of the distinction, not possible in Hebrew, but possible in Greek, between σάρξ and σῶμα.

θάνατος ("death"), σάρξ ("flesh"), αἷμα ("blood"), πνεῦμα ("spirit"), and σῶμα ("body"), constitute a semantic field in which all the terms are interrelated and mutually qualifying. Although in English these terms each denote a *component* of the human being, in biblical usage they each denote the *whole person* from some perspective or under some aspect. Ignoring this difference can result in serious misunderstanding, such as the tendency of many moderns to hear cannibalistic overtones in Jesus' invitation to eat his flesh and drink his blood in John 6:52-58. And mistranslating the terms σάρξ and αἷμα in that passage, i.e., "flesh and blood," as "body and blood," leading to the identification of flesh with body, then leads to an erroneous identification of bodily resurrection with physical resurrection. In other words, it is crucial to understand what these anthropological terms meant in the context of John's first-century Judaism as a basis for understanding how they function in the FG.

John uses the terms for life, ψυχή and ζωή, very consistently. Ψυχή refers to the person as a living human being. In John 10:17-18 Jesus speaks of freely laying down and taking up his ψυχή, meaning his natural human life.[13] Ζωή, which also means life, is virtually always explicitly or implicitly qualified in John with the adjective αἰώνιος ("eternal"), not in the sense of indefinite temporal extension of natural life but as a qualitatively different kind of life. "Eternal life" is a technical theological term in John meaning God's own life lived by Jesus as the λόγος incarnate and participated in, before as well as after death, by those who, born of God through the Spirit, are now τέκνα Θεοῦ, children of God (cf. John 1:12-13; 3:5-6). Jesus sums up the purpose of the Incarnation: "I have come that they may have ζωή, and have it abundantly" (10:10). The term refers not to some quality or even power possessed by the human being but to the whole person as divinely alive.

Θάνατος, the opposite of life in both its natural and its divine sense, is a richly ambiguous term in John. It means the human person without life. But, as Jesus' lapidary self-revelation to Martha in 11:25 makes clear,

---

[13] Andrew T. Lincoln, " 'I Am the Resurrection and the Life': The Resurrection Message of the Fourth Gospel," in *Life in the Face of Death: The Resurrection Message of the New Testament*, ed. Richard N. Longenecker (Grand Rapids, MI/Cambridge, UK: William B. Eerdmans, 1998), 129, makes the important point that Jesus could not have been speaking of laying down his divine life. He immediately slips into the mistaken identification, however, of ψυχή with σάρξ, leading to an understanding of bodily resurrection as fleshly or physical resurrection.

there is death and death. Those who die, as all humans must, may, like Jesus' opponents in 8:24, "die in their sins," i.e., be finally dead, denizens of Sheol where they are cut off from all meaningful personal and communal existence and especially from communion with the living God (cf. Ps 6:6). Or, conversely, even though they die, they may, like Jesus, live with eternal life in the glory of God. In John 11 Lazarus is a symbolic instrument on which are rung all the changes and interrelations of which the concept of θάνατος as opposition to both ordinary human life and eternal life is susceptible.[14] In John, Jesus' death was simultaneously real human death and his Glorification as Son of Man (cf. 12:23 and elsewhere).[15] But once again, death is not simply an event; it is a condition of the whole human subject.

Σάρξ and αἷμα, usually translated as "flesh" and "blood," respectively, are closely related terms. For moderns these terms denote substances that are separable components of a human being. Flesh, in John's anthropology, is not a part of the human but the human being as natural and mortal.[16] To say that in Jesus the Word of God (λόγος) became flesh (σάρξ) is to say that he became fully human, i.e., subject to death.[17] In the Psalms especially we see "flesh" used to speak of humanity in its weakness and mortality: "God remembered that they were flesh, a passing breath that returns not" (Ps 145:21; see also 56:5; 65:3; and elsewhere). In John 6:51 Jesus says that he *is* the living bread come down from heaven and that the bread which he will *give* for the life of the world "is [his] flesh." Jesus is not talking about a physical part of himself. He is saying

---

[14] I have dealt with this topic in greater detail in "The Community of Eternal Life (John 11:1-53)," in *Written That You May Believe: Encountering Jesus in the Fourth Gospel*, 2nd ed. (New York: Crossroad, 2003), 171–83.

[15] Francis Moloney, "The Johannine Son of Man Revisited," in *Theology and Christology in the Fourth Gospel* (Leuven: University Press, 2005), 177–202. His understanding of the Johannine use of "Son of Man" for the revelation of God in the human event of Jesus Christ, esp. in his being "lifted up" on the cross, is very helpful for understanding resurrection in John.

[16] "Flesh" is a good translation of σάρξ, which is a more differentiated term than the Hebrew *bāśār*, which denotes the human in his or her infirmity or weakness (Wolff, *Anthropology*, 26–31). But the Hebrew term covers the territory of "body" almost completely whereas Greek distinguishes *sarx* from *sōma*, a crucial distinction for John's theology of resurrection.

[17] For a very rich treatment of the meaning of flesh in John, see Lee, *Flesh and Glory*, 29–64.

that in giving himself totally in death, which is only possible because he is flesh, i.e., mortal, he gives life to the world.

If flesh denotes the human as mortal, "blood" used in combination with flesh focuses on the mortal as living. Blood is not simply a part of the human being but the "livingness" of one vulnerable to death. In Genesis 9:4 God says to Noah that all living creatures are given to humanity as food but "flesh with its lifeblood still in it you shall not eat." Blood, then, can stand for life itself and "flesh and blood" means the living human being. When Jesus, in John 6, says that believers must consume his flesh and blood, he is talking not about eating and drinking physical substances but of receiving as food his living human self in the community's eucharistic meal.

The rich ambiguity of the word θάνατος, which can refer to physical or eternal death, is reflected in the ambiguity of the word πνεῦμα. Spirit can mean the breath of life, i.e., God's creating gift to every mortal that returns to God when the creature dies, or the Spirit of God who came to rest permanently on Jesus (cf. John 1:31-33), who gives this Spirit without measure (cf. 3:34) to those who believe in him making them children of God whose divine life death cannot touch. Jesus says in 6:63 that "the flesh" is futile, i.e., doomed to death, but that "the spirit" gives life (πνμεῦμά ἐστιν τὸ ζωοποιοῦν). When he then goes on to say that his words are "S/spirit and life" (πνμεῦμά . . . καὶ ζωή), he plays on the ambiguity of spirit as both human life and divine life.

The most important term in this anthropological semantic field in relation to the Resurrection of Jesus, and the one John uses in a subtle way that marries Semitic and Hellenistic understandings of the human, is σῶμα, "body."[18] Because moderns tend to think of the body as a distinct substance in the human composite, the physical component as distinguished from the spiritual, they tend to equate it with flesh, itself misunderstood as the soft, solid component in distinction from blood and bones. In other words, body is understood as a physical substance that is integral to but only a part of the person.[19]

---

[18] Here I disagree with Lee, *Flesh and Glory*, 45–46, who suggests that there is no significant difference between σάρξ and σῶμα. I will argue that there is a critically important difference. Jesus rises not as "flesh" but as "body."

[19] It is interesting that psychosomatic medicine is discovering in various ways how completely the whole human is "body," not in the reductive sense of being nothing but material, but in the sense of being, as a whole, a "bodyperson." This understanding is closer to the biblical understanding than the reductionistic anthropology

For John, body is the person in symbolic self-presentation. The person may be living or dead,[20] but it is the whole self, the bodyself, who is living or dead. In Semitic thought, once the dead body begins to decay, to fall apart, the person is no longer a person. Whatever trace of the individual may survive in Sheol, it is not a human being because it does not enjoy subjectivity, community, or union with God.[21] The body is quintessentially the person as self-symbolizing, i.e., as numerically distinct, self-consistent, and continuous, a subject who can interact with other subjects and who is present and active in the world.[22] A corpse, in John's vocabulary, is also called a body (John 19:31, 38, 40) precisely because it symbolizes the whole person, the bodyself, in its transition from being to nonbeing or from presence to absence. It is the symbolic (i.e., perceptively real) person in the process of becoming absent, and when the person is finally and fully absent, when the corpse has decomposed (which does not happen in the case of Jesus), it is no longer considered a body. In short, if Jesus as flesh, that is, as earthly human being, is the symbolic presence of God's glory in this world, Jesus as body is his own symbolic presence to his contemporaries. Prior to his death the two, flesh and body, i.e., the human person, are coterminous as they are

---

spawned by the Scientific Revolution and the Enlightenment. Nevertheless, contemporary understandings of the human are still quite dichotomous, as is evidenced by the mechanistic approaches to medical procedures.

[20] The Hellenistic influence on John's thought as well as the exploitation of the possibilities of the Greek language are clear here. *Bāśār* is not used to speak of a corpse (although *nepeš* occasionally is) but only of living creatures, whereas John does not use *sarx* (which the LXX uses for *bāśār*) but *sōma* to speak of the corpses on the cross (19:31) and specifically of the dead body of Jesus (19:38, 40) and of his risen body (2:21-22).

[21] John L. McKenzie, "Sheol," *Dictionary of the Bible* (Milwaukee, WI: Bruce, 1965), 800, says, Sheol "is less a positive conception of survival than a picturesque denial of all that is meant by life and activity."

[22] I have dealt at length with the concept of symbol, especially as it functions in John's gospel, in *Written That You May Believe*, 63–77. See also Lee, *Flesh and Glory*, 9–28. A still very important work on symbol in theology and especially on the body as the primary symbol by which a person is present to him- or herself as well as to others is Karl Rahner, "The Theology of the Symbol," *Theological Investigations*, vol. 4: *More Recent Writings*, trans. Kevin Smyth (Baltimore: Helicon Press, 1966), 221–52, esp. 245–52 on the body. It is especially interesting that the term "body" does not seem to play a distinct enough role in Semitic thought to merit a term of its own in distinction from "flesh." The only bodies known to human experience were fleshly ones, either the potential human, the "earth creature" (*hāādām*) of Gen 2:7, or the living person, *nepeš* or *bāśār*.

in all humans in this life. The issue of "body" as distinct in some sense from "flesh" only arises when Jesus dies and the two are no longer strictly coterminous.[23]

The issue of Jesus' real presence in and after his passage through death dominates the Last Supper in John (chaps. 13–17) as well as the Resurrection Narrative (chap. 20). Where is the Lord? Has he gone where his disciples cannot follow? Are they orphans, deprived of the glory of God that had been present in the flesh of Jesus? Are future believers condemned to a faith based on hearsay about events in which they did not and do not participate? Unless Jesus is bodily risen, i.e., unless he is alive in the full integrity of his humanity symbolized in his body, he is not present, either as the presence of humanity in God or as God's divinely human presence to us.

The crucial anthropological-theological issue for the topic of resurrection is, then, the relation of flesh to body, i.e., of the pre-Easter person of Jesus as mortal human being to the post-Easter person of Jesus as glorified Son of Man. By way of anticipatory summary, I will propose that the relation of flesh to body is precisely what is altered by Jesus' Glorification. In his pre-Easter existence as flesh, the body of Jesus, i.e., his personal symbolic presence, was conditioned by his mortality. He was subject to death and to the limitations of space, time, and causality that natural human life entails. In his Glorification Jesus goes to the Father as a human bodyself, and in his Resurrection he returns to his own in the full integrity of his humanity. His body is real, both continuous and discontinuous with his earthly body. He is numerically distinct, a personal subject who can be intersubjectively present and active,[24] but he is

---

[23] I find very suggestive the point made by Mary Coloe in "Like Father, Like Son: The Role of Abraham in Tabernacles—John 8:31-59," *Pacifica* 12 (February 1999): 1–11. "In speaking of Jesus as both Temple and Tabernacle there is no dichotomy as the two are intrinsically related as the flesh (1:14) is related to the body (2:21). The Tabernacle and the Temple serve the same symbolic function even though they recall different historical eras" (p. 4, n. 6). I think that, in fact, flesh and body denote different and subsequent modes (analogous to historical eras) of the presence of Jesus to his disciples. Flesh indicates his career as a mortal and body his glorified life. But the two terms denote the same person and the same presence of the glory of God among humans in that person.

[24] See the fascinating article by Graham Ward, "Bodies: The Displaced Body of Jesus Christ," in *Radical Orthodoxy: A New Theology*, ed. John Milbank, Catherine Pickstock, and Graham Ward (London/New York: Routledge, 1999), 163–81, esp. 168 on the body of Jesus in its displacements, transformations, and resignifications that brings

no longer subject to death nor determined by the spatial, temporal, or causal coordinates of historical existence. And he will be present as this same bodyself throughout post-Easter time in the range of symbols through which his personal presence will be manifest.

IV. Johannine Eschatology

A final preliminary subject that is crucial for a consideration of bodily resurrection in John is eschatology. It has long been recognized that John's treatment of the end of Jesus' earthly life is quite unlike that of the Synoptics. Jesus' Passion and death in the FG are not presented as a *kenosis* that requires divine vindication through resurrection. Indeed, Bultmann suggested in the middle of the last century that "if Jesus' death on the cross is already his exaltation and glorification, *his resurrection* cannot be an event of special significance. No resurrection is needed to destroy the triumph which death might be supposed to have gained in the crucifixion."[25] The Resurrection Narrative in the FG, in such a view, is merely a concession to the tradition that, by the time John was written, considered the Resurrection intrinsic to the kerygma. I would suggest that, while it is true that the Resurrection of Jesus is not understood in the same way and does not play the same role in John that it does in the Synoptics, it is nevertheless essential to John's theological purpose. Integral to understanding John's presentation of the Resurrection is a grasp of his eschatological presuppositions, especially as they differ from those operative in the Synoptic tradition.

As is well known, early Israelite eschatology was a collectivist, national, and this-worldly expectation of Israel's ongoing prosperity if it remained faithful to the covenant (see, e.g., the classic formulation in Deut 30:15-20). The conundrum of the suffering just person and the prosperous sinner (e.g., Ps 73; Job), however, gradually led toward a more universalistic hope for individual vindication beyond death. In the figure of the Suffering Servant of Deutero-Isaiah (Isa 42:1-4; 49:1-6; 50:4-9; 52:13–53:12), Israel achieved a seminal insight into the redemptive

---

a confirming postmodern light to bear on the topic. See also his article, "Transcorporeality: The Ontological Scandal," *Bulletin of the John Rylands University Library of Manchester* 80 (August 1998): 235–52.

[25] Rudolf Bultmann, *Theology of the New Testament*, vol. 2, trans. Kendrick Grobel (New York: Charles Scribner's Sons, 1955), 56.

potential of the suffering of the just person within and for the guilty community. This insight was developed in both the intertestamental literature (c. 200 BCE to 100 BCE)[26] and within the latest books of the Jewish Bible, notably Daniel, as well as in 2 Maccabees and Wisdom of Solomon, where we find traces of two strands of eschatological speculation, each of which supplied categories for the Christian interpretation of Jesus' death and Resurrection.[27]

The Synoptic Gospels operate primarily within the earlier of these two strands that, for convenience, I will label "resurrection eschatology," which developed in the context of the Syrian persecutions and the Hasidean-Hasmonean controversies in Palestine in the second to first centuries BCE. Faithful Jews were being persecuted and even martyred for their fidelity to Torah, but they were strengthened by the hope that they would be vindicated by God after death. The clearest Old Testament expression of this eschatology is found in Daniel 12:1-3 and 2 Maccabees 7, both of which are influenced by the Suffering Servant image, in which the martyrs are assured that they will be restored even in their bodies, that Israel will be reconstituted, and that the unjust will be finally punished.

The eschatology that functions in the Synoptic treatment of resurrection, like that of Daniel and 2 Maccabees, is fundamentally futuristic and apocalyptic. It envisions an "end of the world" at which all the dead will be bodily raised to appear before the glorified Christ, the divine judge, who will assign them to eternal reward or punishment on the basis of

---

[26] Although the dating of the "intertestamental" period as well as the category itself is debated, I am using it here to suggest the overlapping of late pre-Christian Jewish thought and the development of the canonical New Testament. My thanks to my colleagues John Endres, Barbara Green, and Gina Hens-Piazza as well as to GTU research librarian, Kristine Veldheer, for help with this and other sections in the chapter.

[27] I have explored the historical development of eschatological thought in Israel in the postexilic and intertestamental periods at some length in my doctoral dissertation, *The Johannine Resurrection Narrative: An Exegetical and Theological Study of John 20 as a Synthesis of Johannine Spirituality*, 2 vols. (Ann Arbor, MI: University Microfilms International, 1983), 76–89. The treatment offered here is a very brief and oversimplified synopsis whose purpose is simply to contrast apocalyptic and sapiential eschatology in order to account for the distinctive Johannine treatment of the death and Resurrection of Jesus. For a succinct treatment of NT eschatology, see Adela Yarbro Collins, "Eschatology and Apocalypticism," in Raymond Brown, Donald Senior, John R. Donahue, and Adela Yarbro Collins, "Aspects of New Testament Thought," *NJBC*, 81:25–56.

their comportment in this life (cf. Matt 25:31-46). This final event is conceived in apocalyptic terms as an unexpected cosmic cataclysm (see Matt 14:15-44; Mark 13:1-37; Luke 17:22-37). Those who die before the final event are judged at death and go to an interim reward or punishment, like Lazarus and Dives in Luke 16:19-31, or perhaps even to purgative suffering (see, e.g., Matt 18:23-35), while awaiting the universal judgment at the end of time when individual fates will become definitive. This is essentially the Pharisaic eschatology of Jesus' own time. The role of bodily, even physical, resurrection in this eschatology is essentially functional. It renders the just and the unjust present for final vindication.

John operates within the other strand of late pre-Christian Jewish eschatology, which I will label "exaltation eschatology."[28] It developed in the Hellenistic context of Diaspora Judaism, probably in the late second to first century BCE. Jews who had remained faithful to Torah even far from Palestine were being persecuted not only by non-Jewish authorities but also by their assimilated and worldly coreligionists. Once again, there is appeal to a post-death solution to the problem of the intra-historical victory of the unjust. The clearest (deutero)canonical expression of this eschatology occurs in Wisdom 1–6, probably written in Greek by an Alexandrian Jew. In these chapters a Torah-loving "wisdom hero"[29] is persecuted by the foolish who mock his fidelity to the Law, repudiate his claim to be God's son, and are infuriated by his accusation that they are unfaithful to their training and tradition (cf. Wis 2:10-20). Unlike the traditional wisdom hero, e.g., Joseph or Susanna, who is rescued before death, the Jews for whom Wisdom of Solomon is written were being killed. Thus, it became necessary to introduce the possibility of post-death salvation. The influence of the LXX version of the fourth Suffering Servant Song from Isaiah 52:13–53:12 and of the Daniel 7 figure of the Son of Man on the hero in Wisdom of Solomon is virtually certain.[30] The

---

[28] For an excellent, and provocatively suggestive, treatment of the Wisdom of Solomon, its eschatology in relation to its *Sitz-im-Leben*, and possible relation to the NT, see Barbara Green, "The Wisdom of Solomon and the Solomon of Wisdom: Tradition's Transpositions and Human Transformation," *Horizons* 30 (Spring 2003): 41–66.

[29] For the development of the extrabiblical literary genre of "wisdom tale," within which we meet wisdom heroes in noncanonical dress who resemble Joseph, Daniel, and Susanna whose "wisdom," however, is fidelity to Torah, see G. W. Nicholsburg, *Resurrection, Immortality, and Eternal Life in Intertestamental Judaism* (Cambridge, UK: Harvard University Press, 1972), 49–55.

[30] See Schneiders, *The Johannine Resurrection Narrative*, vol. 1, 98–101, for the textual evidence supporting this position.

theme of exaltation for judgment is combined with the theme of entering into an intimate relationship with God in a nonterrestrial realm. The text tells us that even though the hero is killed, "the souls of the just are in the hand of God. . . . They seemed, in the view of the foolish, to be dead . . . but they are in peace. . . . God took them to himself" (Wis 3:1-6).

Bodily resurrection does not figure explicitly in this sapiential understanding of the destiny of the just and unjust because the judgment of the ungodly takes place in their very choice of evil by which they "summon death" (cf. Wis 1:16) and the just are exalted by and/or assumed to God in their seeming death. The assumption or exaltation of the just, however, is not simply immortality of the soul in the Greek philosophical sense, that is, the natural indestructibility of a spiritual substance. It is life in the Jewish sense, i.e., a gift from God, who alone possesses it by nature[31] and who freely bestows it on those who are loyal to the covenant. And life, even after death, in which the body did not participate in some way would have been inconceivable to the Jewish imagination. So, while nothing is said of bodily resurrection in sapiential eschatology, it is fundamentally susceptible to it.[32]

The predominantly realized, nonapocalyptic eschatology of John's gospel as well as John's presentation of the Resurrection of Jesus reflect this exaltation eschatology. In the FG, a person's fundamental option to believe or not to believe in Jesus (cf. John 5:29) situates her or him, even in this world, in eternal life or eternal death (cf. John 3:15-19; 5:24, in relation to Wis 1:16).[33] People are thus divided into two groups: the children

---

[31] This was explained well by Joseph Moignt, "Immortalité de l'âme et/ou résurrection,"*Lumière et Vie* 21 (1972): 65–78, who takes essentially the same position as Oscar Cullmann in his classic text, "Immortality of the Soul or Resurrection of the Dead: The Witness of the New Testament," The Ingersoll Lecture, 1955, *Harvard Divinity School Bulletin* 21 (1955–56): 5–36.

[32] It is important, however, but beyond the scope of this essay, to note that Jewish anthropology was influenced by Hellenistic philosophy in the immediate pre-Christian period. This is evident in the use of terms such as "incorruption" (ἀφθαρσία) in Wis 2:23 and "immortality" (ἀθανασία) in Wis 3:4. On the other hand, the biblical influence appears in the notion that death is not intended by God but entered the world through the envy of the devil (cf. Wis 2:23-24) in contrast to the notion of death as natural passage into nonexistence that the enemies of the wisdom hero enunciate in Wis 2:1-22.

[33] This "moral dualism" of the FG is not absolute, and 1 John 2:19; 3:4-10, in relation to 5:16-17, suggests that the historical Johannine community had trouble with it. It seems to stem, however, from the "two-way theology" that appears pervasively in the OT (e.g., in Hos 14:9; Amos 5:14-15; Mic 4:2, 5; Jer 5:4; Ps 1:1, 6; Prov 2:12-15; and

of God and the children of the devil (John 8:41-47). Death is not a moment of judgment but a definitive establishment in that state of life or death in which the person has been living before death (cf. 8:2 in relation to 11:25). Judgment is neither a universal nor a future phenomenon, for those who believe are never judged (5:24), and those who do not believe are already judged, not by Jesus but by their very choice of unbelief (3:18-19).

Two conclusions can be drawn about sapiential exaltation eschatology in relation to the Gospel of John.

First, bodily resurrection is compatible with, perhaps even implicit in, but not explicitly affirmed in sapiential eschatology. It *could* easily become explicit, however, if the right pressures were brought to bear upon it, e.g., by the Easter experience of the first followers of Jesus.

Second, if bodily resurrection *did* become explicit within a sapiential eschatology, it would not have the same meaning it has in a future, apocalyptic eschatology. It would not be seen as vindication of the persecuted, since this vindication takes place in the very death/exaltation of the just one, or as a victory over death, because death never has any real power over the one who is a child of God. It would be essentially a manifestation of the meaning for the whole person of life in God now lived in all its fullness. And in the case of Jesus it would be a condition of possibility for his post-Easter personal presence to his disciples and his continuing action in the world.

I would suggest that the bodily Resurrection of Jesus in John is presented in terms of the sapiential anthropology and eschatology of the Wisdom of Solomon. The Resurrection Narrative in John 20 is, therefore, not a concession to the constraints of early Christian tradition but a narrative-theological exploration of the Easter experience of the first disciples and its implications for the spirituality of the Johannine community. This entails making a distinction between the Glorification or exaltation of Jesus on the cross (i.e., the passage of Jesus to God) and his Resurrection (i.e., his return to his own), which, though related, are not strictly identical in John.

---

elsewhere) but that comes to very explicit articulation in the Wisdom of Solomon (e.g., 1:4-8, 14; 2:24; 3:7-19; 5:6-7). Interestingly, Nichelsburg, *Resurrection, Immortality, and Eternal Life*, 165–66, says that the "two-way theology," which is perfectly compatible with an eschatology of immediate assumption at death, was combined with a notion of bodily resurrection only after 70 CE, e.g., in *IV Ezra* and *Epistle of Barnabas*.

V. The Textual Framework for John's Resurrection Narrative

Bearing in mind the gospel's narrative unity and against the background of John's sapiential anthropology and eschatology, we turn now to the text of the FG with our original question: what is John's contribution to our understanding of the bodily Resurrection of Jesus? Pertinent texts occur in virtually every chapter of the gospel, but since I intend to concentrate on John 20:19-23, Jesus' appearance on Easter night to his disciples, I will briefly situate that passage in relation to the texts most important for understanding it and make reference in passing to other texts.

The Prologue[34]

John 1:1-18, the Prologue, differs notably in form, content, and function from the rest of the gospel, which is concerned with the career of the Word incarnate. The Prologue begins in eternity, in the bosom of God, from whom the Word came forth to tent or tabernacle among us (ἐσκήνωσεν ἐν ἡμῖν) by becoming flesh (σάρξ ἐγένετο), i.e., human, in Jesus Christ. The term λόγος, designating the pre-incarnate Word, never appears again in the gospel even though the activity and speech of Σοφία, the Word personalized as divine Wisdom, are ubiquitous in the earthly career of Jesus. Jesus, the human being, has become the symbolic presence of God in history that the Word is in eternity.

An analogous linguistic strategy occurs in the other direction at the end of the gospel when the earthly Jesus becomes the risen Lord. Jesus says, "I came forth from the Father and have come into the world; again I leave the world and go to the Father" (John 16:28). As the Word through incarnation became flesh, i.e., assumed the existential mode of humanity in time, so the human Jesus through his Glorification assumes a new mode of being in God that transcends history and that, without repudiating his humanity, transforms it. John 20 is a narrative exploration of this new mode of presence and its significance for Jesus' followers.

---

[34] See Coloe, *God Dwells with Us*, 15–29, for a very good treatment of the structure and content of the Prologue, particularly in relation to the issue of the presence of God in Jesus, which is our concern here. Coloe also summarizes other influential theories concerning the structure and dynamics of the text.

The Textual Framework for the Symbolic Use of Body

Two nested prophecy-fulfillment schemas with parallel structures culminate in the central event of the Resurrection Narrative, the raising of the New Temple of Jesus' glorified body in the midst of his community. The major schema is constituted by the logion of Jesus in the temple during his first Passover in Jerusalem, John 2:19-22, and its fulfillment in the appearance to his disciples on Easter evening, John 20:19-23. Nested within that overarching schema is another with the same structure: the logion of Jesus in the temple at the feast of Tabernacles in 7:37-39 and its fulfillment in the piercing of Jesus' side in 19:34.

The first prophecy-fulfillment schema: Jesus as Temple. Jesus' first public act in John, which has the programmatic significance of his appearance in the Synagogue of Nazareth in Luke 4, is his prophetic gesture in the temple. Mary Coloe, correctly in my opinion, sees this not as a cleansing of the temple in which valid worship was still possible but rather as a termination of the temple and its cult, which Jesus would replace.[35] "The Jews"[36] demand an authenticating sign. Jesus replies, " 'Destroy this temple [ναός] and in three days I will raise it" (2:19). "The Jews" take him literally, a clear Johannine indication that Jesus was not speaking of the physical temple in which they were standing. The Evangelist clarifies, "He [Jesus] was speaking of the temple of his body [σῶμα]," which his disciples would understand only after his Resurrection (cf. 2:20-22). This is the first time the word σῶμα, "body," is used in John, and it is explicitly identified with ναός, "temple."[37] Σῶμα will not be used again until Jesus

---

[35] Mary Coloe's interpretation of Jesus as replacement of the temple, the place of divine glory, with Jesus as the locus of the glory of Yahweh is strongly reinforced by the article of Carey C. Newman, "Resurrection as Glory: Divine Presence and Christian Origins," *The Resurrection*, 59–89. Carey convincingly argues that the real cause of the break between the early Christian community and Judaism was "that the resurrection of Jesus, as depicted in early Christian creeds, confessions, and hymns, was interpreted as his investiture with, and inauguration of, eschatological divine presence—that is, the Glory of Yahweh" (87).

[36] I will use the convention of placing "the Jews" in quotation marks when the expression denotes the so-called Johannine Jews, that is, the collective representative figure in the Fourth Gospel that signifies rejection of the light, in order to warn the reader not to equate this literary stereotype with actual Jews, either those of Jesus' time or those of later periods.

[37] Lincoln in " 'I Am the Resurrection and the Life,' " 126, says of the temple episode, "It is made clear that not only will the incarnate Logos die, but also that he will rise and the *bodily* form of his resurrection will continue to be an essential feature of his

has been glorified on the cross (19:31, 38, 40). Like the use of λόγος in the Prologue, which looks back to eternity and is not used of the historical Jesus who is the Word made σάρξ, "flesh," σῶμα is used here in prediction and will not be used again until Jesus is glorified. In other words, what flesh is to λόγος, its symbolic locus in the pre-paschal dispensation, σῶμα is to the glorified Jesus, his symbolic locus in the post-paschal dispensation.

This prophetic logion, which occurs in Jesus' first public appearance, is balanced by a narrative at the end of the gospel that fulfills it. In John 20:19 we are told that the glorified Jesus "stood into the midst" or "rose up in the midst" of his disciples, who were behind closed doors.[38] This image of Jesus arising in the midst of the community evokes the raising of the New Temple, the new presence of God in their midst, which Jesus had promised in chapter 2.

The second prophecy-fulfillment schema: Body as Temple. Between these two scenes is another prophecy-fulfillment schema, this time constituted by the logion of Jesus in the temple at the feast of Tabernacles in John 7:37-39 balanced by the narrative that fulfills it, the scene at the cross as Jesus dies in John 19:25-34.

The context is again the temple in Jerusalem, this time at the joyful feast of Tabernacles celebrating the Sinai covenant. It is the last and the "great day" of the feast, the eighth day evoking both creation and eschatological fulfillment, just as the Sabbath that follows Jesus' death is a

---

identity" (emphasis added). On pages 128 and 141, however, Lincoln seems to equate risen *bodiliness* with *physicality*, which may reflect a lack in his philosophical repertoire of a notion of materiality that is not physical rather than a conscious position on the nature of glorified bodiliness. His evident concern is to affirm the bodiliness of the risen Jesus.

[38] I am indebted to my colleague, David Johnson, who pointed out to me that the Greek "ἔστη" was rendered in the Peschitta (Syriac version from the fifth century CE but related to the much earlier Old Syriac) by the term *qâm* from the root *qom*, which means either "stand" or "arise as from sleep or from death," as well as "to stand up" or "to be present." See R. Payne Smith, *A Compendious Syriac Dictionary, Founded upon the* Thesaurus syriacus *of R. Payne Smith*, ed. J. Payne Smith (Oxford: Clarendon, 1903). John's construction, Jesus "stood into " (ἔστη εἰς), suggests that the more dynamic translation is to be understood since simply appearing or standing would not suggest motion. I am inclined to think that "stand into" is best translated as "arose among," esp. in light of John 2:19 and 21-22, where Jesus predicts that he will "raise up" (ἐγερῶ) the new temple and the Evangelist clarified that Jesus was referring to the temple of his body, which the disciples will understand after he "was raised from the dead" (ἠγέρθη ἐκ νεκρῶν).

"great day," namely, Passover (cf. John 19:31).[39] The symbols used in the feast of Tabernacles are water from the pool of Siloam and light from innumerable torches shining in the darkness,[40] both Johannine symbols for Jesus.[41] Jesus now identifies himself as temple. He cries out to all who thirst to come to him and drink, again, as in chapter 2, citing Scripture.

The translation as well as the source of the Scripture text Jesus evokes in this scene are much debated.[42] Two translations are grammatically possible. Following the argumentation of Germain Bienaimé, and without denying that the ambiguity in the text may have been intentional on the part of the FE, I prefer, for the theological reasons given below, the translation that would make Jesus, rather than those who believe in him, the originating source of the living water.

> If anyone thirst, let [that one] come to me
> And let the one who believes in me drink
> As the Scripture said, "Out of his interior [κοιλία; or from within him]
> Will flow rivers of living water. (7:37-38)

The Evangelist, as in chapter 2, clarifies Jesus' saying: he was speaking of the Spirit, which "was not yet [given]" because Jesus was not yet glorified. Once again, Jesus' word can only be understood after "the hour" of the paschal mystery.

---

[39] P. Van Dieman, in his 1972 Rome dissertation, *La semaine inaugurale et la semaine terminale de l'évangile de Jean: Message et structures*, proposed a modification of É. Boismard's thesis of the "weeks" of Jesus' life as a structure of the FG. Van Dieman argued that, in John, the first and last weeks of Jesus' life are actually composed of six days and an eighth day while the seventh day, the Jewish Sabbath, is passed over in silence. The eighth day is both the first day of creation and the eschatological day of the New Creation. Consequently, this "last and great day of the feast" of Tabernacles is a day symbolic of both the New Creation and the Resurrection while the day after Jesus' death is Passover, the silent end of the old dispensation, and the Resurrection, inaugurating the new, occurs on the eighth day.

[40] See Coloe, *God Dwells with Us*, 119–22, for description of the rituals of Tabernacles in relation to John 7–8.

[41] The Evangelist will identify Jesus, the Sent One, with the waters of Siloam in John 9:7, and Jesus will identify himself as "the light of the world" in 8:12 and 9:5. This is not the only time that the FE "recalls" something that has not yet happened.

[42] Germain Bienaimé, "L'annonce des fleuves d'eau vive en Jean 7,37-39," *Revue théologique de Louvain* 21 (1990): 281–310, 417–54, summarizes and evaluates virtually every recent study of this passage in regard to punctuation, the provenance of the citation, and the relation of v. 39 to vv. 37-38. He includes an exhaustive bibliography.

The search for the Old Testament source of Jesus' citation, which would clarify the meaning of the "rivers of living water," has led scholars to Exodus 17:6 where God tells Moses to strike the rock in the desert and water will flow (and Pss 78:14-16 and 105:41, which celebrate that event); Zechariah 14:8, which predicts that in the eschatological day living waters will flow from Jerusalem (and Ps 46:5-6, which celebrates the streams that gladden the holy city); Isaiah 55:1ff., which invites all who are thirsty to come to the water.[43] Given John's symphonically allusive use of the Old Testament, I would not reject any of these texts as part of the background for the logion in John 7:38, but I think the most important text, which controls the use of the others, is Ezekiel 47, where the prophet is shown the abundant streams of life-giving waters that flow from the side of the temple, beginning as a trickle (47:2) and growing to a mighty river giving life, health, and freshness to all living things. This is certainly a description of the Spirit promised in John 7:37-38 that is unleashed in the world as a trickle of water from the pierced side of the glorified Jesus, specifically identified now as "body" (19:31).

The translation of κοιλία has also exercised exegetes. It means, literally, the inner cavity of the human body, whether the breast, the womb, or the belly, and consequently, symbolically, the interiority of the bodyself. Rivers of living water, the Spirit, will come from within the body of Jesus glorified, as the water sprang out of the cleft rock in the desert to give life to the historical people and will flow from within the eschatological temple to give life to the world.

The text that fulfills the prophetic logion in John 7 is 19:34, which recounts that a soldier opened the side of the glorified Jesus with a lance and blood and water flowed out. Throughout the FG water is symbolic of or closely associated with the Spirit, as it is in John 7. Blood, as we saw earlier, is the locus or bearer of the life of the person as mortal. Just before the dead body of Jesus is pierced, he had "handed over the Spirit" (v. 30), an expression used nowhere in Scripture or secular Greek to refer to death. Consequently, most commentators agree that John used it to

---

[43] Ibid., 422–31, discusses the positions of C. C. Torrey and A. Feuillet among others on these suggestions. He himself regards Exod 17:6 as the "texte fondamental de la citation" (431–32), which is enriched by Pss 78 and 105 and Ezek 47. He concludes, however, that the primary point of the evocation of Ezek 47 is to recall that the water flowing from the temple is the water of the new paradise and thus that the text in John 7 is more about the New Creation than about Jesus as the New Temple (454). I would place the emphasis the other way around.

convey the coincidence of Jesus' physical death, i.e., his Glorification, and the outpouring of the Holy Spirit.[44] Blood (symbolizing his human life, given for the life of the world [cf. 6:51]) and water (symbolizing the Spirit) flow from the New Temple to give life to the New Israel, the community gathered at the foot of the cross. The Evangelist, in 19:37, cites Zechariah 12:10, "they shall look on him whom they have pierced," which evokes the Suffering Servant but also Zechariah 13 and 14, which describe the messianic gift of purifying and flowing waters of which Jesus had spoken in John 7:38. Jesus' body on the cross is both the New Paschal Lamb slain to give life[45] and the New Temple from which that life pours forth.

In summary, the schemas we have examined weave a symbolic tapestry within which the glorified Jesus can be discerned as the New Temple raised up in the midst of the New Covenant people. From him flows the Spirit who will be, in them, the promised presence of Jesus throughout all time.[46]

---

[44] James Swetnam, "Bestowal of the Spirit in the Fourth Gospel," *Biblica* 74 (1999): 556–76, cites E. Hoskyns (*The Fourth Gospel* [London: Faber, 1947], 532) on the peculiar language for the death of Jesus (παραδιδόναι τὸ πνεῦμα). In Mark Jesus "gave up the ghost," or expired (ἐξέπνευσεν); in Matthew he "yielded up his spirit" (ἀφῆκεν τὸ πνεῦμα); in Luke he "gave up the ghost," or breathed his last (ἐξέπνευσεν). Swetnam says John's expression is "unparalleled in the Greek language as a description of death" (564). Hence his conclusion, following Hoskyns, is that the primary meaning of the account is the "bestowing of the Spirit" rather than simply Jesus letting go of his human life. Nevertheless, it also, obviously, means that Jesus died.

[45] See Maarten J. J. Menken, "The Old Testament Quotation in John 19,36: Sources, Redaction, Background," in *The Four Gospels 1992: Festschrift Frans Neirynck*, ed. F. Van Segbroeck, C. M. Tuckett, G. Van Belle, J. Verheyden, 3 vols. (Leuven: University Press, 1992): 2101–18, for an investigation of the sources for the citation. Menken concludes that the citation identifies Jesus as both the Suffering Servant and the Paschal Lamb.

[46] Raymond E. Brown, in *The Gospel according to John*, Anchor Bible 29 and 29a (Garden City, NY: Doubleday, 1966–70), 2:1139, says, "It is our contention that John presents the Paraclete as the Holy Spirit in a special role, namely, as the personal presence of Jesus in the Christian while Jesus is with the Father." It is unusual for Brown to label a position as his personal opinion rather than presenting it as a convincing conclusion from the data he has provided. I think he understood the originality of his "contention." He may be suggesting that Spirit is the mode of bodiliness of the glorified Jesus, which is my position. But because the dichotomous Western mind tends to equate "spirit" with "disembodied," as in "pure spirit," it is difficult for this term to function clearly in discussing bodily presence. The fact that Brown entitled one of his books *The Virginal Conception and Bodily Resurrection of Jesus* [emphasis added] (London/Dublin: Geoffrey Chapman, 1973) suggests that he considered

VI. The Glorified Body of the Risen Jesus in John 20

The Significance of the Resurrection of the Body for Christian Faith

We turn finally to the Resurrection Narrative in John 20 to explore the role of the body of Jesus in the post-paschal dispensation. I have suggested that just as the term "flesh" functioned throughout the lifetime of the historical Jesus to denote his real presence in his mortal humanity, "body" functions after the Glorification to speak of his real, divinely human, presence as risen Lord in and among his disciples. If Jesus ceased, at his death, to be a living human being, then Christian faith as Christian has no real object. Bodiliness, the condition of possibility and symbolic realization of human self-identity and continuity, intersubjective presence, and action in the world, is integral to the meaning of real, living humanity. But if bodiliness can only be understood in terms of the physical materiality that characterized the earthly Jesus, then it is imaginatively implausible and consequently incredible for many, if not most, people today as it was for Paul's listeners in Athens (cf. Acts 17:32) and some of his converts at Corinth (1 Cor 15:12ff.).

In what follows I am proposing that the Resurrection Narrative in John functions not primarily to proclaim or explain what happened to *Jesus* after his death (since, in John, he was glorified on the cross and has no need of vindicatory restoration) but to explore what his Glorification meant and means for his *followers*. In other words, the Glorification in John is Jesus' passage to God, and the Resurrection is Jesus' return to his own. This twofold destiny of Jesus is not a chronological succession of separate events but two dimensions of his post-paschal life. As Jesus promised on the eve of his death, "I go away [ὑπάγω] and I come to you [ἔρχομαι πρὸς ὑμᾶς]" (14:28), both verbs in the present. The bodily Resurrection is the condition of possibility for the fulfillment of that promise.

Structure and Content of John 20

Proposed structures—historical, chronological, literary, theological, and spiritual—for John 20 are legion.[47] Any well-crafted literary work is

---

Jesus/the presence of the glorified and risen Jesus as bodily. Hence the importance of the statement above.

[47] Robert Crotty, "The Two Magdalene Reports on the Risen Jesus in John 20," *Pacifica* 12 (June 1999): 156–68, lists some of the more interesting recent proposals:

susceptible to diverse structurations depending on how it is read. So, without disagreeing with most of those that have been proposed, I will offer a layered literary-theological-spiritual structure that I think can help us address the question of the body of the risen Lord.[48]

Literary structure. On the surface level the chapter is *narratively* divided into two parts: 1-18 and 19-29, each unified by place and time (see fig. 1, p. 183). In part 1, which takes place on Easter morning in the garden of the tomb, we read of Mary Magdalene's discovery of the open tomb (vv. 1-2), the Beloved Disciple coming to believe on the basis of what he and Simon Peter saw in the tomb (vv. 3-10), and Jesus' appearance to and commissioning of Mary Magdalene (vv. 11-18). In part 2, which takes place in Jerusalem, where the disciples were gathered on Easter evening and again the following Sunday, we read of Jesus' appearance to and commissioning of his assembled disciples (vv. 19-23) and his appearance a week later to Thomas (vv. 24-29). In verses 30-31, the Evangelist concludes both chapter 20 and the gospel as a whole by telling his readers that henceforth the gospel text will function for them as the signs of Jesus

---

Brown, *The Gospel according to John*, 2:965; F. J. Moloney, *The Gospel of John*, Sacra Pagina, vol. 4 (Collegeville, MN: Liturgical Press, 1988), 516; B. J. Byrne, "The Faith of the Beloved Disciple and the Community in John 20," *Journal for the Study of the New Testament* 23 (1985): 83–97; D. A. Lee, "Partnership in Easter Faith: The Role of Mary Magdelene and Thomas in John 20," *Journal of Studies in the New Testament* 53 (1995): 37–49; J. Dupont, C. Lash, and G. Levesque, "Recherche sur la structure de Jean 20," *Biblica* 54 (1973): 482–98; D. Mollat, "La foi paschale selon le chapître 20 de l'évangile de saint Jean," in Dhanis, *Resurrexit*, 316–34; I. de la Potterie, "Génèse de la foi pascale d'après Jn 20," *New Testament Studies* 30 (1984): 26–49. More recently, Raymond Brown again addressed the subject in "The Resurrection in John 20—A Series of Diverse Reactions," *Worship* 64 (May 1990): 194–206. A fascinating study of the use of numerical proportions among the verbs in chap. 20 to structure the narrative is J. S. Sibinga, "Towards Understanding the Composition of John 20," *The Four Gospels 1992*, 2139–52. He concludes that 20:16 emerges as the center of gravity of the chapter (2149). John Paul Heil, in *Blood and Water: The Death and Resurrection of Jesus in John 18–21* (Washington, DC: Catholic Biblical Association of America, 1995), 6, structures chap. 20 as six scenes arranged in four "sandwiches" that move the action forward and draw the reader forward by an intercalation: A[1], B[1], A[2], B[2], A[3], B[3], C which correspond respectively to the following scenes: A[1] 20:1-2; B[1] 20:3-10; A[2] 20:11-18; B[2] 20:19-23; A[3] 20:24-25; B[3] 20:26-29; C 20:30-31. Zumstein, "Lecture narratologique du cycle pascal du quatrième évangile," has already been mentioned as an excellent example of narratological structuring.

[48] I developed the structural theory I am proposing here (with slight revisions) in my 1976 doctoral dissertation, *The Johannine Resurrection Narrative*, 189–216.

had for his first disciples, i.e., as mediation of revelation leading to salvific faith.[49]

At a deeper level (see fig. 2, p. 184) the five scenes form a *dramatic* literary whole in which the first two scenes rise from the situation of the earthly disciples to the culminating appearance of Jesus to the community and the last two descend from that appearance toward the post-Easter audience. Each scene has its own revelatory crisis and subsequent resolution that prepares for the succeeding scene. In the first scene this crisis is verse 7, the Beloved Disciple seeing the face cloth; in the second, verse 16, Jesus calling Mary by name; in the third, verse 21, Jesus identifying his disciples with himself in mission; in the fourth, verse 27, Jesus inviting Thomas to believe; and in the fifth, verse 31, the Evangelist identifying the "the things which are written" as the signs for later believers.

Theological and spiritual structure (see fig. 3, p. 185). Most important for our purposes, however, is the *theological* structure of chapter 20, which is a careful answer to the question, "Where is the Lord?" and the resulting response to the *spiritual* question, "How can he be encountered today?"[50] Our primary interest is in the central scene, the appearance to the disciples, but what precedes is crucial preparation and what follows focuses the Easter event on post-Easter disciples.

---

[49] The debate continues about whether the verb in v. 31 is a present subjunctive (πιστεύητε), suggesting that the intended audience is the Christian community itself or an aorist subjective (πιστεύσητε), which would suggest that the gospel is directed to possible converts. Gordon D. Fee, "On the Text and Meaning of John 20,30-31," *The Four Gospels 1992*, 2193–2204, argues convincingly, against D. A. Carson, "The Purpose of the Fourth Gospel: John 20:31 Reconsidered," *Journal of Biblical Literature* 106 (1987): 639–51, that both from a text-critical standpoint and in terms of meaning the present-tense reading is preferable. I agree with this position and assume it in what follows.

[50] A leitmotif of the Christian mystical tradition is the question of how to find, how to encounter, the seemingly absent Lord. John of the Cross begins his classic poem on the mystical life, *Cántico Espiritual*, with the anguished address of the bride-soul to Jesus, "Where have you hidden, Beloved, and left me groaning?" (See *The Collected Works of Saint John of the Cross*, rev. ed., trans. Kieren Kavanaugh and Otilio Rodriguez [Washington, DC: Institute of Carmelite Studies, 1991], citation from 44.) But the question predates John of the Cross by centuries, e.g., Augustine's famous "interrogation of the creatures," and continues up to the present. The path runs from the Song of Songs in the OT through the Gospel of John in the NT into the Jesus mysticism (sometimes called "bridal mysticism") of the subsequent tradition.

The first scene opens with Mary Magdalene coming to the tomb early on Easter morning and seeing the *stone* taken away. She concludes instantly, "They have taken the Lord out of tomb and we do not know *where* they have put him" (20:2). She voices the position of one who has not grasped the meaning of "the hour," Jesus' transition from the dispensation of the flesh to the dispensation of glory. She is seeking "the Lord" whom she equates with his corpse. The equation of person with body and body with flesh, therefore of person with flesh, is precisely what Easter faith must transcend. Mary Magdalene personifies the theological problem of how the earthly Jesus (the Word made flesh) is related to the glorified and risen Lord. And at the end of the chapter the Thomas scene will suggest that this is precisely the problem for Jesus' disciples of all time.

At Mary's report, Simon Peter and the Beloved Disciple (BD) run to the tomb and examine its contents. Both see in the tomb the abandoned burial cloths and the veil (σουδάριον) that had been on Jesus' face not lying with the cloths but carefully and definitively wrapped up and placed aside. We are told that the BD (not Peter) "saw and believed" (20:8). In John, to see and believe is to respond in faith to a revelatory sign (σημεῖον). But the question is, "What did he believe?" since the next verse tells us that "as yet they did not know the scripture that he must rise from the dead" (20:9).

Johannine symbolism as well as the literary structure of the episode suggest to me that the sign that led the Beloved Disciple to believe was neither the open tomb nor the linen cloths but the face veil, linguistically related to the face veil that Moses wore to protect the Israelites from the glorification of his face by his encounter with God on Sinai (cf. Exod 34:27-35).[51] Jesus, the New Moses, had definitively left behind the veil

---

[51] Σουδάριον is the Greek transliteration of a Latin loanword, *sudarium*. The root suggests that it was a towel or a handkerchief. Most significantly, it appears in the Aramaic of Targums pseudo-Jonathan and Yerushalmi (Codex Neofiti I) as *soudârâ*, סודא or סודר, to translate מסוה, a unique word for the face veil of Moses in Exod 34:33-35. It has the same sense in Syriac. In other words, σουδάριον in the FG is probably equivalent to the LXX's in Exodus 34, meaning "veil," and if John's community was originally Aramaic-speaking and read or heard the OT in Aramaic they would have heard σουδάριον as equivalent to the LXX's κάλυμμα in reference to the face veil of Moses. Σουδάριον, however, would be preferable to the very common word κάλυμμα if the intention was to call attention to the unique character of Jesus' face veil, as Moses' face veil was designated by a unique word. That Jesus' face veil was not simply a normal burial cloth seems to be suggested by the notation that it was not

of his earthly flesh as he returned to the glory he had as Son with God before the world was made (cf. 17:24).[52] The first installment of the answer to the question "Where is the Lord?" has been supplied: Jesus is with God, i.e., he has been glorified. Neither the fact nor the meaning of the Resurrection as Jesus' return to his own is yet available.

The next scene, redolent of allusions to both the garden of the first creation (cf. Gen 2:8ff. and 3:8-10) and the Song of Songs (esp. Song 3:1-4),[53] brings the lover, Mary Magdalene, to the garden of the tomb search-

---

lying with the burial clothes but wrapped up into a place by itself. Paul's use of the face veil of Moses (2 Cor 3:6-18) to speak of the passing away of the Old Covenant and the establishment of the New suggests that this symbolism was not unfamiliar in early Christian circles. Jesus, in John, is the mediator of the New Covenant. The relation of מסוה to סודאר was pointed out decades ago by F.–M. Braun, *Le Linceul de Turin et l'évangile de S. Jean: Étude de critique et d'exégése* (Tournai and Paris: Casterman, 1939), 34–35.

[52] Brendan Byrne, in "The Faith of the Beloved Disciple and the Community in John 20," *Journal for the Study of the New Testament* 23 (1985): 83–97, also proposes that the *soudarion* is the sign, but he explicitly disagrees with me about the meaning of the sign. He locates its meaning in the contrast of Jesus' face veil with Lazarus's: Lazarus had to have the veil removed by others whereas Jesus removed his own. I would not reject that interpretation, but I think that there is considerably more involved, namely, the evocation of the Mosaic-covenantal motif. Byrne's thesis concerning the relation of the "seeing and believing" in the 3-10 episode to that in 24-29 is, however, a real contribution. In a sense, the whole of chap. 20 is an exploration of the "absence" (I would say the absence/presence) of Jesus and the role of signs, historical signs and ecclesial ones, in the handling of that experience. I am in substantial agreement with his conclusion: "The Gospel of John seems to me to be composed very largely to give subsequent believers access to the central events of Jesus' life, death, Resurrection and return to the Father and to assure them that in this access they can have an encounter with Jesus every bit as valid and indeed more fruitful than that of those who actually saw him" (93). I am, however, not persuaded that there is a hierarchical comparison, explicit or implicit, in 20:29.

[53] The influence of the Song of Songs on John 20 was suggested by A. Feuillet, "La Recherche du Christ dans la Nouvelle Alliance d'après la Christophanie de Jo. 20,11-18: Comparaison avec Cant. 3, 1-4 et l'épisode des pélerins d'Emmaüs," in *L'Homme devant Dieu: Mélanges offerts au père Henri de Lubac*, Théologie 56 (Paris: Aubier, 1963), 93–112. John, in chap. 20, uses κῆπος for "garden." In the LXX the garden of creation is παράδεισος, while the garden in the Song of Songs is κῆπος, suggesting that the stronger allusion is to the Song. There is, however, a progression in the OT from the paradise in which humanity was created in union with God and from which it was expelled because of sin, through the alternating possession and loss of the land (a garden or a desert) because of Israel's fidelity or infidelity to the covenant, to the garden of union in the Song of Songs. So the allusion in chap. 20 is probably to both paradise regained, i.e., the New Creation, and the New Covenant. For a different

ing for her Beloved and refusing comfort or enlightenment from anyone, even angels, who cannot tell her where he is. No one doubts that the center of this episode is the recognition scene in which Jesus, whom Mary takes for the gardener, directly addresses her, "Mary." He is indeed the Divine Gardener inaugurating the New Creation, the Good Shepherd calling his own by name, and the Spouse of the New Covenant reward-ing the search of the anguished lover. Mary recognizes him as her Teach-er.[54] But she is still struggling out of the darkness of her pre-paschal literalism into the light of Easter. Jesus forestalls her attempt to touch him, to encounter him in the flesh as his disciples could and did prior to his Glorification. Jean Zumstein helpfully provides a paraphrastic translation of verse 17a, the famous "Do not touch me" verse, as "*For you*, I am not yet ascended to the Father."[55] Jesus, glorified on the cross, has indeed gone to the Father, but in Mary's perception he has not yet ascended, for she has not yet integrated the fact that he has also been glorified into her realization that Jesus is risen. Jesus redirects her to the community of his brothers and sisters, which is, in a mysterious way, his glorified body. Mary understands that the "brothers and sisters" means "the disciples," and she arrives as the first apostle of the Resur-rection announcing, "I have seen the Lord" (20:18).

Furnished with the essential knowledge that Jesus is both glorified (from the first scene) and risen (from the second scene), that is, with the theological answer to the question, "Where is the Lord?" the reader is prepared for the chapter's central scene, which will answer the question, "How are post-paschal disciples to encounter the risen Lord?" The nega-tive answer from the first two scenes is that it is not through physical sight or touch of his earthly body, that is, not in the flesh, but somehow in his disciples. Scene three narratively explores this cryptic answer.

The central scene is the shortest and least circumstantial in the chapter. Its depth derives largely from the fact that it is suffused with the Last Discourse(s) material, which itself is suffused with the themes and even

---

interpretation of the use by John of κῆπος, see J. N. Suggit, "Jesus the Gardener," *Neotestamentica* 33, no. 1 (1999): 166.

[54] "Teacher" is the quintessential identity of the historical Jesus in John as the pri-mary relationship to him is that of "disciple." This address by Mary, with her attempt to touch him physically, suggests that she is still short of full Easter faith, which, somehow, she seems to possess by the time she reaches the disciples where she an-nounces not that she has seen the Teacher or even Jesus but that she has seen the Lord.

[55] Zumstein, "Lecture narratologique du cycle pascal du quatrième évangile," 7.

the language of the New Covenant from Isaiah 51–56 and 65–66, Jeremiah 31, and Ezekiel 36–37.[56] These themes include the sealing of the New Covenant itself and its gifts of peace, joy, seeing the Lord, knowledge of the Lord, purification from sin, a New Spirit, and a new heart. The New Covenant will unite Yahweh with his purified and faithful spouse, the New Israel, and the sign of their mutual belonging will be the New Tabernacle, God's own presence, raised up in their midst.

When the scene is displayed structurally (see fig. 4, p. 186), it is clearly perfectly balanced, with one all-important exception. The scene falls into two parts, evoking the two dimensions of the Sinai covenant, the theophany followed by the gift of Torah (cf. Exod 19:16–20:17). Each part of John 20:19-23, the christophany and the giving of the Spirit who is the New Law placed in their hearts, opens with a solemn declaration, "Peace be to you," the fulfillment of Jesus' promise that he would see them again and give them a peace that the world cannot give or take away (cf. 14:27).

Part 1, the christophany, is the revelation of the risen Jesus to the community of his disciples. The Jesus standing in their midst is no shade from Sheol. He is Jesus, the One who had been crucified and pierced, who had died and whose body had been buried. His body, marked with the signs of his Glorification through death and its life-giving fruit of the Spirit, establishes both his identity in himself and his capacity to reestablish his presence to and relationship with them. But the Jesus standing in their midst is not simply resuscitated. He is alive with a new life that is bodily but no longer subject to death or to the laws of historical space, time, and causality. He is the same person, Jesus, but in a new mode of being and presence.

Part 2 of the scene is the giving of the New Law, i.e., the Spirit, promised in Isaiah 55:7, Jeremiah 31:33, and Ezekiel 36:26-27 and 37:1-10, 14, 24. This Spirit both unites them to Jesus and empowers them for a new life in which, sent as Jesus was sent by the Father, they will continue his mission as the Lamb of God who takes away sin of the world (cf. 1:29

---

[56] I was impressed by the paper delivered by Rekha Chennattu, " 'If You Keep My Commandments': Exploring Covenant Motifs in John 13–17," at the August 2003 convention of the Catholic Biblical Association of America, in which she used the account of the covenant renewal in Josh 24 to highlight the covenant themes she proposes that John used to structure his presentation of discipleship as a covenant relationship. If John presents discipleship as a covenantal relationship, there is all the more reason to think that his understanding of the post-paschal community's relationship with God in Jesus is the realization of the New Covenant.

with 20:21-23). Jesus bestows the Spirit of the New Covenant by breathing on his disciples, as God had breathed the first human into life and new life into the dry bones in Ezekiel's vision, a clear indication that this *New People*, the community, with whom this *New Covenant* is made is indeed a *New Creation*.[57]

This brings us back to the one notable exception to the perfectly balanced structure of the passage. Except for verse 19c, "Jesus came and stood [or rose up] in[to] the[ir] midst," every member in the passage has a corresponding member. We have just been told that the doors where the disciples were gathered had been closed (κεκλεισμένων) for fear of "the Jews." Suddenly Jesus arises among them.[58] (He does not, as some have naïvely pictured it, come through the doors or walls!) The preposition εἰς with the accusative suggests motion to the interior. But the interior in this text is not a physical place. It is "where the disciples were gathered together" (20:19).[59] Jesus arises in the midst of the community. The verb "to stand" or "to arise" evokes Jesus' promise in chapter 2 to raise up the New Temple, his body, which his enemies will have destroyed. In the OT the sign of the New Covenant was to be that Yahweh would establish his tabernacle in the midst of the renewed people:

> I will make with them a covenant of peace; it shall be an everlasting covenant with them, and I will multiply them, and put my sanctuary among them forever. My dwelling shall be with them; I will be their

---

[57] Ἐνεφύσησεν (ἐμφυσάω) in v. 22 is a NT *hapax legomenon*. There are only three uses of the term in the OT, all directly connected with creation: Gen 2:7, the enlivening of the "earth creature" with God's breath; Wis 15:11, which refers to that event; Ezek 37:9, in which the prophet is told to breathe upon the bones of the house of Israel that it might be re-created. The use of the word in the LXX of 1 Kgs 17:21 is either a mistranslation or a reinterpretation of the verb יתמרר ("stretched" or "measured") in the Hebrew text.

[58] See n. 38 on the possible meaning "arise" for "came and stood."

[59] C. H. Cosgrove, "The Place Where Jesus Is: Allusions to Baptism and the Eucharist in the Fourth Gospel," *New Testament Studies* 35 (1989): 522–39, presents a fascinating argument for the community as the "flesh" of Jesus and the "hard saying" in John 6 as directed at the crypto-Christians in the Johannine community who want a faith that does not express itself in public community participation. Because "the life of the Spirit is present nowhere else but in the concrete fleshly existence of the community" (535), it is only by participating in the Eucharist (and thus identifying oneself publicly with Jesus) that one can have life. I think this is a very thoughtful suggestion. The community in its historical existence would be the flesh of the glorified Jesus who is, in himself, glorified body.

God and they shall be my people. Thus the nations shall know that
it is I, the Lord, who make Israel holy, when my sanctuary shall be
set up among them forever. (Ezek 37:26-28)

This New People will worship not in a physical place, whether temple
or mountain, but in Spirit and in Truth (cf. John 4:21-24). Jesus the Truth
now pours out on them his Spirit.

What is structurally exceptional about this line, "Jesus came and stood
in[to] the[ir] midst," is that there is no corresponding member at the end
of the scene. Literarily there should be a notice that, having finished that
for which he came, Jesus left, or that he vanished from their sight (cf.
20:2 in relation to 1, and 20:10 in relation to 3). But even though Jesus
will come again, he never leaves suggesting the new mode of Jesus'
presence to his disciples.

Two further points, which cannot be explored in depth here, must be
made before leaving this central scene. First, the *group* to which the risen
Jesus comes in John 20 is not the Twelve; the seventy-two; the apostles;
Peter, James, and John; or any other select group.[60] He comes to "the
disciples," which, in John, is an inclusive group of men and women;
itinerants and householders; Jews, Samaritans, and Gentiles.[61] Believers,
the Church as community not as hierarchical institution, are the foundational symbolic expression of the risen Jesus. The Church is his Body.[62]

---

[60] James Swetnam, "Bestowal of the Spirit in the Fourth Gospel," represents well
the position, with which I am here disagreeing, that the Spirit was given in 20:22 to
"a restricted group of disciples, possibly only to the 'Twelve'" as "an agent of empowerment to help [the restricted group] to act with regard to the forgiveness of sins"
(572). I agree with Raymond Brown, *The Gospel according to John*, 2:1044: "We doubt
that there is sufficient evidence to confine the power of forgiving and withholding
of sin, granted in John xx 23, to a specific exercise of power in the Christian community, whether that be admission to Baptism or forgiveness in Penance. These are
but partial manifestations of a much larger power, . . . given to Jesus in his mission
by the Father and given in turn by Jesus through the Spirit to those whom he commissions. . . . John does not tell us how or by whom this power was exercised . . .
[but] that it was exercised."

[61] The gospel, especially chap. 4, which includes the story of the conversion of the
Samaritans at Sychar and of the (probably Gentile) royal official and "his whole
household," suggests that at least after the Resurrection the community included not
only Jews but Samaritans and Gentiles.

[62] John's use of body is quite different from Paul's, which is an image for the unity
and mutuality of the "members" within the Church of which Christ is the head. In
John, the Church is a mode of Jesus' presence, his bodyself, present and active in the
world.

Second, the *commission* in John is to continue the work of Jesus who came to take away the sin (singular) of the world, i.e., the fundamental sin of unbelief. The disciples will carry on this mission by forgiving sins (plural), the expressions of unbelief that are renounced by those who come to believe in Jesus. Sometime after the third century a linguistic anomaly, in which "retention of sins" was gratuitously paired with "forgiveness of sins," found its way into the translation of verse 23 and was eventually enshrined dogmatically in the decrees of the Council of Trent.[63] The exegetical basis for this move was interpreting John 20:23 as a parallel of Matt 16:19 and 18:18 on binding and loosing through interpretation of the law, thus reading John 20:23 as an elliptical antithetical parallelism. The apologetic basis was the establishment of the Catholic discipline of confession as a sacrament against its rejection by the Reformers.[64]

Whatever might be said about the apologetic motive, it is highly questionable to read John in terms of Matthew, but especially when the respective contexts differ completely. In any case, the text of John 20:23 does not say anything about "retaining sins." Translated literally, it says, "Of whomever you forgive the sins, they are forgiven to them; whomever you hold are held fast."[65] In the second member there is no direct object, "sins," nor indirect object, "to them." The verb "to hold," κρατέω, does

[63] The pertinent decrees were made in the fourteenth session of the Council of Trent (1551). See H. Denziger and A. Schönmetzer, *Enchiridion Symbolorum: Definitionum et Declarationum de Rebus Fidei et Morum*, 34th ed. (Freiburg-im-Breisgau: Herder, 1965), 1703, defining John 20:23 as the institution of the sacrament of penance, and 1710, concerning the requirement of an ordained minister for the sacrament.

[64] Raymond Brown takes a judicious position on the Tridentine declarations that John 20:23 is the establishment of the Roman Catholic penitential discipline as a sacrament that can only be administered by the ordained. He distinguishes between what the text (or the text's author) intends, which could hardly be what Trent defined, and the legitimate and diverse disciplines developed by various Christian communities. See Brown, *The Gospel according to John*, 2:1044–45.

[65] Raymond Brown, "The Resurrection in John 20," 194–206, accurately translates this text: "If you forgive people's sins, their sins are forgiven; if you hold them they are held fast." He takes it for granted that "them" refers to sins, which is not really what the text suggests since there is a real, textual parallel between ἄν τινων in 23a, which he reads as "people," and ἄν τινων in 23b, which he reads as "sins" (implied). He says, however, that whatever positions patristic or Tridentine writers took, "there is no requirement to think that the evangelist had them in mind" (204, n. 16). I suspect that this is one of the cases in which Brown tries to walk a tightrope between the results of his scholarship and official Church teaching based on approaches to Scripture before *Divino Afflante Spiritu*.

not mean, in secular or biblical Greek, "retain." It means "hold fast," "grasp," even "embrace" (cf. Matt 28:9 where κρατέω is correctly translated "held" or "embraced"). And it normally takes an objective genitive, as it does in this case, τινων, "whomever." In other words, the text as it stands is a synthetic or progressive parallel. The community that forgives sins must hold fast those whom it has brought into the community of eternal life. This may be a reference to baptism but hardly to penance.[66] But whether or not there is an explicit sacramental reference, translating this text as it stands rather than by supplying supposedly missing words to create a parallel to Matthew, accords well, in both form and content, with Jesus' own descriptions of his mission from the Father, which he is here committing to his disciples.

> All that the Father *gives* me will come to me and the one who comes to me I *will not cast out*. (6:37)

> It is the will of the One who sent me that I should *lose nothing* of all that he has *given* me. (6:39)

> I *give them eternal life* and they shall *never perish*, and *no one shall snatch them out of my Father's hand*. My father, who has *given* them to me, is greater than all, and *no one is able to snatch them out of the Father's hand*. I and the Father are one. (10:27-29)

> While I was with them, I *kept* them in your name those whom you have *given* me, and I guarded them, and *not one of them is lost*. (17:12)

> This was to fulfill the word which he had spoken, "Of those whom you have *given* me I have *not lost* any." (18:9)[67]

---

[66] T. Worden, "The Remission of Sins," *Scripture* 9 (1957): 65–79, 115–27, is a study of virtually all patristic references to the possibility of forgiveness of sins committed after baptism. In the first three centuries, when this was a hotly debated issue, there is no reference to John 20:23 as warrant for such a practice, even by those fathers who held adamantly to this possibility. This argues strongly that John 20:23 was not understood by those closest to its composition as having anything to do with the sacrament of penance, which, in all likelihood, did not exist in any form in the Johannine communities.

[67] It is interesting to note that there is only one passage in the OT where ἀφιήμι and κράτεω occur together in reference to an object. It is Song 3:4, a passage whose influence on John 20 has already been noted. The words constitute a negative and a positive expression of the union between the spouse and the Beloved (Israel and Yahweh). "I held [ἐκράτησα] him and would not let him go [ἀφῆκα]."

The importance of this point lies in how John understands the community of the New Covenant. The community is the ongoing bodily presence of Jesus in the world. As the Father had sent him, so he sends his disciples (v. 21). They are to live by his Spirit, which he breathes upon them (v. 22), and to carry on his mission of receiving those whom the Father gives them and holding them fast in the community (v. 23) as Jesus received his disciples from the Father and held them fast amid the evils and dangers of the world. Jesus (in the flesh) is no longer in the world, but they (his body) are in the world (cf. 17:11). They are to do his works, and even greater works than he had done in his earthly career (cf. 14:12). The community is not, according to John, an agent of a departed Jesus exercising judgment, which Jesus explicitly said he was not sent to do and does not do (12:47). The community in all its members is Jesus at work in the world, and his work is to take away sins by giving life in all its fullness.

There is no indication in the text, as this Church founding scene ends, that the reader should expect anything further. So the next scene opens unexpectedly with the news that one of the Twelve, Thomas, was not with the community when Jesus came. Significantly, Thomas is called "the twin." He has a double identity: he is both a disciple of the earthly Jesus and he shares the experience of later disciples who were not present on Easter.[68] Narratively, the Evangelist establishes the identity of pre-Easter and post-Easter disciples for whom the structure of faith is essentially the same.

The glorified Jesus, not bound by earthly conditions of physicality, is again sensibly, i.e., bodily, present even though the doors are closed, and he knows of Thomas's refusal to believe on the basis of the disciples' witness, "We have seen the Lord." Jesus invites Thomas to touch him even as he challenges him to renounce the unbelieving demand to do so

---

[68] When, two decades ago, I suggested this symbolic significance to the identification of Thomas the Twin in *The Johannine Resurrection Narrative*, 579–85, it seemed "too symbolic" for some readers. Recently, however, perhaps as literary approaches have made scholars more amenable to symbolic material in the gospel, J. N. Suggit, in "Jesus the Gardener," 161–68, proposed that Thomas is the twin "to remind disciples that Thomas is *their* twin. Thomas, the twin, the representative of every disciple, was prepared to accompany Jesus to share in his death," referring to 11:16 (162; emphasis in original). Interestingly, Suggit feels he still has to justify this type of interpretation (167)!

and become believing (v. 27).[69] Thomas rises to the challenge. He confesses what he cannot see with his bodily eyes, that the Jesus who addresses him is "My Lord and my God" (v. 28).

Jesus' response is all-important. He accepts Thomas's confession of what he cannot see based on what he has seen, both in his pre-paschal experience of Jesus and in this Easter experience. But Jesus equates Thomas's "seeing" to the "not seeing" of all disciples down through the centuries who will not have seen Jesus in the flesh or in Easter appearance (20:29).[70] Their believing will be based on "seeing" him in sacramental signs, "hearing" him in the community's witness, and especially in the "things written" in the gospel. Following Jesus' turn in blessing to his future disciples in verse 29, the Evangelist addresses the readers directly by equating the signs of the earthly Jesus with the gospel text itself. Just as his first disciples had to discern in his ambiguous historical signs the revelation of God in Jesus, and the Easter community had to discern their Lord and God in the mysterious person risen in their midst whom they are not to touch physically, so all later disciples must discern the new bodily presence of Jesus in the ecclesial community, Eucharist, and Gospel. In all these cases, Jesus as the locus and revelation of God's glory is perceptible only to the eyes and ears of faith responding to the symbolic modes of his presence.

John 20 as a whole, and especially the contrast between the Mary Magdalene and Thomas scenes in light of the central scene of the raising of the temple of Jesus' body in the midst of the New Covenant people, tells us something crucial about the body of the glorified and risen Jesus. It is human and material but not physical.[71] In other words, mortal flesh has become glorified body. In the Mary Magdalene scene Jesus restrains Mary from trying to touch him physically, not because he is a ghost, or because he disdains her love and desire. It is because she does not completely grasp that he has not been resuscitated like Lazarus to life in the flesh. Jesus redirects Mary's attempt to relate to him by pointing her to

---

[69] Brown, "The Resurrection in John 20," 205, says that Jesus turns the tables on Thomas. Thomas demanded to probe Jesus physically, and Jesus now probes him spiritually by inviting him to do what he demanded.

[70] There is no basis in the text for reading a hierarchy of "blessedness" in Jesus' macarism. Thomas is blessed for his believing based on seeing; later disciples are blessed for their believing although they have not seen.

[71] Ward, "Bodies," 176, says, "The body of Jesus Christ [after the Resurrection and ascension], the body of God, is permeable, transcorporeal, transpositional." I find this an intriguing way of expressing the mode of being of the glorified Jesus.

his presence in the community where she will touch him, encounter him, in a new way corresponding to his new mode of being and presence.

In the Thomas scene Jesus invites Thomas to touch him. The glorified Jesus can self-symbolize quasi-physically if that is necessary, but this is not how he ordinarily chooses to be present, to Thomas or to us. Thomas becomes "not unbelieving but believing" when he, like Mary, moves from the dispensation of the flesh to the dispensation of glory. He recognizes Jesus as the person he knew in the flesh but who, while remaining himself, is no longer in the context of history.

These two seemingly contradictory facts, that Jesus is himself in the full integrity of his humanity and that he is no longer subject to the historical coordinates of space, time, and causality, are mediated by the concept of body as symbol. In the context of history the human person self-symbolizes in and as her or his mortal (i.e., fleshly) bodyself. Person as subject, body as symbolic self-expression, and flesh as physical, i.e., mortal, locus of the person as bodyself are coterminous, which leads us to spontaneously identify them without distinction. John's Resurrection Narrative suggests (as does Paul in 1 Cor 15 and Luke in the Damascus road event in Acts 9:5) that the glorified person, Jesus himself in his divine humanity, continues to self-symbolize, that is, to be bodily present and active but no longer in mortal flesh. He can be present when, where, and how he wills: in the community itself and in its actions of preaching the Word, celebrating Eucharist, and ministering to the needy. He can be present to the individual believer in prayer or even in vision, although John, like spiritual writers down through the centuries, warns that this is an exceptional and always ambiguous occurrence that is not to be sought or privileged. Materiality as the condition of symbolic self-expression is what bodiliness connotes. It is that which marks the person, Jesus, as distinct from other persons and self-continuous, as a subject who can relate to other subjects, and as one who can act effectively in the world even though not conditioned by it. Materiality, which is the condition of possibility of sensibility, is no longer equated with physicality. The glorified body is a body, Jesus as body, but it is no longer a fleshly, that is, a mortal or historical, body.

VII. Conclusion

In summary and conclusion, the bodiliness of Jesus' Resurrection is crucial to Christian faith, theology, and spirituality for a number of reasons. First, only if Jesus is alive in the full integrity of his humanity, which entails bodiliness, *can he be in God the firstfruits of humanity's incorporation into divinity.* Humanity is not a transitory mode of the Word that he abandoned in death.

Second, because body is the symbolic mode of presence, both self-presence as subject and intersubjective presence to others, *the real and personal existence of Jesus as human after his death and his continuing presence to his followers* requires bodily resurrection.

Third, symbols are the perceptibility of what is otherwise not able to be encountered, and because body as material (not as physical) is the condition of possibility of perceptibility, *Jesus can only self-symbolize in various ways* if his post-Resurrection humanity is bodily.

Fourth, body is not exhausted in the notion of "flesh," i.e., humanity as mortal. Jesus as the Word made flesh experienced the condition of mortality, but by his Glorification he transcended that condition and *became capable, in his humanity, of a range of self-symbolization that is not limited by space, time, or causality.*

Fifth, the *Church's faith in the real presence of Jesus* in his ecclesial body, in his eucharistic body, in the textual body of Scripture, is also expressed in the spirituality tradition of those mystics whose direct experience of Jesus as friend, lover, and spouse has been nurtured especially by the Song of Songs and the Fourth Gospel. We see this Jesus mysticism in writers such as Origen, Gertrude of Helfta, Bernard of Clairvaux, Catherine of Siena, Francis of Assisi, Teresa of Avila, John of the Cross, and later writers.

In short, John's gospel is a primary source and resource for the experience in the Church of the glorified human Jesus, personally alive, present, and active throughout all time. The Church's spirituality is an ongoing exploration of the existential meaning of Jesus' promise:

> I will not leave you orphans: I am coming to you. Yet a little while and the world sees me no longer, but you see me, for because I live you also will live. In that day you will know that I am in the Father, and you in me, and I in you. (John 14:18-20)

Part Two

John's Theology and Spirituality of Presence

Chapter 4

The Raising of the New Temple:
John 20:19-23 and Johannine Ecclesiology

I. Introduction

In 1958 Alf Corell called John 20:19-23, the scene of Jesus' Easter appearance to the community of his disciples, part of the most badly treated passage in the Fourth Gospel,[1] a judgment that ongoing conflicts of interpretation suggest still has some validity. Its mistreatment, it seems to me, is due in large measure to the predominant tendency in the history of its interpretation to divide this passage into two separate events and to interpret each in terms of supposed Synoptic parallels. Verses 19-20 are frequently interpreted as John's version of Luke 24:36-43 and thus as an apologetically motivated demonstration of the reality and miraculous qualities of the body of the risen Jesus. Verses 21-23 are often read in terms of Luke's Ascension-Pentecost material (Luke 24:51; Acts 2:1-4) and Matthew's binding and loosing texts (Matt 16:19; 18:18). This leads to a focus on two questions. First, how is this Johannine scene related to Jesus' ascension and is this John's version of Pentecost?[2] Second, is the

Originally published as "The Raising of the New Temple: John 20.19-23 and Johannine Ecclesiology," *New Testament Studies* 52 (July 2006): 337–55.

[1] A. Corell, *Consummatum Est: Eschatology and Church in the Gospel of St. John* (London: SPCK, 1958), 36. His comment applies to the whole of John 20:19-29.

[2] See T. R. Hatina, "John 20,22 in Its Eschatological Context: Promise or Fulfillment?," *Biblica* 74, no. 2 (1993): 196–219, arguing against D. A. Carson, *The Gospel according to John* (Grand Rapids, MI: Eerdmans, 1991), 652–54. Hatina rejects Carson's argument that the Lukan Pentecost is the criterion by which other experiences of the

commission Jesus imparts here the Johannine version of the Matthean commissioning of Peter and of the disciples to "bind and loose"?[3] My position on these questions will become apparent, but for the moment suffice it to say that I consider these questions ill-conceived insofar as they are generated by an exclusively historical-critical methodology that is not well suited to the texts in question.

The literary-theological approach I will take to the passage involves four presuppositions. First, unlike Bultmann, who hypothesized that because the Glorification of Jesus takes place on the cross in John's gospel the Resurrection Narrative has no real purpose in this gospel except as a concession to the established tradition,[4] I regard the Resurrection Narrative as a crucial and integral component of the Fourth Gospel even though it plays a very different role in John's theology than it does in the Synoptic Gospels.

Second, I presuppose the theological unity of John 20 and the centrality within the chapter of this pericope, which, I will suggest, is the sealing of the New Covenant with the New Israel, in whose midst has been raised up the New Temple, the glorified Jesus. This implies taking very seriously the Old Testament, especially the prophetic literature, as intertext.

My third presupposition is that this passage has no Synoptic parallels. John probably reflects a common tradition that the risen Jesus appeared not only to individuals but also to groups (cf. 1 Cor 15:5-7; Mark 16:14-18; Matt 28:16-20), one of which he commissioned to carry on his mission. There are substantive thematic similarities between Matthew 28:16-20 and John 20:19-23, namely, Jesus' empowering his disciples with his own authority received from the Father; the modeling of their mission on Jesus' mission to them; Jesus' remaining with them; and the reference, explicit in Matthew and implicit in John, to baptism. There are, however, virtually no verbal contacts that would suggest any textual relationship.

Spirit must be considered. I agree with Hatina's position. See also C. Bennema, "The Giving of the Spirit in John's Gospel—A New Proposal?," *The Evangelical Quarterly* 74, no. 3 (2002): 195–213, who summarizes six currently held positions on the meaning of 20:22 (201–8).

[3] For a clear presentation, which he espouses, of the common position on John 20:23 as a parallel of the Matthean texts, see J. A. Emerton, "Binding and Loosing—Forgiving and Retaining," *Journal of Theological Studies* 13 (1962): 325–31.

[4] R. Bultmann, *Theology of the New Testament*, trans. K. Grobel, vol. 2 (New York: Charles Scribner's Sons, 1955), 56.

Fourth, and following the preceding, I presuppose that the entire passage is to be interpreted in terms of the theology and spirituality of the Fourth Gospel itself, especially as expressed in the Last Discourses (John 14–17), which are pervasively influenced by the Old Testament themes of creation/new creation in Genesis 2:7 and Ezekiel 37:9-10, covenant/new covenant in Exodus 19–20 and Jeremiah 31:31-34 with Ezekiel 37:26-28.

By way of proleptic summary, I will conclude that the passage as a whole is a narrative-theological synthesis of Johannine ecclesiology in which the Church appears as the body of the risen Lord who is in its midst as the glory of God and which is commissioned to be in the world the presence of the post-Easter Jesus as the pre-Easter Jesus had been the presence of God in the world.[5]

Since I will be using a predominantly literary-theological rather than exegetical-historical approach to this text, the structure of the chapter as a whole and the pericope in question have special importance. Numerous structural theories, some incompatible with each other and many complementary, have been proposed for chapter 20.[6] For our purposes I offer two narrative structurings of chapter 20, one concerned with the theology of the Resurrection and the other with the spirituality of Jesus' post-Easter disciples. (See figs. 1 and 3 in the appendix.)

A first narrative structure suggests a theological division of the chapter into two interconnected parts, each governed by a thematic question to which the text responds. Part 1, verses 1-18, which takes place in the garden of the tomb, responds to the concern of the traumatized community, voiced by Mary Magdalene, "Where is the Lord?" after his crucifixion. The two-step answer is that Jesus is glorified, i.e., that he has, as he predicted, *returned to the Father*. This is intuited in faith by the Beloved Disciple who, confronted with the sign of the face veil definitively laid

---

[5] I came to this conclusion before reading the article by R. Kysar, " 'As You Sent Me': Identity and Mission in the Fourth Gospel," *Word and World* 21, no. 4 (2001): 370–76, which gives an excellent short summary of this position. I disagree strongly with the position of J. Meier, "The Absence and Presence of the Church in John's Gospel," *Mid-Stream* 41, no. 4 (2002): 27–34, in which he maintains that "High christology is the black hole in the Johannine universe that swallows up every other topic, including the church" (29). His argument seems to be driven by an understanding of Church as necessarily hierarchical in nature and essentially if not primarily a structure rather than a mystery of relationality.

[6] R. Crotty, "The Two Magdalene Reports on the Risen Jesus in John 20," *Pacifica* 12 (June 1999): 156–68, summarized and criticized a number of the major attempts to decipher the structure of John 20.

aside in the tomb, "sees and believes" that the predicted Glorification of Jesus has indeed occurred even though, as yet, neither he nor Simon Peter understands the Scripture that Jesus must rise from the dead.[7] The Resurrection, i.e., Jesus' promised *return to his own* (cf. 16:16-22), is revealed in the next pericope in Jesus' encounter with Mary Magdalene, who is commissioned to announce it to the disciples. In John's Resurrection Narrative, in other words, there is a subtle but significant distinction between the *Glorification*, i.e., what happened to Jesus on the cross, and the *Resurrection*, which is the communication of the effects and significance of Jesus' Glorification to his disciples.[8]

Part 2, verses 19-31, responds to the question, "How can the glorified and risen Lord be encountered?" by his post-Easter disciples. The answer is that this encounter can take place in the community of those who are now Jesus' brothers and sisters (cf. 20:17), those who have seen the Lord (cf. 20:18, 20:24), who participate in his life through the Spirit they receive from the open side of the glorified Jesus (cf. 20:20-22), and who proclaim the Gospel, the "things that are written" that all may believe and through believing have life in Jesus' name (cf. 20:31).[9]

A second narrative structure, which suggests the spiritual dynamics of the scene, complements the first structure and depends on it. It is a concentric exploration of the changed mode of Jesus' presence to his disciples as the physical, mortal mode of his pre-Easter presence gives way in their experience to his new, equally real and personal, ecclesial

---

[7] I have presented my interpretation of the σουδάριον as a Johannine σημεῖον in chap. 12 of *Written That You May Believe: Encountering Jesus in the Fourth Gospel*, 2nd ed. (New York: Crossroad, 2003), 202–10.

[8] I am suggesting a *theological* distinction between the two aspects of the paschal mystery, not a *chronological* distinction, as does Hatina in "John 20,22," between two different phases in the gift of the Spirit. See the article by M. J. J. Menken, "Interpretation of the Old Testament and the Resurrection of Jesus in John's Gospel," in *Resurrection in the New Testament: Festschrift J. Lambrecht*, ed. R. Bieringer, V. Koperski, and B. Latair (Leuven: Peeters, 2002), 189–205, who follows C. H. Dodd in making a distinction somewhat akin to mine. Dodd suggested two modes of the event of Resurrection, one occurring outside history in Jesus' death on the cross (what I am calling Glorification) and the manifestation of this reality within history in the experience of the disciples (what I am calling Resurrection).

[9] R. Kysar, "As You Sent Me," 375, says, "In the context of the Fourth Gospel, we are correct . . . to think of the community of believers as the continuing incarnation of the Word (1:4)." See also the insightful article of M. L. Coloe, "Raising the Johannine Temple (John 19:19-29)," *Australian Biblical Review* 48 (2000): 47–58, on the community as the New Temple.

mode of presence. The first and fifth scenes take place in what we might call "ordinary time." The first scene, verses 1-10, involves nothing numinous or miraculous. Mary Magdalene, Simon Peter, and the Beloved Disciple are confronted with the kinds of signs that believers of all time will experience, ones in which Jesus is not physically present as he was when he healed the man born blind (John 9) or raised Lazarus from the dead (John 11) but through which he continues to reveal his presence and to act in their midst. The three disciples manifest the range of possible responses to such non-miraculous but revelatory signs. Mary, *seeing* (βλέπει) the sign of the open tomb, misinterprets it to mean that the Lord has been taken away (20:2, 13, 15); Simon Peter *examining* (θεωρεῖ) the grave clothes and face veil in the tomb draws a blank (20:6-7); the Beloved Disciple *contemplating* (εἶδεν) the face cloth sees and believes (20:8).

The balancing fifth "scene" is the conclusion to the chapter in which the Evangelist addresses directly the readers of all time. The implied author tells them that the sign that will be for them what the signs of the pre-Easter Jesus had been for his contemporaries is "these things that have been written" (20:31), i.e., the Gospel as Scripture. Scripture, like the open tomb and the face cloth, is the kind of non-miraculous sign through which later disciples will encounter the risen Jesus in faith.

Moving inward, we read two scenes that take place narratively in the mysterious in-between time of Easter, the time of transition, of conversion from the physically mediated faith encounter with the pre-Easter Jesus to the ecclesially mediated faith encounter with the post-Easter Jesus. In these scenes Jesus is present-absent. Mary Magdalene recognizes her "Rabbouni" but must be converted from a desire to touch him physically as she had in the pre-Easter dispensation to true communion with "the Lord" whom she, with Jesus' other sisters and brothers, will encounter in the community.

In the balancing fourth scene, we meet Thomas the Twin. His double identity as "one of the Twelve," i.e., one of Jesus' earthly contemporaries, and as one "who was not with them" at Easter, i.e., one of Jesus' post-Easter disciples who must respond in faith to the witness of the apostolic generation, "We have seen the Lord," works narratively to carry the reader through the Easter transition from physical sight to spiritual insight. Thomas, challenged by Jesus to abandon his faithlessness and believe, is converted from his stubborn fixation in the pre-Easter dispensation of physical sight and touch and confesses precisely what he cannot see or touch physically—that the risen Jesus is indeed his "Lord and God."

At the center of the chapter is the scene that narratively presents the establishment of the real presence of the glorified and risen Lord with his disciples of all time. The conditions of possibility, nature, mode, and effects of this new presence are symbolically unfolded. In this scene the transitional presence-absence of the Easter Jesus is resolved into the definitive covenant presence of the risen Jesus in his ecclesial mode. Jesus definitively returns to his own, manifests himself to them but not to the world (cf. 14:18-22), and gives them the peace the world cannot give (cf. 14:27), which overcomes their fear of persecution and fills them with the eschatological joy of the woman who has come through the labor of the hour (16:20-22). He communicates to them the Spirit of truth whom the world cannot receive. This Spirit will realize in them the abiding presence of the Father and the Son, bring to their minds all that Jesus had taught them, and lead them into all truth while convicting the world of sin, justice, and judgment (cf. 14:16-22, 25-27; 15:26; 16:7-11, 12-15).

In short, this pericope stands at the very center of the Johannine Resurrection Narrative. In it, the characteristic "realized eschatology" of John's gospel takes on its full ecclesial significance. The long-anticipated "hour" has occurred. The work that the Father had entrusted to Jesus has been consummated. Jesus has been fully glorified through his return to the Father and now takes up his promised abode, with the Father, through the Spirit, in his own, those who believe in him, love him, keep his commandments, and abiding in him as branches in the Vine (cf. 15:1-11) will bear the fruit he commissions them to bear in the last verse of this scene.

II. The Structure of John 20:19-23

A more detailed look at the structure of John 20:19-23 will facilitate our closer reading of this central pericope (see fig. 4, p. 186). Verse 19a clearly parallels the opening verse of the chapter, which narrates that Mary ran to the tomb near Jerusalem early on the first day of the week.[10]

---

[10] Although Jerusalem is not mentioned in chap. 20, the opening scene takes place at the tomb, which was in a garden "in the place where he was crucified" (19:41); Mary is able to run to the place where Simon Peter and the Beloved Disciple were and was able, after seeing Jesus on Easter morning, to go to the disciples with Jesus' message before his appearance to them on Easter evening. These details establish that the place of the Johannine Resurrection Narrative is Jerusalem, the scene of the "hour," which is now being completed. This roots the resurrection experience in history while suggesting its history-transcending character, which grounds its universality.

This scene takes place in Jerusalem on the evening of that same day, the first of the week. Part 2 is thus tightly integrated with part 1 in the unity of the chapter.

The first part of the pericope, verses 19b to 20c, is framed by the contrasting states of the disciples: at the beginning they are locked behind closed doors for "fear of the Jewish authorities," and at the end, having received from Jesus the peace that the world cannot take away (cf. 14:27), they are free of fear, rejoicing "in seeing the Lord."

Between the contrasting states of fear and joy is the reason for the disciples' transformation, a verse that has no corresponding element in the structure of the pericope. Jesus has risen in their midst (v. 19c). We would expect the pericope to terminate, as does the Mary Magdalene scene and the scene of Simon Peter and the Beloved Disciple, with a closure. The disciples, having come to the tomb and played their respective roles, went away. But there is no verse 23c to the effect that Jesus, having accomplished his purpose in appearing, vanished from their sight (as we see, for example, in the Emmaus scene in Luke 24:31). The risen Jesus is not visiting. He has definitively returned to his own. He will come and come again, but he never leaves. His covenant presence, like that of Yahweh in the temple, is an abiding glory. He has, as he promised, taken up his abode with them (cf. 14:23). The structural singularity of verse 19c marks it as foundational for the meaning of the entire pericope.

Jesus' coming is revelatory in character. Section A, verses 19d-20b, is a two-member christophany, evoking the great theophany on Sinai. The Lord shows them the marks of the Glorification in his wounded hands, and the source of their participation in its fruits through his Resurrection, his open side. Δείκνυμι is a quasi-technical term for revelation in John (cf. 2:18; 5:20; 10:32; 14:8, 9).

The second part of the pericope begins with the rejoicing of the disciples that was the conclusion of the first part, thus integrating the pericope as a unit. Section B closely parallels section A. As section A is composed of the greeting of peace and the revelation of the glory connected by καὶ τοῦτο εἰπών, "and saying this," so section B is composed of the greeting of peace and the gift of the Spirit connected by "and saying this."

The great christophany (A) is followed by section B, verses 21-23, a two-member covenant-commission evoking the giving of the Law at Sinai. Each of the two members of section B is expanded by explication of its essential meaning, sections a and b (vv. 21b-c and 23a-b), respectively. In short, a careful examination of the structure of this pericope strongly suggests that it is a carefully constructed literary-theological unity evoking the Sinai covenant narrative in Exodus 19–20. The christophany is the revelation of Yahweh's glorious New Covenant presence (cf. Ezek 34:25 and 37:26-28) in the person of the risen Lord. The gift of the Spirit fulfills the promise that in this New Covenant the re-created Israel would receive God's own Spirit (cf. Ezek 36:26-28) who would engrave a New Law in their hearts (cf. Jer 31:31-34).[11]

III. John 20:19-20: The Revelatory Christophany

Let us turn now to a closer reading of part 1, the christophany. I would call attention to the three-part time indication that opens the scene. Most commentators recognize the significance of John's use of time, and this instance is particularly important. It situates the New Covenant in respect to history as both immanent and transcendent by its simultaneous evocation of the historical (Easter day), the eschatological ("that day"), and the liturgical, which binds them together (Sunday evening, the first day of the week, the time of Christian Eucharist). Furthermore, by overlapping the three so that they become inseparable and only partially distinguishable the Evangelist involves the reader in the perspective of realized eschatology characteristic of the Fourth Gospel as a whole and now finally established as the permanent time frame of the Church. This event takes place in early evening, the threshold moment. The "day" of the present age, which ended with Jesus' Glorification on the cross, draws to a close as "that day," the eschatological day of the new dispensation inaugurated by Jesus' Resurrection, dawns. The disciples are drawn into the mystery of Jesus' promised new presence to them: "In that day you will know that I am in my Father, and you in me, and I in you" (14:20). This is the mystery experienced anew in Eucharist on Sundays down through the centuries.

The next phrase continues, in terms of place and personae, the mysterious historically rooted but history-transcending character of this scene. Jesus appears not to the apostles or to the Twelve but to "the dis-

---

[11] Although Ezekiel places the New Covenant promises in the context of the Davidic rather than the Mosaic covenant, by the time the Fourth Gospel was written Jesus had come to be seen as the fulfillment of all messianic expectations. This seems clear from the blending of all the New Covenant themes in the promises of the Last Discourses.

ciples," a term that, in John, refers to all Jesus' followers,[12] both those present on Easter and all those who through their word will believe in him (cf. 17:20), those for whom the gospel is written (cf. 20: 31). And Jesus comes not to a designated place, although it is clearly some place in Jerusalem, but simply into the place "where the disciples were," which is where Jesus is always present, namely, in the ecclesial community.[13] The doors are closed, both in this scene and in the following one of Thomas's encounter with Jesus (cf. 20:26). The very significant difference between this verse and verse 26 is that here there is a motive for the closed doors, which anchors the scene in history, namely, "for fear of the Jewish authorities." After Jesus' return to his own, the doors where the community is gathered are still closed, marking it off from the surrounding "world," but there is no mention of fear, for Jesus has given them his peace, which the world cannot give or take away.

Jesus' sudden presence in their midst in verse 19c is not a preternatural demonstration of the miraculous quality of his risen body. (We are not told that Jesus came through the solid doors or walls!) The starkly simple "Jesus came and stood into their midst" (ἔστη εἰς τὸ μέσον) is perhaps best translated in terms of the Aramaic verb קוּם, which the unusual Greek verb construction of motion suggests stands behind this verse. It can

---

[12] Among the standard commentators are those like J. H. Bernard, F. M. Braun, and A. Feuillet who want to equate "disciples" with the "Twelve"; others like M. J. Lagrange, A. M. Hunter, B. Lindars, and B. F. Westcott who hold that the Twelve were among those present but not the only ones; the majority, e.g., C. K. Barrett, R. E. Brown, R. Bultmann, A. Cassien, F. Godet, E. C. Hoskyns, H. Klos, X. Léon-Dufour, R. H. Lightfoot, J. M. Sanders, B. A. Mastin, and most later commentators of a nonfundamentalist bent who believe that "the disciples" means the community, whomever it includes. Most recently, J. Swetnam, "Bestowal of the Spirit in the Fourth Gospel," *Biblica* 74 (1999): 556–76, revived the suggestion that the gift of the Spirit in John 20:22 was to "a restricted group of disciples, possibly only to the 'Twelve'" (572). His argument on this point is clearly motivated by his interpretation of 20:23 as a conferral of juridical authority parallel to Matt 18:18. R. Kysar, on the other hand, in "As You Sent Me" (371), cites with approval Käsemann's distinction between "disciples" and the "Twelve" in John and his conclusion that those who are sent as Jesus is sent are all the disciples (E. Käsemann, *The Testament of Jesus: A Study of the Gospel of John in the Light of Chapter 17* [Philadelphia: Fortress Press, 1968], 30–32).

[13] C. H. Cosgrove, "The Place Where Jesus Is: Allusions to Baptism and Eucharist in the Fourth Gospel," *New Testament Studies* 35 (1989): 522–39, says that the risen Jesus is present only in the community and "nowhere else" (529). I think this is a slight overstatement, but the Church is certainly the normal and habitual place of Jesus' presence in the post-Easter dispensation.

mean "stand up" or "rise up," whether from sleep or from death. In John 2:19-21, Jesus' opponents had challenged him to show them a sign of his authority over the Jerusalem temple, the place of Yahweh's abiding presence in Israel. Jesus replied, "Destroy this temple, and in three days I will raise it up," and the Evangelist clarifies, "he was speaking of the temple of his body," a saying that his disciples would understand, in the light of Scripture, after Jesus was raised from the dead. Jesus, bodily risen, is the New Temple raised up in the midst of the community that will constitute the New Israel. As Ezekiel had prophesied:

> I will make a covenant of peace with them; it shall be an everlasting covenant with them; and I will bless them and multiply them, and will set my sanctuary in the midst of them forevermore. My dwelling place shall be with them; and I will be their God and they shall be my people. The nations shall know that I the LORD sanctify Israel, when my sanctuary is among them forevermore. (Ezek 37:26-28; cf. 34:25 and Isa 54:10)

In 20d it is precisely this New Covenant peace that Jesus bestows on his disciples, his own peace that the world cannot give, which he had promised them on the night before his death (14:27; cf. also 16:33 in relation to the "fear of the Jews").

The connective phrase "and saying this" or "having said this" is frequently used in John (e.g., 9:6; 11:43; 13:21; 18:1, 38; 20:14) to mark the close causal relation of what follows to what has just been said. In this case, it marks the dependence of the New Covenant of peace on its source in the death/Glorification of the Son. Jesus immediately "shows" them (δείκνυμι) the marks of his Glorification in his hands and the source of its fruits, his open side. The verb δείκνυμι signals the revelatory rather than apologetic character of this action of Jesus. It is not a parallel of Jesus' proof, in Luke 24:36-43, of the reality of his body. It is a revelatory identification of himself as the one who was glorified on the cross and whose Glorification is the source of the peace he has just imparted and the Spirit he is about to bestow.

The significance of Jesus' showing his open side (not his feet as in Luke) lies in the relation of temple, water, and Spirit in the Fourth Gospel. This symbolism is too extensive and complex to be detailed here,[14] but

---

[14] This entire complex of texts is treated in some detail in the preceding chapter. See pages 77–81.

it is important to recall the three key texts that illuminate this revelation of the open side in 20:20b. Jesus had predicted in the temple in 2:19 that his risen body would be the New Temple. In 7:37-39, again in the Jerusalem temple at the feast of Tabernacles commemorating the making of the Covenant and the Dedication of the temple, and in a clear allusion to Ezekiel 47:1-12 describing the life-giving water that would flow from the side of the New Temple, Jesus offers the living water that would flow from within him and that the Evangelist says refers to the Spirit that will be given when Jesus is glorified.[15] Finally, in 19:34-37, after Jesus has "handed over his Spirit" at his Glorification, blood and water flow from his side.[16] In this scene, Jesus' manifestation of his open side reveals the full significance of Jesus as the New Temple. He is the presence of God's glory in their midst[17] and the source of the life-giving water of the Spirit.

The character of this christophany as the New Creation is evident in the response of the disciples. They exult with the joy Jesus had promised them in 16:20-22—that their weeping would be turned to rejoicing as is

[15] G. Bienaimé, "L'annonce des fleuves d'eau vive en Jean 7,37-39," *Revue théologique de Louvain* 21 (1990): 281–310; 417–54, supplies a thorough review of the scholarly discussion of this passage and convincingly defends the position that the water of which Jesus speaks in 7:37-39 flows from his (Jesus') side. Bennema, "The Giving of the Spirit in John's Gospel," 200, takes the opposite position. I believe that the primary reference is to the Spirit flowing from within Jesus, but a deliberate ambiguity need not necessarily be ruled out since the effect of the gift of the Spirit is assimilation of the post-resurrection disciples to Jesus and their participation in his life-giving mission.

[16] J. Kremer, *Die Osterbotschaft der vier Evangelien: Versuch einer Auslegung der Berichte über das leere Grab und die Erscheinungen des Auferstanden* (Stuttgart: Katholisches Bibelwerk, 1969), 104, made this point unequivocally over thirty years ago.

[17] See the excellent article of C. C. Newman, "Resurrection as Glory: Divine Presence and Christian Origins," *The Resurrection: An Interdisciplinary Symposium on the Resurrection of Jesus*, ed. S. T. Davis, D. Kendall, G. O'Collins (Oxford, UK: Oxford University Press, 1997), 59–89, in which he argues that it was the early Church's faith in the Resurrection as the assigning to Jesus of the glory of Yahweh, rather than high Christology as such, that precipitated the alienation between Christianity and Judaism. See also A. T. Lincoln, "'I Am the Resurrection and the Life': The Resurrection Message of the Fourth Gospel," in *Life in the Face of Death: The Resurrection Message of the New Testament*, ed. R. N. Longenecker (Grand Rapids, MI/Cambridge, UK: William B. Eerdmans, 1998), 122–44, who says that "believing that the divine glory is manifest in the temple of Jesus' risen body makes possible the attaching of that glory to the whole of Jesus' mission (cf. 1:14, 2:11), as well as, specifically, to his death as the supreme moment of glory rather than shame" (127).

the sorrow of a woman giving birth when life has come forth.[18] In Isaiah 66:7-14 the New Creation was described as the birth from Jerusalem of a New People whom God will cherish as a mother comforts her child. The prophet says, "You shall see, and your heart shall rejoice," a prediction taken up by Jesus in 16:22, "I will see you again and your hearts will rejoice, and no one will take your joy from you." It is fulfilled here in the birth of the New Israel in whose midst stands the New Temple and which will be enlivened by the gift of the Spirit and commissioned to carry on Jesus' mission.

If this interpretation of part 1 as the great christophany of the New Covenant has any merit, it implies that the questions often raised about whether Jesus, in this scene, has or has not yet ascended are misconceived.[19] Ascension, in the Lukan sense, is not a Johannine category. Jesus is exalted to God in his Glorification on the cross. There is no time interval in which Jesus is risen but not yet ascended. On the contrary, his Exaltation/Glorification is the condition of possibility of his rising up into the midst of his disciples. In John, the Glorification on the cross is the condition of possibility of the Resurrection, not the other way around. The relevant distinction is between Jesus' Glorification on Good Friday and his Resurrection, that is, his revelatory return to his disciples, on Easter. The time interval is in the experience of the disciples who are still conditioned by history and who require time to experience Jesus' death as real before they can fully assimilate the reality of the Resurrection.

IV. John 20:21-23: The Sealing of the New Covenant

Part 2 of the pericope, verses 21-23, parallels in structure part 1. It begins with a second conferral of peace. The first gift of peace and result-

---

[18] See also John 15:11; 16:24; 17:13 on the fullness of joy that Jesus predicts and promises to his disciples.

[19] For example, Bennema, "The Giving of the Spirit in John's Gospel," 198, 203–4, argues that Jesus cannot fully confer the Spirit/Paraclete in 20:22 because one condition for the gift of the Paraclete is that Jesus has "gone away" (16:7), which requires an ascension like that in Luke 24:51 and Acts 1:8. This position, held with various nuances by many scholars of more conservative bent, contrasts with that of the majority of scholars, typified by Hatina, "John 20,22 in its Eschatological Context," who hold that this scene is a "Johannine Pentecost" in which the giving of the Spirit on Easter night is the fulfillment of the Last Discourses promises of the gift of the Spirit/ Paraclete.

ing joy overcame the fear that had gripped the disciples at Jesus' death. The second gift is the peace that will undergird their mission, which he is about to confer.[20]

Verse 21b-c, i.e., section α, is the foundation of the great commission. As Bultmann pointed out, καθώς in John often has a foundational rather than simply comparative function.[21] De Dinechin, decades later, did a detailed and persuasive study of all the occurrences of the καθώς–καθώς (κἀγω), the "as . . . so" construction in John, and concluded that it is Johannine theological language, a "privileged synthesis "of the entire revelatory dynamic in the Fourth Gospel.[22] The relation of the Father to the Son, in this case God's sending of the Son into the world as salvific revelation of God, is the foundation and pattern of the incarnate Son's sending of his disciples into the world. In other words, their mission, like his, will be one of salvific revelation.

Most commentators have taken some position on the significance or lack of significance of John's use of two different words for "send." In 21b-c ἀποστέλλω is used for Jesus' sending by the Father, and πέμπω for Jesus' sending of his disciples. It would lengthen this paper unduly to summarize the debate on this subject, but, differing from Francis Gignac's recent statement on the subject,[23] I subscribe to the position that sees a significant distinction between the two words in the Fourth Gospel. In classical as well as Koine Greek there does seem to be a difference of

---

[20] This gift of peace follows the pattern of those Old Testament passages such as Judg 6 (the Gideon vision) and Dan 10–11 in which a terror-inducing theophany is followed by a gift of peace that reassures the recipient and serves as prelude to or confirmation of a difficult commission. Here, there is no experience of religious terror because the theophany is the coming of Jesus who is now their "brother." The fear is of persecution, and Jesus' gift of peace overcomes it. E. Coye, "Sent to Be Scarred: John 20:19-23," *Expository Times* 113, no. 6 (March 2002): 190, says the first greeting of peace is to allay their fear, the second to prepare them for missionary suffering. His point is that persecution is a prominent theme in John, and it continues after Jesus' Resurrection.

[21] R. Bultmann, *The Gospel of John: A Commentary*, trans. G. R. Beasley-Murray et al. (Philadelphia: Westminster, 1971), 382, n. 2. The English translation says that καθώς in John often has an "explanatory" rather than merely comparative sense. I would translate "begründenden Sinn" as "foundational meaning."

[22] O. de Dinechin, "ΚΑΘΩΣ: La similitude dans l'évangile selon saint Jean," *Recherches de Sciences Religieuses* 58 (1970): 195–236.

[23] F. T. Gignac, "The Use of Verbal Variety in the Fourth Gospel," *Transcending Boundaries: Contemporary Readings of the New Testament*, Festschrift F. J. Moloney, ed. R. M. Chennattu and M. L. Coloe (Roma: Salesiano, 2005), see 192–93.

nuance between the terms, and John exploits the philological distinction for theological purposes.[24] Ἀποστέλλω emphasizes the relation of the *sent to those to whom one is sent* with a consequent insistence on the content of the mission to be accomplished and the authority for its accomplishment, whereas τέμπω emphasizes the relation of the *sent to the sender* or the representational character of the mission. The ambassador, in other words, is not only an agent of the sender's will but also the presence of the sender in the midst of the recipients. Most often it is the second meaning that is emphasized in regard to Jesus. Twenty-four times in John πέμπω is used in participial form to refer to God as "the one sending" Jesus, i.e., the one indwelling him and generating his words and works from within. God is in Jesus doing his works (cf. 14:10 and elsewhere). Whoever sees Jesus sees the Father (cf. 14:9). Jesus is the great symbol who renders God present and active in the world. Only twice, in 5:36 (in which Jesus refers explicitly to the works he was sent to accomplish) and the present verse 20:21, is ἀποστέλλω, in the perfect tense, used of Jesus, and the context suggests that the emphasis is on the fact of the Incarnation, Jesus' being sent from God into the world at a particular point in time to accomplish a specific mission.

In verse 21b-c Jesus, having completed the work for which he was sent into the world hands over to his disciples its continuation. They will do the works he has done and even greater works will they do (cf. 14:12). Only twice in the gospel, in 13:20 and here, is πέμπω used for the disciples. In 13:20 Jesus says that those who receive the disciples, receive Jesus. And those who receive Jesus receive the One sending him. The representational sense of the verb, used for both Jesus' sending by God and the disciples' sending by Jesus, is clear. The situation is the same in this verse. In other words, Jesus' completion in "the hour" of his mission from God in the Incarnation grounds the ongoing representational mission, only now possible, of his disciples: to render him present and active in the world as he had revealed God.

This verse is crucial for understanding the meaning of the commission that follows. The mission Jesus entrusts to his disciples is not, as some

---

[24] See W. F. Arndt and F. W. Gingrich, *A Greek-English Lexicon of the New Testament and Other Early Christian Literature* (Chicago: University of Chicago, 1957): ἀποστέλλω (98); πέμπω (647). G. R. Beasley-Murray, "The Mission of the Logos-Son," *The Four Gospels 1992*, Festschrift Frans Neirynck, vol. 3, ed. C. M. Tuckett, G. Van Belle, J. Verheyden (Leuven: University Press, 1992), 1857, calls attention to the two facets of the sending of a messenger in the ancient world: the representative character of the messenger and the messenger's obedience.

have suggested, a rather anemic version of the Great Commission in Matthew 28:18-20. It is Jesus' conferring upon them of the mission to continue his own mission as the Lamb of God who takes away the sin of the world (cf. 1:29). The καθώς verse is connected to the commission verse by the phrase "having said this," marking the dependence of the commission on its foundation in Jesus' own mission from the Father.

Verse 22b closely parallels 20b. As Jesus *revealed* to them his Glorification manifested in his hands and side, now he *breathes* on them and says, "Receive the Holy Spirit," who could not be given until Jesus was glorified (cf. 7:39). The verb "breathe" (ἐμφυσάω) is a *hapax legomenon* in the New Testament and occurs substantively only twice[25] in the Septuagint. In Genesis 2:7, God at the first creation breathes life into the earth-creature, and it becomes the first living human being. In Ezekiel 37:9-10, God commands the prophet to breathe upon the dry bones "that they may live," i.e., that the people Israel might be re-created. In this Easter scene, Jesus, in an act of New Creation, breathes the promised Spirit of the New Covenant into the community of his disciples, making them the New Israel, in whose midst he is present as the New Temple.

Jesus' symbolic action of breathing, accompanied by the effective word, "receive the Holy Spirit," has suggested to many commentators an explicit sacramental meaning in this verse. Indeed, the institution of five of the seven sacraments (baptism, confirmation, Eucharist, penance, ordination) has been discerned in this verse by various scholars! Discussion of the Johannine sacramentary would take us too far afield, and I tend to be reserved about "institution" claims. The structure of effective word accompanying symbolic gesture does, however, suggest a sacramental allusion here, and in a moment I will take up the question in relation to the forgiveness of sins.

The majority of commentators (with whom I agree) see in this verse the gift of the fullness of the Spirit who is the Paraclete promised by Jesus in the Last Discourses.[26] This Spirit is the substantial gift of the New

---

[25] Actually, the verb appears four times in the LXX, the two instances adduced here, plus Wis 15:11, which recalls the enlivening of Adam and thus is not an independent third instance, and 1 Kgs 17:21, recounting the prophet Elijah's reanimation of the son of the widow of Zarephath. The LXX inaccurately (but perhaps deliberately) translates the Hebrew for "stretched" or "measured" as "breathed," perhaps alluding to the creation narrative.

[26] Hatina, "John 20,22," offers an excellent argument for this position from the texts in the gospel itself that indicate the gift of the Spirit/Paraclete is immanent to the gospel against Carson, *The Gospel according to John*, 652–54, who thinks the Spirit is not given until Pentecost. Bennema, "The Giving of the Spirit," 207–13, suggests a

Covenant promised in the prophets, the New Law written on their hearts, the water of purification removing all sin and uniting them with God and one another. The relation of this account to the Lukan Pentecost scene, however, is not one of literary or theological dependence, and I do not think the term "Johannine Pentecost" is particularly helpful. This is one of a number of accounts in the New Testament of "comings of" or "gifts of" the Spirit, to individuals or to groups, during the first days of the Church's existence. Trying to harmonize these accounts, relativize all of them in terms of the Lukan event, or reduce them to one is neither necessary nor helpful.[27] This scene is important precisely because it gives us the particular Johannine take on the role and meaning of the Spirit's presence in the community.

Verse 23, which explicates the community's mission, has been the subject of vigorous debate among scholars for centuries. Catholic commentators have historically tended to see in it the foundation if not the institution of the sacrament of penance within which the ordained minister has authority to forgive sins or to refuse absolution.[28] Protestant scholars tend to see it as a more general conferral of ecclesiastical authority to give or withhold spiritual benefits. But both tendencies are rooted in what, in my opinion, is a mistaken assumption that John 20:23 is the Johannine parallel of Matthew 18:18,[29] "whatever you bind on earth will be bound in heaven and whatever you loose on earth will be loosed in heaven." Most commentators remain uneasy about this interpretation, but it has proven amazingly tenacious. The problems it presents are formidable.

---

middle position, that the Spirit sustaining the relation between Jesus and his disciples is given in 20:22 but not as Paraclete until Pentecost. Bennema summarizes six theories on the meaning of 20:22 and in n. 36 supplies a list of scholars who hold the position I espouse, that 20:22 is the full and definitive gift of the Spirit/Paraclete. Many of these scholars speak of this scene as the "Johannine Pentecost," a formulation I think is misleading.

[27] See Hatina, "John 20,22," 201, on this point.

[28] This interpretation of John 20:23 was dogmatically defined by the Council of Trent in 1551. (See H. Denziger, *Enchiridion symbolorum definitionum et declarationum de rebus fidei et morum*, 37th ed. [Freiburg: Herder, 1991], 1710, on the ordained minister of the sacrament, and 1703, which defines John 20:23 as the institution of the sacrament of penance.) For a balanced interpretation of the force of these decrees, however, see R. E. Brown, *The Gospel according to John*, Anchor Bible 29 and 29A (Garden City/New York: Doubleday, 1970), 2:1044–45.

[29] In Matt 16:19 the "power of the keys" is given to Simon Peter, but in 18:18 it is conferred on the community. Thus, the latter verse is a clearer possible parallel to John 20:23.

The first member of the verse, 23a, is perfectly straightforward. All the parts of the sentence are explicit and grammatically unproblematic. The second-person plural verb identifies the disciples, mentioned in verse 19 as the subject.[30] The meaning of the verb ἀφίημι, which can mean "cancel, remit, abandon, release, etc." is clearly determined to mean "forgive" by the explicit direct object, "sins," and the presence of the indirect object αὐτοῖς, "to them," makes it clear that τινων is a subjective genitive referring to those forgiven. Thus, the literal translation "Of whomever [or "if of anyone"] you forgive the sins they are forgiven to them" is hardly disputable.

The problem arises in relation to verse 23b in which there is neither a direct nor an indirect object, and the traditional translation of the verb as "retain" is highly questionable.[31] The verse is usually translated on the assumption that 23b is in elliptical antithetical parallelism with 23a, which rests on the hypothesis that John 20:23 is the parallel of Matthew 18:18. Needless to say, this is a clearly circular argument: John 20:23 is the parallel of Matthew 18:18 because κρατέω is the opposite of ἀφίημι and κρατέω is the opposite of ἀφίημι because "bind" is the opposite of "loose" in Matthew 18:18. So, the translations supply from 23a a direct object, "sins," and an indirect object, "to [or in] them," and then construct a meaning for the verb κρατῆτε, which would be antithetical to ἀφῆτε. The weakness of the entire process appears in the translation of κρατέω as "retain" in relation to sins. Virtually everyone admits that there is no such meaning for this verb attested anywhere in classical or Koine Greek. So John presumably assigned this meaning to the term here and never used this meaning again, nor did anyone else before or after. Furthermore, there is the theological problem of what "retaining sins" in another person could possibly mean. The Church might claim the authority to refuse juridical absolution to a sinner or bar a person from membership in the institutional Church by refusing baptism, but the sins of a repentant

---

[30] See n. 12 above on the identity of the "disciples" in John.

[31] J. A. Emerton, "Binding and Loosing—Forgiving and Retaining," *Journal of Theological Studies* 13 (1962): 325–31, is typical of those who argue for the translation "retain" even though he admits that κρατεῖν "is not here used in any of its normal Greek senses" (327). Even A. Feuillet, who represented the most rigid of Catholic positions about this text as the conferral on the hierarchy alone of the power to forgive and retain sins ("Le temps de l'église selon saint Jean," *Études Johanniques* [Bruges: Desclée, 1962], 160), noted that "le sens dans lequel il [κρατέω] est ici utilisé (retenir les péchés) est tout à fait inhabituel" (*Le sacerdoce du Christ et de ses ministres d'après la prière sacerdotale du quatrième évangile et plusieurs données parallèles du Nouveau Testament* [Paris: Editions de Paris, 1972], 138).

sinner are always forgiven by God and those of the unrepentant are not, regardless of juridical ecclesiastical processes. So the notion of "retaining sins" interior to another is both grammatically and theologically highly problematic.[32]

Since neither sins nor sinners are mentioned in 23b and the verb does not mean retain, on what does the traditional interpretation rest? The only textual basis is the anaphora, ἄν τινων, in each member. If, however, one translates the verb according to its normal meaning, namely, "hold fast" or "take hold of," and treats τινων in the second member as an objective genitive, which this verb would normally take (cf., e.g., Matt 9:25 and Heb 4:14), the verse would read, "Anyone whom you hold fast is held fast." In other words, what is held is not sins but people. I would suggest that, if this verse is interpreted not as a parallel of Matthew 18:18 but in the context of Johannine theology and spirituality, this is precisely what the text does mean. It is a synonymous, synthetic parallel. "Anyone whose sins you forgive, they are forgiven to them and those [the forgiven] whom you hold fast [in the communion of the Church] are held fast."

In John's gospel Jesus is identified by John the Baptizer on the first day of his public ministry as "the Lamb of God who takes away the sin of the world" (1:29). In the Fourth Gospel "the sin," in the singular, which Jesus comes to abolish is the refusal to believe in him as the revelation of the Father. "Sins" in the plural, e.g., in 8:21-24 where Jesus tells his opponents, "you will die in your sins unless you believe that I am," are the moral fallout of the foundational "sin" of unbelief. The disciples in 20:23 are commissioned to continue Jesus' mission, not by taking away the "sin of the world," which Jesus has accomplished once for all on the cross, but by making available the results of Jesus' victory over the world (cf. 16:33) in the lives of those who will become members of the community. The distinction between "the sin" and "sins" appears in the gospel itself. The disciples who were already clean because of the word

---

[32] It is worth noting that in the first three centuries of the Church, when there was heated debate about whether sins committed after baptism could be forgiven, none of the Church fathers evoked John 20:23 on either side of the argument. According to T. Worden, whose two-part study of the history of the sacrament ("The Remission of Sins," *Scripture* 9 [1957]: 65–79; 115–27) is still valuable, the first father of the Church to use the text in reference to the sacrament of penance seems to be Cyril of Alexandria (fifth century) in his commentary on the Fourth Gospel (see Worden, "The Remission of Sins," 67, n. 3).

Jesus had spoken to them would nevertheless continue to be pruned by the Father (cf. 15:1-3), and Simon Peter whom Jesus declared clean (cf. 13:10) denied Jesus and had to be forgiven by him (cf. 21:15-17). So, later disciples who have been cleansed from "the sin" by believing in Jesus would have to be purified of their "sins," probably originally a reference to baptism but perhaps also to sins committed after baptism. And, just as Jesus not only called disciples to himself but also held them fast for eternal life, the community not only will admit people to the ecclesial community, i.e., forgive their sins, but must hold them fast in that communion. In John there are thirteen occurrences of the verb ἀφίημι outside verse 23a, and in every case with two possible exceptions (11:48 and 18:8) it is paired with a verb that is not antithetical to but synonymous with it, which suggests that the same would be the case here.[33] To hold fast in the ecclesial community is the ongoing dimension of the punctual forgiving of sins. Furthermore, Jesus repeatedly describes his mission from God in terms of preserving in union those who have come to him.

> All that the Father gives me will come to me; and the one who comes to me I will not cast out. (6:37; my translation)

> This is the will of him who sent me, that I should lose nothing of all that he has given me. (6:39)

> I give them eternal life, and they will never perish. No one will snatch them out of my hand. What my Father has given me is greater than all else, and no one can snatch it out of the Father's hand. The Father and I are one. (10:28-29)[34]

> While I was with them, I kept them in your name. . . . I guarded them, and not one of them was lost. (17:12; my translation)

> I did not lose a single one of those whom you gave me. (18:9)

[33] John 4:3, 28, 52; 8:29; 10:12; 11:44, [48]; 12:7; 14:18, 27; 16:28, 32; [18:8]. In 11:48 the Sanhedrin declare that if they "leave" Jesus doing as he is doing "everyone will believe in him," and in 18:8 Jesus says to the police who come to arrest him, "If you seek me, let these go." Even in these verses the parallelism is more reinforcing than oppositional.

[34] It is interesting that Beasley-Murray in "The Mission of the Logos-Son" (1866) invokes this very text as a special example of the "ontological" unity of the Sent One with the Sender. I am pursuing that line of reasoning in seeing 20:23b as a way of speaking of the "holding fast" of disciples in the Church as an expression of the ontological union between Jesus and the disciples he sends to continue his mission.

If the mission conferred on the disciples is the continuation of Jesus' own mission, it is well expressed as the charge to forgive sins and to hold fast in ecclesial communion those whom the community has received. Consequently, if baptism was the way in which new members were incorporated into the Johannine community, and there are good reasons to hold that it was, and Eucharist was the community's celebration of its communion with Jesus, this could well be a sacramental text. It is wider and deeper in meaning, however, than simply authorizing or instituting particular rituals. It is the establishment of the Church as the ongoing presence of the glorified Jesus in the world carrying on his salvific work throughout all time.

V. Conclusion

This close examination of John 20:19-23 has led to interpreting this passage as integral to the Johannine Resurrection Narrative and as a unified pericope reflecting the structure of the Sinai covenant, i.e., the great theophany followed by the gift of the Law through Moses making Israel God's people. In this scene the christophany of the Easter Jesus is followed by the gift of the Spirit, the New Law that constitutes the sealing of the promised New Covenant with the New Israel. Jesus, glorified and risen, has raised up the New Temple of his body, the dwelling place of the glory of God, in the midst of this New People. It presents the Johannine understanding of the Church not as an institution replacing the departed Jesus, nor even as his commissioned representative or agent, but as the ongoing presence and action of Jesus in the world through his corporate body, the ecclesial community, which will salvifically reveal him as he revealed God. Jesus had prayed to his Father that "they may be one, as we are one . . . *so that the world may know that you have sent me*" (17:22-23; emphasis added). As the Father has sent Jesus, so Jesus sends his disciples to do the works that he has done and even greater works through which the Father will be glorified (cf. 15:8).

Chapter 5

"Whose Sins You Shall Forgive . . .":
The Holy Spirit and the Forgiveness of Sin(s)
in the Fourth Gospel

I. Introduction

When I was invited to give this lecture I was asked to speak about the Holy Spirit in relation to my own research interests, namely, the Resurrection Narrative in the Gospel of John in relation to what I consider the most pressing issue in our world today, namely, violence. My overarching question is the following: what are Christians called to be and do in the face of the escalating violence in our world? In this lecture I am focusing on John 20:19-23, the scene in which Jesus appears to his disciples on Easter evening and commissions them to carry on his reconciling work in the world. I will focus on the second half of the pericope, verses 21-23:

> Jesus said to them again, "Peace be with you. As the Father has sent me, so I send you." When he had said this, he breathed on them and said to them, "Receive the Holy Spirit. If you forgive the sins of any, they are forgiven them; any you hold fast are held fast."[1]

Originally published as "'Whose Sins You Shall Forgive . . .': The Holy Spirit and the Forgiveness of Sin(s) in the Fourth Gospel," The Dusquesne University Fifth Annual Holy Spirit Lecture and Colloquium, Pittsburgh, Pennsylvania, June 2009.

[1] The translation of the Greek text of John 20:19-23 throughout the paper is my own, which is often identical to that of the NRSV. The translation of other texts of the

Some Catholic readers think that this text recounts the institution of the sacrament of penance in which ordained ministers exercise a power to grant or refuse forgiveness of sins confessed by penitents. As we will see shortly, this text is not about the sacrament of penance.[2] There is nothing in the Greek text about "retaining sins." And the commission is not given to some specialized group among the baptized. Rather, this text is about the human conundrum of sin and the resources Christians have received, through the paschal mystery of Jesus and the gift of the Holy Spirit, for addressing it. I will be suggesting that the conundrum of sin is deeply rooted in violence.

So my question is the following: according to the Fourth Gospel, what is our mission as Jesus' disciples and what has the Holy Spirit to do with that mission? The text, *prima facie*, says that whatever our mission is, it is a *continuation of Jesus' mission* from God ("as the Father has sent me, so I send you"). This mission has to do with handling *the problem of sin* ("if you forgive the sins of any, they are forgiven them"). And carrying out this mission *requires the gift of the Holy Spirit* ("he breathed on them and said, 'Receive the Holy Spirit'").

I will attempt to answer this question by making three interrelated moves in relation to the text. In part 1, I will raise two exegetical questions necessary for us to understand John 20:21-23 in its own context in

---

Old and New Testaments is that of the NRSV, unless otherwise noted. The NRSV, as well as most others, translates John 20:23b: "if you retain the sins of any, they are retained." I will argue later that this translation is not well grounded in the Greek text and is theologically problematic. At times I will elide texts, supplying only what is necessary for the clarity of the argument, but all such elisions are indicated.

[2] John 20:23 is one of the very few texts in the NT that have been the object of a conciliar definition. The Council of Trent (1551) in session 14 (Denziger and Schönmetzer, *Enchiridion Symbolorum*) 1703 and 1710, respectively defined the ordained as minister of the sacrament of penance and John 20:23 as the institution of that sacrament. These definitions arose in the polemical context of Trent in its reaction to Reformation positions on the sacraments, and there is much reason today, not only theological, but also historical and especially exegetical, to apply to these decrees the hermeneutical principle that texts must be read in terms of their intention in their own context and not as if words have some absolute meaning that remains identical through time. Their purpose at the time was to insist, against the Reformers, that there is a sacrament (besides baptism) through which sins are forgiven and that the Roman Church's penitential discipline at the time was binding. Trying to root these positions in an institution text from the NT was an understandable move at the time but is highly questionable today.

For a balanced Catholic position on this matter as it touches John 20:23, see R. E. Brown, *The Gospel according to John*, Anchor Bible 29 and 29A (Garden City, NY: Doubleday, 1970), 2:1044–45.

the Fourth Gospel, namely, who are the disciples whom Jesus commissions and who or what is the Holy Spirit who will empower them to fulfill that commission? In part 2, I will make what might appear at first sight to be a detour through the thought of the French philosopher and anthropologist René Girard. His work on violence and religion will provide a lens or a filter through which to read John's theology of Jesus' salvific work in which we are called to share and for which we are empowered by the gift of the Holy Spirit. In part 3, I will establish an *inclusio* relationship[3] between John 20:21-23, the Easter evening commissioning scene, and John 1:29-34, the inaugural scene in which Jesus himself is commissioned by God. By this I hope to clarify the meaning of Jesus' mission and how his mission is both unique to him and foundational for our mission. This will lead to an interpretation of the final verse, "Whose sins you shall forgive . . ." in a way that is historically and exegetically plausible, theologically sound, and, I hope, spiritually challenging in regard to the issue of violence in our world.

II. Meaning of "Disciples" and of the "Holy Spirit"

Our first two questions, then, are the following: according to the Gospel of John, whom did Jesus commission on Easter evening, and who or what is the Holy Spirit by which Jesus empowers those he commissions?

A. *The Disciples*

The first verse of our text, John 20:19, says, "when it was evening on that day, the first day of the week, the doors being closed where the *disciples* were for fear of the Jews, Jesus came and stood among them and said, 'Peace be with you.'" This is the same group to whom Jesus, in the immediately preceding scene, had sent Mary Magdalene to announce the Easter kerygma. Jesus told her to "Go to my *brothers and sisters*."[4]

---

[3] *Inclusio* is a literary device in which a "bookend" structure is created by the use of similar material at the beginning and end of a literary unit often suggesting the meaning of the intervening text. In this case, the intervening text is the public life of Jesus as a whole.

[4] The Greek text has πρὸς τοὺς ἀδελφούς μου, which is usually translated "go to my brothers." Greek, like English, uses the masculine plural, however, both for a group of male siblings and for a mixed-gender group of siblings. In other words, ἀδελφούς,

The next verse says that "Mary Magdalene went . . . to the *disciples*" (see John 20:17-18), thus equating the two designations. In the Fourth Gospel, "disciple" is a category that includes both women and men, is more extensive than "the Twelve," and is not equivalent to "apostles." As Raymond Brown points out, "disciple" is the Fourth Gospel's primary category for followers of Jesus.[5] Apostles are never mentioned in this gospel. And, although the Fourth Evangelist knew of the group of "the Twelve" (see John 6:67, 70-71), there is no account of a calling of "the Twelve" in John and no list of them. Jesus called five disciples at the beginning of his public ministry (John 1:35-51). One of them, Andrew's companion, remains anonymous, and one of them, Nathanael, is not in any list of the Twelve anywhere in the New Testament. The term "the Twelve" is used in only two texts in John (John 6:69-71 and 20:24), and in both instances the term is used to emphasize the greater gravity of sins committed by those disciples. It is never used to suggest that they enjoy special prerogatives or status among the disciples.[6]

The group to whom Jesus appeared on Easter evening, "the disciples," certainly included at least some whom we know were among the Twelve, e.g., Simon Peter, as well as people prominent among the disciples in

---

like the English "brethren," can mean either "brothers" or "brothers and sisters." The argument for translating the term "brothers and sisters" here is not linguistic inclusivity but the fact that Mary Magdalene understands herself as sent to "the disciples," a group that in John clearly includes women as well as men.

[5] See Raymond Brown, *The Community of the Beloved Disciple* (New York/Ramsey/Toronto: Paulist Press, 1979), 191–92, on women as well as men being identified as "Jesus' own" and as "beloved" disciples.

[6] After the multiplication of the loaves in John 6 many of Jesus' disciples turned away and ceased to follow him. When Jesus asked "the Twelve" if they also wished to go away and Simon Peter replied, "To whom shall we go? You have the words of eternal life," Jesus responded: " 'Did I not choose you, the twelve? Yet one of you is a devil.' He was speaking of Judas, son of Simon Iscariot, for he, though one of the twelve, was going to betray him" (John 6:70-71). The other text occurs right after the commission to forgive sins in chap. 20. The next pericope, 20:24-29, begins: "But Thomas . . . one of the twelve, was not with them when Jesus came" on Easter evening. So, one reference to "the Twelve" is to Judas, a devil, whose betrayal is all the worse because he is one of the Twelve, and the other is to Thomas who, contrary to our tendency to regard him as one caught in understandable doubt, the Fourth Evangelist presents as categorically refusing to believe the community's witness to the Resurrection, which is the post-Easter equivalent of Peter's denial of Jesus before the Passion. Jesus has to reintegrate Thomas into the group of the disciples in John 20:29 as he has to rehabilitate Peter in 21:15-17. In other words, "the Twelve" seems to designate a responsibility that, when not met, makes the offense particularly serious.

John whom we know were not among the Twelve, such as the Beloved Disciple, Nathanael, Martha and Mary of Bethany, Mary Magdalene, and others. Significantly, one of the Twelve, Thomas, we know was missing when Jesus commissioned the disciples to forgive sins, and he receives no special commission after his rehabilitation in the following scene. If the commission were intended specifically for the Twelve and involved some exclusive power bestowed on them, Thomas would have to have received the commission he missed.

Nor can we reason backward that since this scene was the institution of a sacrament whose administration today is limited to ordained ministers, the Easter evening community consisted of their forebears. The sacrament of penance in our sense did not exist until about nine centuries later,[7] and there is no indication in the gospels that Jesus "ordained" anyone. Our passage, in short, is about the commissioning of the ecclesial community, the community of Jesus' disciples. This is important for our purposes because we, the baptized, are that community of disciples, and Jesus' commission to his disciples in this scene describes our mission today. In part 3 we will take up the question of what exactly the ecclesial community, which will eventually be called the Church, is commissioned to do.

B. *The Holy Spirit*

Our second exegetical question is who or what is the Holy Spirit that Jesus breathes upon his disciples in the commissioning scene, John 20:21-23? John uses a number of terms for this mysterious reality that are equivalent in what they denote but diverse in theological connotation. The Evangelist speaks of the Spirit, the Holy Spirit, the Spirit of Truth,

---

[7] The earliest provision for any ritual of individual reconciliation, which was not universal or even widespread in the early Church, is referred to in the writings of Hermas around 140. But that extremely severe ritual existed only for the three capital sins (publicly known adultery, apostasy, and murder) and could only be received once after baptism. In fact, many churches during this period maintained that these sins, if committed after baptism, could not be forgiven at all. Sacramental theologian Kenan Osborne summarizes his treatment of the history of the sacrament of penance during the first nine centuries by saying, "Most Christians spent their entire life without ever receiving the sacrament of reconciliation" (Kenan B. Osborne, *Reconciliation and Justification: The Sacrament and Its Theology* [1990; reprint, Eugene, OR: Wipf and Stock, 2001], 82).

the παράκλητος (transliterated as "Paraclete" and variously translated as "Advocate," "Counselor," "Helper," "Comforter"), and each term has particular nuances. Furthermore, the Spirit language moves in a complex and highly symbolic semantic field of Old Testament evocations and technical Johannine theological vocabulary. Spirit is associated symbolically with wind and water, with breath and breathing, with creation and re-creation, with the original covenant with Israel and the New Covenant with the New Israel. Given our space constraints, much of this rich spirit material will have to be passed over. Our purpose here is simply to grasp why the Spirit is so important in Jesus' commissioning of his disciples and in our understanding of what we, as the community of Jesus' disciples, are commissioned to do.

First, "Spirit" is a way of talking about Jesus' special relationship with God, which, by the time this gospel was written, was understood as divine filiation. When Jesus begins his ministry in the Fourth Gospel we are not told that he is baptized by John or tempted by the devil. Rather, John testified that, "The one who sent me to baptize with water said to me, 'He on whom you see the Spirit descend and remain is the one who baptizes with the Holy Spirit.' And I myself have seen and have testified that this is the Son of God" (John 1:33-34). Later, in 3:34, as John's ministry is drawing to a close, the Fourth Evangelist says that Jesus is the one who speaks the words of God because God has given Jesus the "Spirit without measure."[8] So the Spirit is, first of all, a way of speaking about Jesus as Son of God, the repository of the Spirit in all its fullness, who therefore speaks the words of God and is able to give the Holy Spirit to his disciples, making the community his presence in the world.

Second, there is a series of Spirit texts in John 2, 7, and 19 that establishes a close connection between Jesus, the Jerusalem temple and its bloody sacrifices, the bloody sacrifice of Jesus on the cross, and the gift of the Holy Spirit to the Church. This connection is central to our concern.

In John 2:13-22, at the outset of his public life, Jesus performed a powerful prophetic sign in the temple in Jerusalem during the feast of

---

[8] This is my interpretation of this notoriously difficult text. Grammatically, it could mean that God gives Jesus the Spirit without measure or that Jesus gives the Spirit without measure. I have opted for the first under the influence of my reading of the context, but this could be a case of deliberate Johannine ambiguity because the very purpose of Jesus' plenary possession of the Spirit is his gift of the Spirit to those who believe in him.

Passover. He drove out the large animals used for sacrifice and spilled out the Jewish coins that worshipers needed in exchange for their Roman coinage in order to perform legitimately their sacrificial obligations in the temple. Unlike the Synoptics—Matthew, Mark, and Luke—who place this scene at the very end of Jesus' public life where it functions as a "last straw" in the provocation of the authorities to arrest Jesus, John places this scene at the very beginning of Jesus' public life as a kind of interpretive dramatization of what he has come to do. John does not present Jesus as "cleansing the temple," that is, correcting abuses in order to restore the temple to its proper function. In John, Jesus is declaring the end of temple worship through blood sacrifice.[9] He is announcing prophetically that all substitutionary sacrifice, all killing to give glory to God, all trafficking in blood to obtain God's favor or forgiveness would be ended with his death and Resurrection. This is clear from the dialogue that follows the action.

When the temple authorities demanded a sign legitimating this stunning action, Jesus replied, "Destroy this temple and in three days I will rebuild it" (John 2:18). They thought he was predicting the destruction of the physical temple, but the Evangelist intervenes with the explanation that the reader will need to understand Jesus' death and Resurrection as the end of bloody sacrifice: "But [Jesus] was speaking of the temple of his body. After he was raised from the dead, his disciples remembered that he had said this" (John 2:21-22). The risen Jesus will be a New Temple, as he explains to the Samaritan Woman in chapter 4 when she inquires where true worship is to take place, in Jerusalem or on Mount Gerizim. In both places God was worshiped by sacrifice. But Jesus tells her that this dispensation is over. In neither place will true worshipers worship the true God who is Spirit. Rather, Jesus will be the "place" where people will worship God, not by sacrificial slaughter as in the temple, but in Spirit and in Truth (see John 4:19-24).

In chapter 7 Jesus again goes to Jerusalem, this time for the feast of Tabernacles in which water as a source of life played a major symbolic role:[10]

---

[9] See Mary Coloe, *God Dwells with Us: Temple Symbolism in the Fourth Gospel* (Collegeville, MN: Liturgical Press, 2001), esp. chap. 4, "The Temple of His Body: John 2:13-25."

[10] For a fuller description of the feast of Tabernacles, the role of water symbolism, and its relation to the Johannine presentation of Jesus as the source of living water, see Craig R. Koester, *Symbolism in the Fourth Gospel: Meaning, Mystery, Community*, 2nd ed. (Minneapolis: Fortress Press, 2003), 187–200. In this section Koester shows

On the last day of the festival, the great day, while Jesus was standing there, he cried out, "Let anyone who is thirsty come to me, and
let the one who believes in me drink. As the scripture has said, 'From
within him shall flow rivers of living water.'" Now he said this about
the Spirit, which believers in him were to receive; for as yet there
was no Spirit, because Jesus was not yet glorified. (John 7:37-39)[11]

Jesus here evokes the vision in Ezekiel 47:1-12 in which the prophet saw
an ever more abundant river of living water pouring forth out of the side
of the eschatological temple, the New Temple of the New Covenant,
giving life to all the world. The Evangelist, again, breaks in to interpret
what Jesus is saying through the symbol of water: "Now [Jesus] said this
about the Spirit." Jesus is the New Temple from whose open side will
flow living water, that is, the Spirit, but only after Jesus is glorified, which
is John's term for Jesus' death on the cross.

In chapter 19, at the moment of Jesus' death, we have a symbolic fulfillment of this prophecy. According to John, Jesus' last words are, "It is
finished" (John 19:30). And having said this, Jesus "handed over his
Spirit." "It is finished" evokes the creation story in Genesis 2:1-2 when
God finished the work he was doing, namely, the creation of the world,
including humanity, and rested on the seventh day. But God's work,
begun in creation, was not finally finished until humanity was reunited
with God through the sacrifice of Jesus who then rested in the tomb on
the seventh day, the Great Sabbath.[12] Only then can Jesus, through his
Glorification, "hand over" his Spirit. The expression "handed over
[παρέδωκεν] his Spirit" is not a euphemism for "die." Jesus, according

---

the relationship between this Johannine text and a number of other OT passages. See
also Larry Paul Jones, *The Symbol of Water in the Gospel of John*, JSNT Supp. Series 145
(Sheffield, UK: Sheffield Academic Press, 1997), esp. 148–61.

[11] For a fuller exegesis of this text and a discussion of the difficult question of
whether the one from whom living water will flow is Jesus (my position) or the believer, see chapter 3 above, pages 78–81.

[12] In John 5 when Jesus is challenged by the authorities because he healed a para-
lyzed man on the Sabbath, he defends his action by saying, "My Father is still working, and I also am working." In other words, God's work, of which the Jews saw the
Sabbath rest as signifying the end, was, in fact, not finished and would not be until
Jesus rests from the work of re-creation after his death. That his questioners understood the significance of what Jesus was saying is attested by the next verse: "For this
reason the Jews were seeking all the more to kill him, because he was not only break-
ing the Sabbath, but was also calling God his own Father, thereby making himself
equal to God" (John 5:17-18).

to John, is not simply expiring. He is literally giving, bestowing his Spirit that, until now, only he possessed in all its fullness. And immediately a soldier pierced Jesus' side and, out of the body that the Evangelist had told us will arise in three days as the New Temple, flows the water and blood (John 19:34) that will give life to all the world as did the water that flowed from the side of the temple in Ezekiel's vision.

So, when Jesus on Easter evening "rises up" in the midst of his disciples, it is as the New Temple in the midst of the New Israel to inaugurate the New Covenant. He shows them his hands, the sign of his saving death, and his side from which the life-giving water and blood flowed and bestows on them the Spirit. We were told in chapter 2 that it was not until Jesus was risen from the dead that the disciples were able to understand what he had said about raising the temple in three days. In chapter 7 we were told about the water of the Spirit that would flow from within that living temple once Jesus is glorified in death. Now, the disciples (and the readers) are able to connect the dots and understand that, through the bloody death and bodily Resurrection of Jesus, a whole new order of reality, a New Creation, is coming into being. The community is being constituted as a New People of God in whose midst is the New Temple, the risen Jesus.

Third, chapters 13–17 of John's gospel comprise a series of discourses[13] by Jesus in which he prepares his disciples for his "going away." Soon, they will see him physically no longer but "[i]n that day you shall know that I am in My Father, and you in Me, and I in you (John 14:20; NAB translation). This mutual indwelling of Jesus and his disciples is effected by the gift Jesus will give them from the Father, or the Father will give them in Jesus' name, which Jesus calls "the Paraclete" or the "spirit of truth." The Paraclete, as Raymond Brown beautifully wrote, is the Holy Spirit in a special role, namely, as the presence of Jesus after Jesus has gone to the Father.[14]

The Paraclete has a number of functions among the disciples, but the one that is most important for our purposes has to do with understanding

---

[13] Most scholars, though not all, believe that there is more than one discourse in this five-chapter section, e.g., an introduction, two discourses to the disciples, and the long prayer of Jesus to his Father in chap. 17. This question of composition is not significant for our purposes here.

[14] See Brown, *The Gospel according to John*, 2:1141. This remark occurs in Brown's appendix 5, "The Paraclete," 1135–44, which retains its value even four decades after its composition.

Jesus' violent death at the hands of his persecutors. Jesus predicts that his disciples will share his fate. They will be hated and violently persecuted by the world as he was (see John 15:18-19). Jesus warns that "an hour is coming when those who kill you will think that by doing so they are offering worship to God" (John 16:2) just as those who kill Jesus think they are honoring God. This mistaken connection between bloody sacrificial violence and the worship of God is precisely what Jesus will bring to an end by his own death and Resurrection.

When the Paraclete comes, Jesus says, he will act as the defense attorney for the persecuted. The Paraclete will do for the disciples what he does in relation to Jesus' death and Resurrection, namely, reveal the truth about what is really going on under the mythical disguise of sacred violence, of giving glory to God by the murder of a scapegoat. The Paraclete will prove the world wrong about *sin*, about *justice*, and about *judgment* (John 16:7-11), that is, about the whole sacrificial system of judging and killing sinners in order to restore unity and peace in society and between society and God. The Paraclete will reveal that killing Jesus was not a religious sacrifice that gave glory to God and saved the Jewish nation but was a vicious lynching carried out under the prompting of Satan, the false "prince of this world." Executing Jesus, the quintessential expression of rejecting the revelation of the God of love in Jesus, is not only not pleasing to God; it is the real *sin*. Indeed, as we will see, it is "the sin of world" that Jesus came to take away. Furthermore, murdering Jesus was not a restoration of justice by expiating sin through the death of the sinner. The real *justice* was precisely God's vindication of Jesus through resurrection. Finally, the judgment they thought they had rightly rendered against Jesus the blasphemer will be revealed as false judgment. The true *judgment* falls on Satan, the "original liar," who is revealed as the "murderer from the beginning," the one orchestrating this and all sacralized killing (see John 8:44).

This role of the Spirit/Paraclete in unmasking the evil and futility of the sacrificial system for reconciling humans with God and with each other will be key to understanding the alternative to sacrifice that Jesus will inaugurate on Easter night by the gift of the Spirit and the commission to forgive sins.

A fourth and final clue to the meaning of the Holy Spirit in our passage comes from the Old Testament resonances we hear in the Easter evening pericope. The Greek word in this text for Jesus' action of "breathing on" his disciples as a way of gifting them with the Holy Spirit is ἐνεφύσησεν (ἐμφυσάω), a New Testament *hapax legomenon*, that is, a word that occurs nowhere else but here in the whole New Testament. It occurs only twice, once in Genesis and once in Ezekiel, in the Septuagint, the Greek translation of the Old Testament.[15] Because it is such a rare word in the Old Testament, it would immediately evoke the right associations for John's community reading or hearing this narrative.

"Breathed on" occurs for the first time in the Old Testament in Genesis 2:7, where God breathed into the face of the human creature, the ἄνθρωπος created from lifeless clay, the breath of life, and the ἄνθρωπος became "a living being" (Gen 2:7). The second occurrence is in Ezekiel 37, the famous dry bones passage. God shows the prophet a vast valley of dead bones, the decimated house of Israel whose unfaithfulness to the covenant has brought them to total ruin. At God's command Ezekiel prophesies to the bones, and they begin to come together to form skeletons that are then covered with flesh and skin. But they are zombies, the walking dead, because there is no breath in them. Then God tells Ezekiel to prophesy to the breath or the wind or the spirit (breath, wind, and spirit are the same word in Greek: πνεῦμα), and the spirit breathes into the dead house of Israel and they come to life; they rise up as a new people (v. 10). With this re-created Israel God will make a New Covenant:

> I will make a covenant of peace with them; it shall be an everlasting covenant with them; and I will bless them and multiply them, and will set my sanctuary [or temple] among them forevermore. My dwelling place shall be with them; and I will be their God, and they shall be my people. Then the nations shall know that I the Lord sanctify Israel, when my sanctuary [or temple] is among them forevermore. (Ezek 37:26-28)[16]

The scene on Easter evening picks up every element of this promise of the New Covenant to a New Israel. Jesus rises up in their midst as the *New Temple* predicted in John 2 and greets them with *"Peace to you."* He *gives them his Spirit* predicted in John 7 and handed over in John 19 by

---

[15] Actually it occurs also in Wis 15:11 (ἐμπνεύσαντα) in a reference to the Genesis event and in 1 Kgs 17:21 (ἐνεφύσησεν) where it is probably a (deliberate?) mistranslation of the Hebrew that means "stretched" but carries, in this narrative, the same sense of "giving life." So substantively, there are only two uses: creation of humanity and re-creation of the house of Israel.

[16] The LXX has τὰ ἅγιά μου, which is translated "sanctuary" but is equally well translated by "temple." But particularly important for the connection between this passage and the Gospel of John is the use in the LXX of the Ezek passage of ἡ κατασκήνωσίς μου for "my dwelling place." In the Prologue (1:14) ὁ λόγος σάρξ ἐγένετο καὶ ἐσκήνωσεν ἐν ἡμῖν describes the Word made flesh taking up his "dwelling" among humans.

means of which he will dwell with them always, being their God as the community will be his people. The New Covenant promised repeatedly in the Old Testament is realized when the risen Jesus returns to his own to establish them as his ongoing *presence among the nations forevermore.*

In summary, then, the Holy Spirit in John is the Spirit of Jesus, the principle of his divine sonship, which he came into the world to share with all who would believe in him (see John 1:12-13). His public life unfolds as a progressive revelation of what the Spirit, who will be poured forth from the New Temple of Jesus' body when he is glorified on the cross, will be and do for his community. The Spirit will be a stream of life-giving water, a defender when they are being sacrificed as Jesus was, and a revealer of where true justice lies and why human violence can never bring it about. The Spirit will make them a New People of God, a place where the presence of Jesus will be encountered as the presence of God once was in the temple of Jerusalem. The Spirit that Jesus gives them will enable them to find another way to create justice and peace in this world, a nonviolent way of reconciliation that will consist in extending to all people, through forgiveness of sins, the peace Jesus brings to them and breathes into them.

III. René Girard and Followers on Religion and Violence

We turn now to the theory of René Girard and his biblical and theological colleagues, which will provide a lens through which to interpret John's presentation of Jesus' saving work that he commissions his disciples to continue and make effective throughout time and space.

René Girard is a French scholar, born in 1923, who began his academic career in medieval cultural studies. He has become best known for his interdisciplinary studies in literature, cultural anthropology, and religion. Girard discovered in literature, especially in the Greek tragedies and the works of Shakespeare and Dostoevsky, an anthropological pattern that he, and those who have followed him, believe is virtually universal, namely, the intimate connection by means of violence between religion and culture. It is a theory about the use of scapegoating sacrifice, that is, of violent religious ritual, to keep cultures from self-destructing. Good (i.e., sacred) violence, the killing of the scapegoat for the glory of God, is the means of keeping bad (i.e., social) violence under control. Biblical scholars concerned with the issue of violence in both Old and New Testaments and theologians concerned with the violence in the substitutionary atonement theory of redemption[17] saw the significance of Girard's thought for their fields.[18] It is important to realize that Girard's theory, like other major theories in fields like psychology or sociology, is not really "his," something he invented. It is something he discovered in the material he was studying. What we owe the theorist, like Jung, Weber, or Girard, is not the truth of the theory (which has to be determined by its explanatory power) but its discovery and explication. How we use such theory depends on our own ability to see connections between the theory and our own fields of inquiry. In my case, I have found Girard's theory extremely helpful in dealing with the question of how Jesus' violent death, which can be seen only as evil, can be understood as saving the world and how we, his followers, can participate in that saving work in a nonviolent way.

I will first synthesize Girard's very complex thought[19] and then exploit the synthesis in relationship to a single problem, albeit a very central one, namely, the "paradox of the Cross."[20] Feminists, liberation theologians, postcolonial thinkers as well as students of such unspeakable human tragedies of violence as slavery and the Holocaust have charged, in ever more convincing and disturbing ways in recent decades, that the Christian teaching that we are saved by the violent death of Jesus has contributed to the justification of violence in society and to the effort by oppressors to render victimized people passive in the face of their suffering.[21]

---

[17] For an excellent study of the relationship of Girard's theory to a theology of the cross, see S. Mark Heim, *Saved from Sacrifice: A Theology of the Cross* (Grand Rapids, MI: Eerdmans, 2006), 64–104, and throughout the book on violence in Scripture, and 297–329 on Anselm's penal substitutionary theology of atonement, which has held sway in traditional soteriology since the Middle Ages.

[18] Some of the major figures in the biblical and theological academy who explicitly use Girardian theory in their work are James Alison, Gil Bailie, Robert Hamerton-Kelly, S. Mark Heim, Raymund Schwager, and, more recently, Rowan Williams.

[19] For a more detailed summary of Girard's thought, see Michael Kirwan, *Discovering Girard* (Cambridge, MA: Cowley, 2005), or James Alison, *The Joy of Being Wrong: Original Sin through Easter Eyes* (New York: Crossroad, 1998), esp. chap. 1, "René Girard's Mimetic Theory."

[20] I will be particularly dependent in this section on the work of Heim, *Saved from Sacrifice*. See esp. chap. 4, "The Paradox of the Passion: Saved by What Shouldn't Happen," on this subject.

[21] See ibid., 20–33, on the liberationist challenge and critique of mainstream theologies of the cross.

The paradox of the cross is that immeasurable good, namely, the salvation of the world, was brought about by something that was unqualifiedly bad, namely, the murder of Jesus. How is it possible that a totally evil cause produced an infinitely good effect? And how do we explain the fact that a good God either decreed or at least approved of Jesus' death, which was evil? The notion that God was somehow pleased, pacified, or rendered benevolent toward sinful humanity by an act of sheer evil, namely, the murder of God's own Son carried out by God's permission, is increasingly experienced as a theological brick wall. More descriptively perhaps, it is a theological/spiritual Gordian knot, a problem that cannot be solved on its own terms. Every intellectual move toward a solution seems to make the problem worse. Incomprehension before this contradiction is exacerbated by the fact that the Passion of Jesus is often presented as motivation for innocent victims to bear their sufferings in mute imitation of the victimized Jesus.

The understanding of two interconnected dynamics is at the heart of Girard's thesis. The first dynamic is *mimetic or imitative desire*, which causes social and cultural breakdown, and the second is *scapegoating sacrifice*, which provides the religiously sanctioned remedy for the social breakdown. Social reconciliation is achieved through the exile, punishment, or death of the victim.

Put very simply, we find in literature of all ages and cultures and in our own experience at every level that we humans do not simply desire things because we see them as good. Rather, we learn to see something as desirable because someone else has or desires that object. The mother evinces infinite delight as she tastes the spoonful of orange mush, and the baby opens wide its mouth to share in the delicacy of mashed carrots. The child in the playpen drops the toy with which he was contentedly playing when he sees his companion enjoying her toy that now he must have. The teenager must have a particular brand of sneakers only because that is what the coolest kid in the class wears. The same dynamic drives adults' competition over houses, cars, jobs, and salaries. The fuel of the advertising business is mimetic desire, which stimulates the compulsion to acquire what the model possesses. Envious greed leads to rivalry, competition, and eventually conflict. Business and military conflicts evince the same dynamic of envy leading to rivalry that escalates into violence, overt or covert, in the effort of each to obtain what some other has. But winning only incites retaliation against the victor, which keeps the cycle of violence going.

Imitative desire and the resulting acquisitive rivalry in a society leads inevitably toward the war of all against all as everyone struggles to be at the top of the mimetic pileup. As violence escalates, social chaos threatens the survival of the group. Enter the second dynamic in Girard's theory, the remedy for contagious violence, namely, scapegoating sacrifice. Something must be done to divert everyone from mutual destructiveness and channel their violent energy into a common and unifying effort. The age-old and universal remedy for social chaos, for the disunity of "all against all," is the unification of "all against one." Nothing unites like a common enemy. The scapegoat is simply the designated enemy.

The scapegoat ritual has a simple structure and dynamic. And what is vitally important is that it really does work. It is effective. In the group convulsed by mimetically inspired social chaos, someone, by the mere fact of being somehow different from the majority, is identified as responsible in some way for the social disunity. The coming together to expunge that foreign element restores peace. Almost any kind of difference will do: skin color, sexual orientation, a speech defect, poor grooming, "uncool" clothes, a foreign-sounding name, "nerdy" glasses, living in the wrong part of town, even just being "new" in the neighborhood or schoolyard. The point is that someone must be responsible for all the trouble in the group, and it cannot be anyone like "us" because that would suggest that "we" might be the source of our problem, that "we have met the enemy, and he is us."[22]

As antagonism toward the scapegoat spreads through the crowd it becomes a mob, a single collectivity moved by motives for which no one is responsible, at least until the next morning when some individuals begin to wonder how they ever could have participated in "what happened" (not "what we did") last night. But the renewed peace that miraculously descends on the group now that the victim is gone proves that the destruction of the scapegoat was something that "needed to happen." Everything is back to normal. The scapegoat principle is vindicated: "it was expedient that one person die to keep the whole group from perishing" (cf. John 11:50).

Historically, and still in many societies, the scapegoat mechanism is orchestrated within the context of religious sacrifice. The victim is offered to the god or gods whom the people have somehow offended, and the deity, pacified by the offering, responds by restoring peace and unity to the community. Once the sacrificial murder had united the people, they were able to disguise the violence and injustice of the victimization by

---

[22] This remarkable line was written by cartoonist Walt Kelly (1948–75) for an anti-pollution poster published in 1970. It may be one of the most subversive lines in Western literature.

creating a myth or sacred story that retold the event not as murder but as sacrificial service of the divine necessary for the survival of the people. They then created a ritual or sacred drama that allowed the sacrifice to be reenacted, through either bloody or unbloody repetition, whenever social chaos, infertility, crop failure, plague, or war made renewal necessary.

The function of sacrificial myth was to render the scapegoat's victimization invisible either through vilification of the scapegoat as one who deserved to die or through posthumous exaltation of the victim as the selfless savior of the people who willingly went to death for them. In some cases, the myth began as vilification and was later transmuted into divinization. Jesus enraged his opponents by pointing out to them how often they had killed the messengers God sent to them and buried them in unmarked graves, thus bringing together the group that had been fractured by the prophet's troublesome proclamation that God was not pleased with sacrifices but demanded justice. Later, the vilified and murdered prophet was acclaimed as a voice crying in the wilderness even as the descendants of the murderers claimed that they would never have done what their ancestors did. Jesus, of course, was warning them that they were already plotting to do to him precisely the same thing they had done to the prophets before him (see Matt 23:29-39 and Luke 11:47-51). Scapegoating is always a temporary fix. It has to be renewed again and again because the cure is identical with the disease. Violence is used against violence begetting more violence. It is well known, for example, that jurisdictions in which capital punishment is used against murderers have higher murder rates than those in which capital punishment is not used.

Wherever one might be on the political spectrum, or how one feels about the Bush-Cheney presidency, it is easy to discern this mimetic desire and scapegoating mechanism in the cultural upheaval in the United States following the September 11, 2001, terrorist attack in New York City. Society was thrown into chaos by the attack on the World Trade Towers. We were all glued to the television, feeding our terror on endless reruns of the hijacked planes crashing into the towers and the feverish speculation of pundits about who was responsible. In such a case of social destabilization, someone must be responsible or the whole society remains vulnerable to forces totally beyond its control. The scapegoat was quickly identified, a man who was different from us religiously, racially, culturally, linguistically. We were told that he hated us because he did not share our love of freedom and our respect for human rights, that he was insanely jealous of our high standard of living and civic virtue. He was a madman possessed of weapons of mass destruction that, unlike us (the only nation that, in fact, has ever used weapons of mass destruction on a civilian population), he was prepared to use. The traumatized society, feeling ultimately vulnerable, united quickly in a single-minded march to war to hunt him down regardless of the human "collateral damage" incurred in the process. It was expedient that one man die rather than that the whole nation perish.

His capture unleashed the socially unifying euphoria of "mission accomplished," ecstatic cheers as his statue was toppled, presaging his imminent personal destruction for guilt already established beyond a shadow of a doubt on the basis of evidence we were assured existed even though it could not be, and never was, found. And in the surge of social unity expressed in flying flags and yellow ribbons it was essential to suppress any trace of dissent, to silence any "unpatriotic" voice that might suggest that beneath it all could be mimetic desire for oil, or that our own cultural imperialism might have provoked a desire for revenge. The newly unified society did not address the truth or falsity of such suggestions. They were simply rejected out of hand, not as untrue but as "unpatriotic," as taking the side of the scapegoat and thus weakening the newfound unity of all against one. Of course, and this is quite instructive, this particular instance of scapegoating fizzled because someone got to the scapegoat before we did. The sacrificial ritual could not be carried to completion. This left us in a state of widespread indecisiveness and mounting disunity as some people called for reevaluation of the whole project while others called for "staying the course" because, they assured us, there was an even worse scapegoat on the loose. A major obstacle to socially effective scapegoating today, for reasons I hope will become clear, is that for Christians the whole dynamic has lost its legitimating basis in religion precisely because of the execution of Jesus, the innocent scapegoat.[23]

No great stretch of imagination is necessary to see how this Girardian analysis applies to the Passion and death of Jesus. Both the civil and the ecclesiastical establishments in Jerusalem were in chaos on the eve of Passover that year. Pilate was the representative of the Roman Empire

---

[23] Perhaps the best analysis of how the cross of Jesus illuminates and makes ever less compelling the argument for sacrificial victimization in our time is Gil Bailie's *Violence Unveiled: Humanity at the Crossroads* (1999; reprint, New York: Crossroad, 2004).

in a fractious Jewish province[24] that was prone, especially at religious holidays, to riot. Caiphas was the Jewish high priest, basically kept in power by that Roman governor. Jesus was a provincial preacher whose teaching challenged both the political and religious power structures and thereby stirred up the Jewish people. If the people got out of order, for any reason, Pilate would turn against the Jewish leadership whose job was to keep the people pacified. As Jews from all over, domestic and foreign, poured into the Holy City for Passover, both empire and temple were sitting on a social powder keg.[25]

Jesus was "different" enough to make him an ideal scapegoat. He was from the Galilean "boonies," despised by the Jerusalem religious pure-bloods. He was very possibly illegitimate. He was in his thirties and not married, which could have several unsavory explanations. Someone had heard him say something threatening about the temple, although they could not remember exactly what, and his claiming to be God's son was certainly blasphemous. Who needed a trial? Obviously, the riot simmering in the streets was due to this "odd man out," this messianic pretender.

Pilate knew that Jesus was innocent, and in John's gospel announces it three times.[26] So did Caiphas, who had declared to his colleagues the real reason Jesus had to be stopped: if he was allowed to go on, the whole world would follow him, and the Romans would wipe out the Jewish nation (see John 11:48). The scapegoat principle was clearly enunciated by Caiphas, "It is expedient that one man die rather than that the whole nation perish" (see John 11:50 and 18:14).

Pilate and the Jewish elders play off each other in the scenes in John 18–19. They whip the Passover crowd into a mindless mob screaming for the death of someone against whom most have not even heard charges and for the release of Barabbas, already convicted of the very crimes of which Jesus stands accused. The scapegoat is offered to them, dressed as a fool, so brutalized that he in no way resembles their respectable religious selves (see John 19:5). The path to civil and religious peace clearly lay in the unification of all against one.

A few hours later, after the lynching on Calvary, calm descends over the land. In all three Synoptic Gospels one of the executioners acknowl-

---

[24] Pontius Pilate was prefect or governor of the Roman Province of Judea from 26 to 36 CE.

[25] For an illuminating exposition of this situation as it engulfed Jesus in his Passion, see Warren Carter, *Pontius Pilate: Portraits of a Roman Governor* (Collegeville, MN: Liturgical Press, 2003).

[26] John 18:38; 19:4; 19:6.

edges that their victim was innocent, a Son of God (Matt 27:54; Mark 15:39; Luke 23:47). Luke says the crowd dispersed beating their breasts (Luke 23:48). Pilate is relieved to get Jesus' body out of sight before people come to their senses and realize what they have done. The religious go "off to church," home for the solemn celebration of Passover, while the Roman soldiers wash their hands of another gruesome tour of duty, just following orders. The important thing is to relish the restored order, the closure, that the scapegoating sacrifice has accomplished and try not to think too much about the details.

IV. The Meaning of Jesus' Commission of His Disciples

In this third part we will read the paschal mystery of Jesus through the lens of Girardian mimetic theory in order to understand how his violent death and Resurrection brought about the salvation of the world and how his disciples' mission to forgive sins is a nonviolent continuation of that saving mystery. The scene at the end of the gospel in which Jesus sends his disciples as his Father had sent him forms an *inclusio* with the scene at the very beginning of the gospel in which Jesus is commissioned by God.[27]

In John 1:29-34 emissaries from Jerusalem were sent to ask John the Baptizer, who was attracting a crowd, who he was, what he was doing, and by what authority. John emphatically denied being Elijah, the Mosaic prophet, or the Messiah. He was merely a voice crying in the wilderness, one sent to bear witness to someone coming after him whose status far surpassed his own.

> The next day [John] saw Jesus coming toward him and declared, "Behold, the **Lamb of God** who *takes away the sin of the world!* . . . [T]he one who sent me to baptize with water said to me, 'He on whom you see the *Spirit descend and remain* is the one who *baptizes with the Holy Spirit.*' And I myself have seen and have testified that this is the Son of God." (John 1:29-34)

John's witness to Jesus at this inaugural moment, seen in light of the commissioning of his disciples in John 20:19-23, shows the continuity between his vocation and theirs: here the Spirit descends and remains on Jesus, empowering him for his mission to "take away the sin [singular]

---

[27] See n. 3 above on the literary device of *inclusio*.

of the world." When he has accomplished this great work through his life, death, and Resurrection, Jesus will "baptize," that is, empower his followers with the Holy Spirit for their mission to "forgive sins [plural]."

So we need to ask three questions: (1) What is the "sin of the world"? (2) How does Jesus take away the sin of the world? (3) How does the empowerment of the disciples to forgive sins continue Jesus' salvific work? Central to answering these questions is the identification of Jesus by John as the "Lamb of God" (ἀμνὸς τοῦ θεοῦ), a mysterious title that appears nowhere else in the New Testament.[28] Scholars recognize three Old Testament passages as possible background for this title:[29] the "sacrifice of Isaac" in Genesis 22:1-20 in which God provides the lamb for Abraham's holocaust; the Suffering Servant in Isaiah 53:7-8 who is silent like a lamb led to slaughter;[30] the paschal lamb whose blood saves the Hebrews in Egypt and whose flesh becomes their Passover meal (Exod 12:1-14). This Old Testament typology and symbolism will illuminate our investigation of Jesus' mission.

A. *The "Sin of the World"*

First, what is the "sin of the world" that Jesus came not just to forgive but to definitively take away? Jesus, in the Last Supper discourses, says that the Paraclete will convict the world of sin (in the singular), that is, will reveal the true nature of sin. Jesus says that the world, meaning

---

[28] Jesus is associated with the paschal lamb in 1 Cor 5:7, which refers to Christ as τὸ πάσχα ἡμῶν (our Passover [lamb or meal or feast]), and in 1 Pet 1:19, which says that we were ransomed τιμίῳ αἵματι ὡς ἀμνοῦ ἀμώμου καὶ ἀσπίλου Χριστοῦ (with the precious blood of Christ, like that of a lamb without defect or blemish), a clear evocation of the paschal lamb. There is no reference to the "lamb of God."

[29] C. K. Barrett, *The Gospel according to St. John: An Introduction with Commentary and Notes on the Greek Text*, 2nd ed. (Philadelphia: Westminster, 1978), 176–77, gives most of the relevant exegetical data. For a more developed interpretation of the symbol of the "Lamb of God," see Koester, *Symbolism in the Fourth Gospel*, 216–24.

[30] The "Songs of the Suffering Servant" are poems describing the scapegoat death of an innocent victim. The four songs are Isa 42:1-7; 49:1-6; 50:4-9; and 52:13–53:12. The Servant, like other "suffering just ones" in the OT, such as Jonah, Susannah, and the Wisdom Hero, suffers unjustly and, in the case of the Servant, is killed but ultimately vindicated by God, and his suffering plays some mysterious role in the salvation of his people, Israel.

those under the influence of Satan, is wrong about sin because it thinks that Jesus is the sinner, a blasphemer whose elimination will give glory to God. But the real sin, which the Spirit of Truth will reveal, is that "they [the world] do not believe in me" (John 16:9), that is, in Jesus.

In his great final prayer to God Jesus says, "this is eternal life, that they may know you, the only true God, and Jesus Christ whom you have sent" (John 17:3). So "eternal life," or salvation, is to believe in God who is revealed in Jesus, and its opposite, "the sin," is to refuse to believe in Jesus and thus reject God.

What Jesus reveals is not some abstract theological proposition to which people are obliged to give intellectual assent but that Jesus and the Father are one, something readily visible in the signs Jesus had been doing, which are clearly beyond human power (see John 10:37-38): opening the eyes of a man blind from birth, healing a man lame for thirty-eight years, feeding a huge crowd of hungry people with five loaves and two fish, raising someone long dead. The person who sees Jesus sees the Father, that is, sees God at work in the world (see John 12:45 and 14:9). In other words, Jesus is the manifestation of God precisely as love: "God so loved the world as to *give* the only Son" (John 3:16). Jesus says to the Samaritan Woman, about himself, "If you knew the *gift of God* and who it is who is speaking to you . . ." (John 4:10). God is love expressed in the Gift who is Jesus. Jesus manifests God's identity as love by doing the loving works of God in their midst (see John 10:37-38; 14:11). The "sin of the world" is not to accept that Gift, not to believe that God is love. Humans refuse that gift, quite simply, when they refuse to love, when they choose other paths to "life" and security, such as rivalry and violence. "The world" includes everyone involved in the Good Friday murder: Pilate the Gentile; the leaders of the Jews; the disciples of Jesus who betray, deny, and abandon him; the Jewish mob screaming for his blood; the Roman soldiers who execute him. When the world seizes the Gift of God and crucifies him they manifest the true nature of the "sin of the world," that is, the rejection of the God who is love.

The story of the binding of Isaac (Gen 22:1-20) probes this perversity of humanity in the face of God's gift of gratuitous love. In the Old Testament, the holocaust or whole burnt offering was the symbol of wholehearted love of God. God must wrench humanity free from the conviction that true holocaust requires destruction of that which is offered, that equates love with violence.

You will recall that God told Abraham to take his only, beloved son Isaac, the gift of God through whom the covenant would be extended to all people, to a mountain God would show him and there offer Isaac as a holocaust. Abraham understands that to respond with his whole heart to God's wholehearted love he must destroy God's gift. Abraham places the wood for the sacrifice on Isaac, the intended victim, and ascends the mountain. On the way, Isaac says to his father, "The fire and the wood are here, but where is the lamb for the holocaust?" Abraham 'replies, "God himself will provide the lamb for the holocaust, my son" (Gen 22:7-8). As Abraham raises the knife to slay Isaac, God stops him and provides a sheep caught in the thicket to replace Isaac as the symbol of Abraham's self-gift. A major point of this story, which at this point loses all interest in the sheep or the slaughter and turns to the relation between God and Abraham, is that God does not desire human sacrifice. God prizes the total self-gift, the holocaust of the heart expressed in Abraham's willingness to offer even his son, that responds to God's total self-gift to humanity expressed eventually in the gift of God's son. But gratuitous slaughter of what is precious, of God's gift, is not the appropriate way to give glory to God.

Like Isaac, Jesus appears as the beloved Son of his Father, the gift of God, the holocaust of God's heart, the Lamb of God provided by God to take away the sin of the world. John alone among the gospels tells us that Jesus carried by himself to the mount of sacrifice the wood upon which he would die (John 19:17). The difference, of course, is that no substitute victim can be provided for Jesus because he is the victim, not of an agonizing father who thinks he is doing God's will, but of scapegoating human violence. He will go to his death as the innocent Suffering Servant, not because God wills his death, but because we do. Jesus' murder has to be read in light of the meaning of the Isaac story, namely, *God does not desire human sacrifice.* God did not send Jesus into the world to be murdered. Rather, God gave the only Son to the world, as God gave Isaac to Abraham and Sarah, that everyone might have eternal life through him (see John 3:16). By giving the only Son, God has indeed supplied the Lamb, as the father of the Prodigal Son provided the inheritance that would be squandered, but it is human malice, not God's will, that turns God's gift into the bloody execution of an innocent victim. As God was pleased with Abraham's willingness to sacrifice his only son so God is pleased with Jesus' willingness to carry God's love for the world into the very heart of human evil. But God wills neither the death of Isaac nor that of Jesus.

B. *Jesus' Death to "Take away the Sin of the World"*

How, then, does Jesus' death "take away the sin of the world," human-ity's refusal to accept that God is love revealed in God's gift of the only Son? Mark Heim in his remarkable book, *Saved from Sacrifice*, says that two features of Jesus' death make it possible for him to confront and defeat, once and for all, the sacrificial dynamic, the scapegoating mecha-nism of reconciliation through violence by the collective murder of an innocent victim. Jesus had to be simultaneously a victim *like all other scapegoats* and completely *unique*. His death had to be real, part of the endless series of murders he came to stop, not some magical escape that was *sui generis* in relation to the deaths of other innocent victims. And it had to be the once and for all sacrifice, so that reconciling violence need not and must not be used ever again. It had to end the need for ceaseless repetition that is built into the scapegoat ritual.

Jesus was *one more victim like all the others* in the line that stretches back to Abel, the innocent victim of Cain's mimetic rivalry. If Jesus was not like other scapegoated victims, framed and lynched, helpless to prevent his murder for crimes of which he was innocent, his death would not be relevant to theirs. Jesus really went through what all such victims go through, and he truly died. And while he freely accepted what happened to him, as do many of the bravest and noblest of humanity's victims, it could only have been prevented by a miracle, something that is not ac-cessible to other victims. He prayed, as many victims do, to be spared his suffering, but prayer in such circumstances often cannot save the victim from resolute human evil. Jesus' prayer, like that of all the others, did not save him.

But at the same time Jesus was *not like other victims* in two important respects. First, Jesus was absolutely, rather than relatively, innocent. All scapegoated victims are, like all of us, guilty of something, even many things. But they are innocent of that for which they are really being persecuted, namely, being the cause of the social disorder to which only sacrifice can bring closure. Scapegoating involves imputing to the victim something of which the persecutors are convinced they are not guilty. The capital crime is something that makes the victim totally different from the executioners and justifies the "all against one" strategy. The purpose of the guilt imputed to the scapegoat is to disguise simultane-ously the innocence of the victim (by imputing to him or her such enor-mous guilt that only death can eradicate it) and the guilt of the persecutors (who think their murder of the victim gives glory to God who can only be pacified by such violence). The absolute difference between them establishes that the victim deserves to die and that the murderers are licensed to kill. The "rightness" of this transaction, this sacrifice, re-establishes social order. The execution of the victim brings "closure."

But, alone among humans, Jesus was actually not guilty of anything. This difference between the person justly accused of a finite offense for which they might actually be justly punished by the state and the innocent victim who is being scapegoated was clearly expressed by the "good thief" on the cross to his partner in crime, "We indeed have been condemned justly, for we are getting what we deserve for our deeds, but this man has done nothing wrong" (Luke 23:41). Jesus as scapegoat is unique in his total innocence. As totally innocent victim he reveals the innocence of all such victims and the guilt of all those who sacrifice them. He exposes the inner mechanism of the scapegoating process, which can only function as long as it is hidden from the eyes of those who are carrying it out. Once it becomes clear, once we "know what we are doing," namely, murdering the powerless in order to unify the fractured society, it becomes more and more difficult to maintain that there is some real difference between the "good violence" of the executioners and the "bad violence" they are supposedly stopping.

Second, Jesus is unique as victim because he does not stay sacrificed. He truly died, but he rose from the dead. In the Resurrection God gave back to us the Gift we had rejected. Jesus returned with forgiveness on his lips to his disciples who had been complicit in his unjust death by their betrayal, denial, abandonment. "Peace be to you," he greets them, and they "rejoiced at seeing the Lord." He comes not to retaliate, to accuse, to extract a confession, to demand contrition, to impose penance, to set conditions for rehabilitation.[31] He comes only to forgive and, by forgiving, to give them, as he had promised at the Last Supper (see John 14:24), the peace the world cannot give. This is the peace that conquers the "sin of the world," something only Jesus can do. No amount of human violence can truly reconcile, really establish the lasting peace for which the human family longs and that cannot be taken away. The grace Jesus imparts outstrips the sin in which they have participated and removes all the sins they have committed (cf. Rom 5:20).

---

[31] For an excellent extended treatment of this point, see James Alison, *Knowing Jesus* (1993; reprint, London: SPCK, 1998), esp. chap. 1, "The Resurrection."

By the time Jesus commissions his disciples to forgive sins, they have experienced what it means to be forgiven, not just for some particular sins, although they are all guilty of something, and not just to the extent that they have earned forgiveness by repentance or reparation, because there is, in fact, no way to make reparation for their participation in the sin of the world. They now know by experience the connection between "sins" and "the sin of the world." God's reversal of Jesus' sacrificial death did not annul or cancel that death. He returns to them bearing the marks of the crucifixion. But his death is integrated into his gloriously alive bodyperson. No other sacrificial victim of scapegoating violence has ever reversed the mob's violence in a victory not only over personal fate but also over death itself. Jesus has put death to death by his Resurrection (see Rom 6:9; 1 Cor 15:26, 54-55).

This is where the mysterious predictions of the ultimate victory of the Suffering Servant, the silent and unprotesting Lamb led to the slaughter, are concretely realized and where the promise of the salvific benefit from the Servant's death as healing for his persecutors is fulfilled.

> He was oppressed, and he was afflicted, yet he did not open his mouth; like a lamb that is led to the slaughter, and like a sheep that before its shearers is silent, so he did not open his mouth. By a perversion of justice he was taken away. Who could have imagined his future? . . . [But] through him the will of the Lord shall prosper (Isa 53:7-8, 10).

The Suffering Servant is killed not by God or according to God's will but by "a perversion of justice," by human malice. God enters the scene to make this atrocity work for the salvation of those who perpetrated it, just as Jesus' return to his own will make their participation in the sin of the world the raw material of forgiveness and peace that they will now be empowered to extend to others. God's will to save can work even through and despite the evil will of humans.

C. *The Empowerment of the Disciples to Forgive Sins*

Immediately after reestablishing his relationship with his disciples Jesus says again, "Peace be with you." This peace, which is first that of forgiveness, now becomes the solid foundation for the challenging mission he is about to commit to them, namely, to make effective in the world Jesus' overcoming of the sin of the world. At the Last Supper he had spoken to them of his death and their defection "so that in me you may have peace. In the world you face persecution. But take courage; I have conquered the world!" (John 16:33). Now he draws them into that work: "As the Father has sent me, so I send you." And, as the Father had poured forth the fullness of the Spirit on Jesus to empower him to take away the sin of the world, so Jesus now breathes into his disciples that same Holy Spirit to re-create them as the New Israel, the community of reconciliation that requires no scapegoating sacrifice to create or maintain it.

Here the third Old Testament reference to the Lamb, namely, the paschal lamb, becomes revelatory. The death and Resurrection of Jesus will remain salvifically effective in his community in the eucharistic celebration whose prefiguration they saw in Israel's Passover meal. On the night before God rescued the Hebrews from slavery in Egypt, each Hebrew household was to take an unblemished lamb, slaughter it, and share it in a communion meal that would prepare them for the exodus journey to the Promised Land. With a branch of hyssop they sprinkled the blood of the slain lamb on the door frames of their houses so that the angel of death who passed through the land that night to slay the firstborn would pass over the houses of the Hebrews. Thus were they saved from death through the blood of the lamb and united as one liberated community through the sharing in its flesh (see Exod 12:1-14).

John's gospel makes several clear connections between Jesus and the paschal lamb. In John's gospel, unlike the Synoptics, Jesus died on Calvary not on the feast of Passover but on the preparation day, just as the Passover lambs were being slaughtered in the Jerusalem temple. The sour wine that is put to Jesus' lips, the symbol of the bitter cup of suffering he had freely chosen to drink (see John 18:11 in light of 12:27-28), is offered to him on a sponge affixed to a hyssop branch (John 19:29). When the executioners come to break the legs of the three crucified in order to hasten their deaths, they see that Jesus is already dead and do not break his legs. The Evangelist says that this was to fulfill the prescription (see Exod 12:46; Num 9:12) that no bone of the paschal lamb was to be broken (John 19:32-36). Jesus in John is the Paschal Lamb.

The paschal lamb symbolism in Jesus' death must be read in light of John 6:26-66, the Bread of Life discourse that Jesus gave after multiplying the loaves for the crowd. Jesus performed this sign in John at Passover time. The Passover meal was not an expiatory rite but a communion sacrifice. The point was not the killing of the lamb but the sharing in the meal. In John 6, Jesus says his flesh and blood, that is, his living self, would become the food and drink of the community. But it is as bread that he gives himself, not as meat as some of his shocked hearers (then and now!) thought. He says, "I am the *living bread* that came down from heaven. Whoever eats of this *bread* will live forever; and the *bread* that I will give for the life of the world is my flesh" (John 6:51).

"Flesh" here, as commonly in Semitic languages, refers to Jesus as mortal. Because he is mortal Jesus can be killed and thereby become the spiritual or living food that gives life to the world. Jesus, like the paschal lamb, must die to become the communion meal of the community, but the point is not his death, and he is not received as dead. He is willing to die as God was willing to give him to the world that would murder him. But his desire, like God's, is not his death but that he might save the world by becoming its living sustenance. Like the manna in the desert that came down from heaven to sustain the Hebrews, so the living bread that comes down from heaven, Jesus dead and risen, is the food for the New Israel. By symbolically eating him, i.e., by receiving him in the communion meal of the community, they will live by him as he lives by the Father (see John 6:57), that is, as children of God (see John 1:12).

The culmination of the lamb symbolism passes through and beyond the intended bloody sacrifice of Abraham and the murder of the Suffering Servant into a communion meal in which all partake of the Risen One who dies no more. The Eucharist is not an unbloody reproduction, like ancient sacrificial rituals, of a bloody sacrifice carried out in the past but a sharing in the life of Jesus by a community that has repudiated all sacrifice, all trafficking in blood, all sacralized scapegoating. We eat the bread and drink the cup in remembrance of his life, death, and Resurrection, and we live by that which we eat; we become what we consume.

This brings us to the formulation of the commission: "Whose sins you shall forgive they are forgiven to them . . ." and then what? The second member of verse 23 (23b) is usually translated, "Whose sins you shall retain they are retained [to them, understood]." But there are multiple problems with that translation. In fact, I will argue that that is not what the text says.

The text reads:

	ἄν τινων	ἀφῆτε	τὰς ἁμαρτίας	ἀφέωνται	αὐτοῖς
20:23a	If of anyone	you forgive	the sins	they are forgiven	to them
	(subjective genitive)				
	ἄν τινων	κρατῆτε		κεκράτηνται	
20:23b	any	you hold fast		are held fast	
	(objective genitive)				

To begin with, in verse 23b there is no direct object (sins) and no indirect object (to them) in the Greek text. Furthermore, the verb κρατέω does not mean "retain" in the sense of keeping the person's sins unforgiven. No one, as far as I can ascertain, has found an instance in sacred or secular Greek where this verb means "retain" in that sense. Translators supply the missing words "sins" and "of those" and (mis)translate the verb κρατέω in order to make verse 23b a juridical opposite of 23a. The underlying presupposition for this interpretive move is the mistaken presumption that this Johannine text is a version of Matthew 16:19: "whatever you forbid [bind] on earth will be forbidden in heaven, and whatever you annul [loose] on earth will be annulled in heaven." In Matthew 16:18 Jesus is speaking to Peter.

In the Johannine text there is no question of correspondence between earthly and heavenly dispensations. Furthermore, the Matthean text refers to human (specifically ecclesiastical) interpretation of laws by religious authorities, not to the forgiveness of sins. And the two members in the Matthean text, "forbidding" and "annulling," are in the reverse order from the Johannine, "forgive" and "hold." Finally, there is the theological problem of what "retaining" someone else's sins could possibly mean. If a person is sorry for their sins, God forgives the sins. No human words, positive or negative, affect God's handling of sin.

What, then, *does* John 20:23b say? The verb κρατέω (which is not the word in Matthew for "forbid," namely, δέω) means "hold fast" or "embrace." Κρατέω is the word used in Matthew 28:9 of the women leaving the empty tomb who encountered the risen Jesus on the road, fell down, "and took hold of [or embraced] his feet." Translated literally, verse 23b says: "Those whom you embrace or hold fast are held fast."

Deliberate ambiguity is often intrinsic to the text in John. Such, I suspect, is the case here. The sentence could be read at the communitarian level and also at the personal level. The communitarian reading would be, "Whose sins you shall forgive they are forgiven to them and those [meaning the *people* whose sins have been forgiven] whom you embrace are held fast." In this case, the verse would refer to admission to the Christian community by baptismal forgiveness of all the "sins" (in the plural) that have been the expression in the catechumen's life of the "sin of the world." The second member of the verse would refer to the Church's task of "holding fast" in ecclesial communion all those who have been baptized into Christ. As Jesus said of his own ministry, "this is the will of the One who sent me, that I should lose nothing of all that he has given me" (John 6:39), or "they [my sheep] follow me. I give them eternal life, and they will never perish. No one will snatch them out of my hand. What my Father has given me is greater than all else, and no one can snatch it out of the Father's hand. The Father and I are one" (John 10:27-30). In summing up the accomplishment of the mission he had received from God, Jesus said, "Of those whom you [Father] have given me I lost not one" (John 17:12 and 18:9). Maintaining in union with himself all those whom the Father gives him is of the very essence of Jesus' mission to the world.[32] It makes sense to interpret this text in which Jesus commissions his disciples to carry on his work to mean that the mission of his disciples has the same structure as his own. Embracing the people whom God calls into the ecclesial community and preserving them in fidelity is the Church's continuation of Jesus' work.

Another interpretation of John 20:23 could refer more directly to the way in which believers personally make Jesus' work of reconciliation effective in the world or, conversely, fail to do so. The text, in this case, would read: "If you forgive anyone their offenses [against you] those offenses are forgiven or released. If you hang on to them, cling to them [i.e., the offenses] they remain held [i.e., in you, against the person]." This is not a matter of manipulating God, obliging God to refuse forgiveness of what we refuse to forgive. We have no influence on the person's status vis-à-vis God. This forgiveness has to do with how *we* handle the offenses of others against *us*. By refusing to forgive another, we embrace the person's sin and reject the person. We keep that person out of our life, keep the community fractured. Our refusal says nothing about how God sees the person. But it does mean that we have lost faith in God's capacity and willingness to rehabilitate the sinner; we have fallen back on the human mechanisms of retaliation and vengeance that are at the heart of the scapegoating mechanism that Jesus' death overcame. We have taken up again "the sin of the world," the refusal to believe that God is love and has no need of our violence against each other to keep order in human society or the Church. This profound failure of faith, this conviction that we honor God by punishing our brothers and sisters, is probably most evident in the infliction of the death penalty or the punitive use of ecclesiastical excommunication because we think only our human violence can bring the sinner to repentance, can right the wrong and bring real "closure."

---

[32] All of these "union" texts express the same twofold character of Jesus' mission, to bring people into union with himself and hold them fast: 6:37; 6:39; 10:27-29; 17:12; 18:9.

V. Conclusion

Whichever way we read this text, on the communal level or on the personal level, it ceases to be about ecclesiastical officers being empowered to execute divine judgment on their fellow human beings and becomes Jesus' commitment of responsibility for the divine work of reconciliation to his disciples as a community. Jesus, by becoming the "last scapegoat," has taken away the foundational sin of the world—the refusal to believe that God is unconditional love. He has made it possible and right for all expressions of that fundamental sin, all "sins" no matter how serious, to be freely forgiven through the loving action of his disciples who, individually and corporately, renounce all recourse to reconciliation by violence.

The Church of Jesus should be the one place where every sinner can feel absolutely safe because there is no condemnation in this community.[33] The one who freely forgave his own murderers because they did not know what they were doing (see Luke 23:34) now empowers his disciples to drop their stones. Our solidarity in sin to which we were once blind and which we now recognize through our experience of being forgiven must become grateful solidarity in forgiveness and reconciliation. Jesus says that unless we forgive we cannot be forgiven (see Matt 18:35), not because God mimics our hardness of heart, but because only by forgiving can we continue to believe in, to accept, being forgiven. Jesus said to the woman he had rescued from stoning, "Has no one condemned you?" She said, "No one, sir." And Jesus said, "Neither do I condemn you. Go . . . and from now on sin no more" (John 8:10-11). The challenge to "sin no more" can only be met in the context of the experience of being freely forgiven. The mission of Jesus' disciples, that is, of us, is not judgment of our fellow sinners or restoring order to society or Church by vengeance and retaliation. It is to make effective in the world Jesus' work of reconciliation through the forgiveness of sins so that the community of the forgiven can gather around the table of the Lamb who has taken away the sin of the world. For this challenging mission we have the gift of Jesus' Spirit: "Receive the Holy Spirit; whose sins you shall forgive they are forgiven."

---

[33] This was the insight that led to the understanding of early Christian churches as zones of asylum for criminals or those accused of crimes or soldiers under siege, as well as the declaration in the twentieth century of certain cities, university campuses, and other places as "sanctuary" against deportation for people fleeing the violent civil wars in their own countries. The churches continue even today to provide sanctuary for the undocumented.

Chapter 6

The Lamb of God and the Forgiveness of Sin(s) in the Fourth Gospel

I. Introduction

This paper on the problem of violence and the possible contribution of Christian Scripture to its solution is an experiment in biblical interpretation. Specifically, it is an attempt to bring biblical material, theological reflection, and contemporary intellectual resources from other disciplines into meaningful interaction around a religious and spiritual issue that is of major importance not only for the Church but also for society as a whole.

Wilfred Cantwell Smith, the late Harvard scholar of comparative religion, titled his immensely erudite study of the role of canonical religious texts and their interpretation in all the major world religions *What Is Scripture?*[1] He concluded, in a nutshell, that canonical texts in any believing community are a privileged medium for engaging, from within a shared tradition with its accepted categories, symbol system, language, and practice, questions of ultimate concern. Scripture, then, is not a thing—e.g., the biblical text—but a process that he called "scripturing." Through its sacred texts, the believing community engages its own

Originally presented as "The Lamb of God and the Forgiveness of Sin(s) in the Fourth Gospel," Catholic Biblical Association of America Presidential Address (Los Angeles, CA, July 2010) and shortened for print in *The Catholic Biblical Quarterly* 73, no. 1 (January 2011).

[1] Wilfred Cantwell Smith, *What Is Scripture? A Comparative Approach* (Minneapolis: Fortress Press, 1993).

current experience in the effort to find life and to live well, which for Christians means to live by the Spirit as the Body of Christ in and for the salvation of the world.

My process, then, will entail engaging a critical contemporary question, the escalation of violence, by bringing the work of two contemporary scholars, the German depth psychologist-theologian-exegete Eugen Drewermann and the French cultural historian, literary critic, and anthropologist René Girard, and their respective followers, particularly in the biblical and theological academies,[2] into dialogue with three clusters of material from the Gospel of John: the Johannine understanding of "the sin of the world"; the identity and role of Jesus as the "Lamb of God who takes away" that sin; and the ecclesial community's participation in this liberation through "the forgiveness of sins," which is the work Jesus committed to his followers in the great commission in the Fourth Gospel—"As the Father has sent me, so I send you. . . . Whose sins you shall forgive they are forgiven" (see John 20:21-23).

II. Violence and Religion

No documentation is really necessary to prove that violence is not only a societal scourge of monumental proportions but also escalating at a terrifying pace domestically, locally, nationally, and globally. And no one seems to have any idea how to stem the increase except to mobilize more and more "good" violence by arming more people, building more prisons, and declaring more wars to combat the "bad" violence.[3]

---

[2] The relevant biblical work of Eugen Drewermann is virtually unavailable in English except in the excellent book-length synthesis of Matthias Beier, *A Violent God-Image: An Introduction to the Work of Eugen Drewermann* (New York/London: Continuum, 2004). René Girard's work, on the other hand, is widely available either written originally in English or translated. For a full bibliography of his books, see Michael Kirwan, *Discovering Girard* (Cambridge, MA: Cowley, 2005), 126–30. This book also contains information concerning Girard's articles and contributions to collections, articles about him, and scholarly discussions of his work. An invaluable resource on Girard is James Williams, ed., *The Girard Reader* (New York: Crossroad, 1996). Among theologians and biblical scholars who have found Girard's contribution critical to an understanding of sin, forgiveness, and especially the theology of atonement, are James Alison, Gil Bailie, Robert Daly, Stephen Finlan, Robert Hamerton-Kelly, S. Mark Heim, Raymund Schwager, Miroslav Volf, and Walter Wink.

[3] I supplied some illustrative data on this subject in my Bellarmine Lecture (delivered at Saint Louis University, St. Louis, Missouri, November 2, 2008), "Before It's

Many people inside and outside the Christian tradition have suggested that monotheistic religion in general and Christianity in particular might be *a* or even *the* primary instigator and legitimizer of violence, at least in the West. Theology struggles to explain the divine violence inherent in the vernacular version of Anselmian soteriology[4] according to which God required Jesus' horrendous death to divert God's just wrath from sinful humanity, which was incapable of expiating its own infinite offense against God. Within this framework of understanding, Jesus, by his silent complicity in his own victimization, which God required as the price of our redemption, appears to condone by example the passive acceptance of violence by the oppressed.

Biblical scholars are also increasingly faced with questions about the seemingly ubiquitous violence in the sacred text.[5] God the warrior king in the Old Testament obliterating peoples and handing their seized lands over to his chosen people and then avenging himself on Israel itself for its unfaithfulness, and God the ruthless sacrificer of his own Son in the New Testament seems to model and encourage violence as a legitimate, necessary, and, finally, only way of handling the human predicament.

As we know, a growing volume of work in both theology and biblical studies is being devoted to trying to untangle this Gordian knot of the implication of God in human violence.[6] Because the dilemma of violence

---

Too Late . . .: Violence, Reconciliation, and the Church," *Theological Digest* 54 (Spring 2010): 5–23, esp. 5–6.

[4] Anselm's own theology is much more subtle and nuanced than the "catechetical" version many Catholics have internalized. Moreover, Anselm's theory, worked out within the framework of medieval feudal law, was carried forward by Luther in his theory of Jesus as representative of humanity in bearing the punishment demanded by God's wrath and especially by Calvin, who made use of the framework of medieval criminal law in which Jesus becomes the substitute who bears the condemnation and punishment God rightly imposes on the human race for its violation of the divine law. All of this development was involved in the formulation of the late medieval theology of salvation by vicarious suffering that held (and still holds) sway in the imagination of many modern believers.

[5] See William W. Emilsen and John T. Squires, eds., *Validating Violence—Violating Faith? Religion, Scripture and Violence* (Adelaide, SA: ATF, 2008), a collection of essays on the violence in, or promoted by, the Scriptures of the three monotheistic world religions, Judaism, Christianity, and Islam.

[6] A particularly fine work on the subject is S. Mark Heim, *Saved from Sacrifice: A Theology of the Cross* (Grand Rapids, MI: William B. Eerdmans, 2006). Heim makes excellent use of both biblical and theological resources and references much of the best work on the subject in the past few years. He supplies an excellent and extensive bibliography.

lies at the very heart of human experience with implications for all of creation, we are not only justified in asking but also compelled to ask if our sacred texts are actually part of this problem or have anything constructive to contribute to its solution.

III. The Divine-Human Drama in the Fourth Gospel: The Structure of the Sin of the World

Although Jesus' identity as the Messiah is affirmed in John's gospel[7] and there are discussions about his relation to Abraham,[8] Moses,[9] and David,[10] the primary identity of Jesus in John is as Son of God or Sent One manifest in and as the Son of Man. Jesus' true origins are "in the beginning" (ἐν ἀρχῇ) as the Word of God in whom and for whom and according to whom all things are made. The Word becomes human in time, but the Word comes from the depths of God's eternity on a divine mission not just to a chosen people but to the whole world, which "God so loved" (3:16). The Word comes into the world not merely to fulfill the hopes of Israel but also to enlighten "*every* human being" (1:9; my translation). Jesus is the "Savior of the *World*" (4:42) who, when he is lifted up, will draw "*all* people to himself" (12:32).[11]

---

[7] Jesus affirms the tentative identification of himself as Messiah by the Samaritan Woman (4:26); Martha confesses Jesus as Messiah just before the resuscitation of Lazarus (11:27); the gospel ends with the statement that its purpose is to bring readers to believe that Jesus is Messiah and Son of God (20:31). Other references to Jesus as Messiah in the gospel are primarily in the context of people arguing over Jesus' identity, challenging him to claim his messianic identity, or denying it.

[8] The discussion in John 8:31-59 ends with Jesus' assertion that "before Abraham was, I am."

[9] See John 9:28-29 as typical of the "greater than Moses" theme in John. Just as his priority in relation to Abraham makes Jesus not primarily a descendant of Abraham from whom he draws his identity but the one from whom Abraham's significance in salvation history is drawn, so Moses is not primarily the one who legitimates Jesus' claim to authority but rather the one whom Jesus surpasses and who thus bore witness to Jesus by word and work even without knowing it.

[10] In John 7:42 there is a question about Jesus' descent from David since he is not from Bethlehem, but no conclusion is drawn. Jesus in John is not a king from David's line but becomes a king when he is glorified on the cross. The question of Jesus' kingship is very important in John, but it is not centered on the Davidic line. Jesus' transcendent kingship offers an alternative to the Davidic understanding of kingship.

[11] See Enno Edzard Popkes, "The Love of God for the World and the Handing over ('*Dahingabe*') of His Son: Comments on the Tradition-Historical Background and the

The Fourth Gospel, then, is structured as a cosmic drama being acted out in history rather than as a historical event with cosmic implications. This cosmic drama is a struggle to the death between God's love for the world and a personal evil agent, who, in John, is called "the Devil" (6:70; 8:44; 13:2), "Satan" (13:27), and the "Ruler of this world" (ὁ ἄρχων τοῦ κόσμου τούτου; 12:31; 14:30; 16:11) and who is a liar and a murderer from the beginning (ἀπ᾽ ἀρχῆς [8:44]). Satan's project, the alienation of all creation from God, began in the Garden of Eden and proceeds toward its goal, the destruction of Jesus who is the incarnation of God's eternal and infinite love for the world, under the designation of what John calls "the sin of world" (ἡ ἁμαρτία τοῦ κόσμου).

In striking contrast with the dramatic launching of his public ministry by Jesus himself in the Synoptic Gospels, e.g., in the synagogue scene in Luke 4, the Johannine Jesus emerges on the stage of history in silence. As Jesus walks by, the Baptizer proclaims, in what has been recognized as a revelation formula in the Fourth Gospel,[12] "Behold, the Lamb of God who takes away the sin of the world" (1:29). The Baptizer then expands eloquently on Jesus' identity and mission as they were revealed to him by the One who sent him to baptize with water. John recognizes the One sent to baptize with the Holy Spirit by the visible and permanent descent of the Spirit on Jesus (see 1:31-34). But Jesus himself says nothing. Somehow, everything is contained, like the oak in the acorn, in this foundational identification, which will be unfolded throughout Jesus' ministry and especially in his Glorification in and by his violent death on the cross.

"Lamb of God" (ἀμνὸς τοῦ θεοῦ) is a NT *hapax legomenon*, appearing only in this verse, John 1:29 (repeated verbatim in 1:36), and nowhere in the Old Testament. The clue to understanding the meaning of the title lies in understanding what the Lamb comes to "take away," namely, "the sin of the world." Raymond E. Brown, expressing the scholarly consensus on this subject, states that in this verse and elsewhere in John "sin" in the singular denotes a "condition" rather than an act.[13] Sin in John is not

---

Theological Function of John 3,16A in the Overall Context of Johannine Theology," in *The Death of Jesus in the Fourth Gospel*, ed. G. Van Belle (Leuven: University Press, 2007), 609–23. Popkes says, "Although the motif of the love of God for the world is unique in the Johannine writings its importance for the overall understanding of Johannine theology can hardly be overestimated" (623).

[12] M. de Goedt, "Un schème de révélation dans le quatrième évangile," *NTS* 8 (1962): 142–50.

[13] Raymond E. Brown, *The Gospel according to John*, Anchor Bible 29 and 29A (Garden City, NY: Doubleday, 1966–70), 1:56.

a juridical concept referring to an infraction or a transgression of law. At the end of the gospel, in John 20:21-23, the risen Jesus will empower his disciples to carry on his mission with the words "As the Father has sent me [i.e., to take away the sin (singular) of the world] so I send you. . . . Whose sins [plural] you forgive, they are forgiven to them."[14] The contrast in this *inclusio* (1:29 and 20:23) that embraces the whole gospel is between Jesus' absolutely unique mission to "take away" definitively a fundamental state of affairs or condition affecting the whole human race, namely, "the sin of the world," and the mission of his disciples throughout subsequent history to deal with the residual effects and contingent expressions of this condition that, in principle, has already been abolished by Jesus whose salvific Glorification has "cast out" (ἐκβληθήσεται ἔξω) or expelled the Ruler of this world (John 12:31).

In what, then, does the fundamental alienation of humans from God consist? In theology this is the classical conundrum of original sin. What is the nature of that fundamental choice by which humans, made in God's own image and likeness, turned away from their Creator and thereby perverted their relation to themselves, to one another, and to the whole created universe?

The story of the Fall in Genesis 3 is a profound mythological exploration of this question, and chapters 4–11, from the fratricide of Cain to the Tower of Babel, picturesquely describe the trajectory of that original disaster unfolding in the "sins" that sprang from it like hydra-heads until God "regretted" having created humanity (Gen 6:5-8). The sin in the Garden of Eden is "original" not because it was chronologically anterior to any other sins but because it is the root, the source, that which gives rise to and basically structures all the sins to follow.

On this subject the thought of Eugen Drewermann is enlightening. Drewermann is a German polymath, born in 1940, who has been the most prominent and probably most controversial Catholic religious intellectual in Europe for the past two decades.[15] His voluminous writings, including more than seventy books and numerous articles and essays

---

[14] Unless otherwise noted, biblical texts are cited from the NRSV. The exception is John 20:19-23, which I translate because the translation is critical to the argument I am making, namely, that the traditional translation of part of this pericope is questionable.

[15] For a brief synopsis of Drewermann's career and a review of his biblical work, see Wayne G. Rollins's review of Beier's *A Violent God-Image* [see n. 2 above] in *Review of Biblical Literature*, http://www.bookreviews.org (April 2005).

on a wide range of topics, have been translated into nearly a dozen languages but unfortunately not into English. That language barrier has been partially overcome by Matthias Beier in his excellent synthesis of Drewermann's work, titled *A Violent God-Image*.[16]

Drewermann's work spans and integrates theology, philosophy, biblical exegesis, cultural anthropology, and depth psychology on a variety of subjects. He is also well known for his antiwar activism, which grows out of his personal concern with the issue of violence. His most important work, a three-volume treatise based on his doctoral dissertation on Genesis 2–11, titled *Strukturen des Bösen*[17] (*The Structures of Evil*), is a search for the real theological-anthropological-psychological meaning of original sin.[18] A single, but central, insight from Drewermann's work illuminates John's perception of the "sin of the world."

Drewermann calls up the "usual suspects" for the motivation of our first parents' sin—greed, lust, pride, disobedience—and finds all these hypotheses incoherent. He proposes that the fundamental motive for the originating sin was fear—existential fear of annihilation born of the ontological "wound" of creaturehood. What humanity rejects, Drewermann says, is contingency, the fact that we are not God. Our existential terror stems from our realization that—even though made in God's image and likeness—we, unlike God, are not the source of our own existence. The serpent, the liar from the beginning, insinuated into the idyllic context of the "original" couple, endowed by a loving God with all the good humans could desire, the suspicion that they were not really safe, that they were vulnerable to the whims of a capricious and untrustworthy but all-powerful deity. God, who had called them out of nonbeing into life, could, at any moment, plunge them back into the abyss of nothingness over which God held them by the thread of the divine will.

---

[16] See n. 2 above.

[17] Eugen Drewermann, *Strukturen des Bösen. Sonderausgabe: Die jahwistische Urgeschichte in exegetischer/psychoanalytischer/philosophischer Sicht*, 3 vols. (Paderborn: Schöningh, 1985–86).

[18] Theologian James Alison, seemingly unaware of Drewermann's development of this theme (since he does not cite Drewermann or enter into dialogue with him in his writings), offers an illuminating complementary analysis, based on René Girard's thought, in *The Joy of Being Wrong: Original Sin through Easter Eyes* (New York: Crossroad, 1998). They differ in that Drewermann is dealing with the biblical account as "myth," which he analyzes primarily in terms of depth psychology, whereas Alison sees the biblical account as pointing in some way toward the actual anthropological/historical origins of mimetic desire and its fallout.

Of course, this fall scene is not a historical description of an actual event. It is a psychologically sophisticated theological analysis of our existential experience in the face of life's uncertainties, our own vulnerabilities, the inevitability of death, and the unknowability of death's aftermath. We might say that Adam and Eve are, in a sense, the pure essence of creaturehood. They have no parents from whom to have inherited anything—life or power or talents or property. They have not achieved or produced anything they can call their own. They, having no history, have literally nothing they have not received. They are not so much the recipients of divine gifts; they *are* gift, totally and exclusively, a fact that can be disguised for their progeny who, in fact, all have ancestors and a history that can supply a causal masquerade. Adam and Eve, completely devoid of anything that can even appear to come from themselves or anything else, are a pure instance of God's causality as self-bestowing love, as love that creates the object of its love in order to love it.

Under the serpent's deceitful tutelage, they begin to realize that God has one thing they do not have, something God wants to keep them from acquiring, lest they should become "like God." Of all the trees in the garden they may eat, but of the tree of the knowledge of good and evil they are not to eat, "lest they die" (Gen 3:2-5). God's seeming protection *of* them from death, the serpent tells them, is, in reality, God's self-protection *against* them. Thus God, the source of life for human beings, becomes, in fallen human consciousness, the ultimate threat to their life. This existential fear, Drewermann suggests, is the origin of the violent God-image. Humans project on God their own desire to violently seize divine autonomy and see God as violently protecting the divine prerogatives. God and humanity become, in human perception, rivals. In Girardian terms, the first case of mimetic rivalry was the first couple's competition with God.

This penetrating analysis of the existential fear born of the ontological condition of creaturehood is strikingly reflected, in reverse, in the hymn in Philippians 2:

> Let the same mind be in you that was in Christ Jesus, who, *though he was in the form of God, did not regard equality with God as something to be grasped at*, but emptied himself, taking rather *the form of a slave*, being born in human likeness. And being found in human form, he humbled himself and became obedient to the point of death—even death on a cross. (vv. 5-9)

Jesus is God's incarnate overture to alienated humans grasping for divinity as the only security against the contingency of creaturehood. In

Jesus, God demonstrates that divinity—equality with God—is not something to be coveted, because divinity is not something God exploits at our expense. In Jesus, God takes on the very form that humanity, instructed by the tempter, regards as slavery, namely, creaturehood, to demonstrate that creaturehood is not a condition of existential peril rooted in ontological deficiency. Even when drunk to the dregs to which humanity can be reduced by evil itself, namely, violent death on a cross, creaturehood remains the locus of Glorification, exaltation, inextinguishable union with God. To be fully human, including experiencing annihilation's "look-alike"—i.e., death—is not a deprivation of divinity but a privileged way to participate in divinity. God conquers death not by avoiding it, as Adam and Eve hoped to do by seizing divinity, but by embracing it. In the outstretched arms of God's love on the cross, death is finally slain. The Ruler of this world, who never actually had any power over Jesus (see John 14:30) but did have power in "the world" (12:31), is finally cast out. The cosmic struggle is over.[19]

The nature of the "sin of the world," illuminated by Drewermann's analysis emerges in the Gospel of John as the refusal to believe that God is infinite self-bestowing love[20] offering eternal life, God's own life communicated to those who are born of God (see John 1:12-13), to all who will accept it. Jesus, in John, is the Gift of God (see 3:16; 4:10), first offered in creation, but now coming as a human being, into the world that God so loved. By his words and deeds he reveals both the fact and the meaning of God's creative love and what creaturely acceptance of that love means. The Incarnation, in John, is not Plan B, God's salvage operation on the wreckage of creation. It is the fulfillment of creation that was always, from the beginning, in and for and according to the Word that is now made flesh.

John's term for accepting God's self-gift, which is Jesus himself, is "believing." It is the self-gift, in Jesus, of the human to God that responds to God's self-gift, in Jesus, to the world. In Jesus himself humans see not just the possibility but the existential reality of human participation in

---

[19] See the very convincing argument in John Dennis, "The 'Lifting up of the Son of Man' and the Dethroning of the 'Ruler of this World': Jesus' Death as the Defeat of the Devil in John 12,31-32," in *The Death of Jesus in the Fourth Gospel*, 677–91, esp. 690–91.

[20] See Popkes, "The Love of God for the World." Popkes evokes John 3:16; 1 John 3:16; 1 John 4:8, 16 in his overall argument that God's motive in the sending of Jesus and of Jesus' self-gift in his death is the love of God for the world, which is not restricted to Israel. See especially his conclusion, 622–23.

divine life that the serpent tempted them to believe was not possible except by seizing what God jealously withheld from them. Jesus is, at one and the same time, in a single person, the presence of the self-giving God ("I and the Father are one" [10:30]; "whoever sees me sees the one who sent me" [12:45]) and the total receptivity of the creature ("the Father is greater than I" [14:38]; I do always the will of the one who sent me [see John 8:29 and elsewhere]). This coincidence of giving that does not diminish the being of the Giver who therefore has no need to defend it against the creature, and receiving that does not endanger the receiver who therefore has no need to seize divinity as self-protection, makes Jesus the Way, the Truth, and the Life (see 14:6) not only for those who know his name and story but for every human being, for the whole world.[21] He, not Satan, is the Savior of the World.

This victory over the "sin of the world" is succinctly summarized by Jesus at the Last Supper in John 16:8-11. Jesus says that when the Paraclete comes to continue Jesus' presence and action in the world through his disciples,[22] the Spirit's witness will be an exposure that "the world," which here means the satanic project as a whole, was radically wrong about the entire human project, that is, about *sin*, about *justice*, and about *judgment*.

---

[21] This approach might help with the problem many have with the Johannine insistence that only those who believe in Jesus can be saved. What of all those, most of humanity, who have never heard of Jesus? Perhaps responding to Jesus means accepting the revelation of the love of God as utterly gratuitous, that is, meeting in one's life the goodness of God without setting limits or conditions on what goodness can mean, without suspicion that life is a trap, without despairing that death is stronger than life, without succumbing to the lie that protecting oneself by endangering others is the answer. Perhaps living from the life of the Vine means bearing fruit, yielding one's life to the work of enabling others to live. If this is the case, then even those who have never heard of Jesus by name but who know him in and through their participation in his loving and life-giving work may, in fact, have encountered him and are being pruned by his Father as they continue to bear the fruit that testifies to the life they are receiving from the one Vine. In other words, "Those who do the truth come to the light" (see John 3:21), and there is only one Source of that Light, whether a person knows his human, historical name in this world or not.

[22] Brown says: "It is our contention that John presents the Paraclete as the Holy Spirit in a special role, namely, as the personal presence of Jesus in the Christian while Jesus is with the Father" (*The Gospel according to John*, appendix 5, "The Paraclete," 2:1139). I think this is exactly right and base my argument at this point on Brown's position.

First, about sin. The Ruler of this world, acting through the leaders of the Jews, declared that Jesus was not the revelation of God's absolute love for the world but a blasphemer (see 19:7). The Spirit reveals that the *real sin* was precisely not to believe that Jesus was God's Gift.

Second, about justice. The world, under Satan's inspiration working particularly through Judas (see 13:2), thought that executing the blasphemer was the just vindication of God's jealous honor. But *true justice* was accomplished in Jesus' Glorification by his going to the Father, which took place right within the crucifixion.

Third, about judgment. The world, acting through Pilate in league with the leaders of the Jews (see 19:7-10), rendered the judgment of execution on Jesus even though he knew Jesus was innocent of any crime. But the *true judgment* was the final condemnation of the Ruler of this world, who was judged by and in and through the death of Jesus. Jesus' death, which in John is his Glorification by God, is the victory not only of Jesus over Satan but of God's love for the world over the satanic "sin of the world."

IV. Mimetic Desire and Violence: The Dynamic of the Sin of the World

If Drewermann discloses the basic *nature and structure* of the sin of the world as the disordered human desire to "be like God" by seizing divinity rather than accepting it as the gift of God, René Girard has offered a remarkably fruitful analysis of the *dynamics* of the sin of the world in his theory of the connection between human desire run amok and violence. Girard, who taught for much of his career in the United States, was born in 1923 and began his academic career in medieval cultural studies, branching out into interdisciplinary studies in comparative literature and cultural anthropology. Beginning in the 1970s Girard's theory of the religious origin and nature of social violence[23] has generated widespread interest among scholars in such diverse fields as literary studies, critical

---

[23] Works by René Girard, specifically on the issue of violence and religion, which have had an enormous influence on religious studies are the following: *Violence and the Sacred*, trans. Patrick Gregory (Baltimore: Johns Hopkins University Press, 1977); with Jean-Michel Oughourlian and Guy Lefort, *Things Hidden since the Foundation of the World*, trans. Stephen Bann and Michael Metteer (Stanford, CA: Stanford University Press, 1987); *The Scapegoat* (Baltimore: Johns Hopkins University Press, 1986).

theory, anthropology, cultural studies, sociology, economics, psychology, philosophy, and especially theology and biblical studies.

The theory Girard has elaborated is not something he invented. Like Darwin's theory of evolution, or Jung's archetypal theory of the unconscious, or Einstein's theory of relativity, Girard's theory of the nature and role of religiously legitimated social violence in cultural evolution was discovered in the material he was studying, particularly in the fields of literature and anthropology. Such theories, although comprehensive, are not totalizing grand narratives, the ideological straitjackets or procrustean beds of which postmodernity is rightly very suspicious. They are extremely illuminating and fruitful insights into the structure and dynamics of particular areas of human experience. They are like Paul's classic and comprehensive description in Romans 7 of the human moral dilemma: the battle of the spirit between the good we espouse and the evil we so often choose and especially our experience of being controlled in such choices by something that both is and is not ourselves. Such comprehensive theories cannot be validated by authority or even by argumentation. They can only validate themselves by their explanatory power.

An extraordinarily wide range of scholars, including some of the most creative biblical scholars in recent years,[24] have found Girard's theory of the role of sacralized violence in the development of human culture extremely illuminating, no doubt partly because an act of horrendous violence, the crucifixion of Jesus, is at the very heart of the Christian religion and this presents serious problems for many believers. The misunderstanding and misuse of this central datum of the Christian story, especially to promote terror of God and blind obedience in the service of the tyranny of human religious authority, to romanticize suffering especially among the powerless, or to encourage passivity in the face of oppression, are so prevalent and so destructive that a new way

---

[24] One of the most developed theories that relies heavily on Girard's work is Walter Wink's trilogy on "The Principalities and Powers": *Naming the Powers: The Language of Power in the New Testament* (1983); *Unmasking the Powers: The Invisible Forces That Determine Human Existence* (1986); *Engaging the Powers: Discernment and Resistance in a World of Domination* (1992), all from Fortress Press. Robert T. Fortna called Wink's third and concluding volume "[a] masterwork [that] combines skillful biblical exegesis with prodigious knowledge of our modern world to produce a radically new understanding of Christianity as victory over the Powers that dominate and enslave."

of looking at the crucifixion, which Girard's theory offers, is more than worth investigation.[25]

I will first synthesize Girard's theory about sacred violence[26] and then exploit that synthesis in relationship to the "paradox (or perhaps we could say the koan) of the cross," namely, that the immeasurable good of the salvation of the world was brought about by unqualified evil, namely, the murder of Jesus.[27] This paradox or enigma is a Gordian knot, because every effort to render it coherent seems to make the problem more intractable. Girard's theory in conjunction with John's unique take on the death of Jesus as exaltation holds, I think, some promise in dealing with this conundrum.

The interconnection of three dynamics is at the heart of Girard's thesis. The first dynamic is *mimetic or imitative desire*, which causes social and cultural breakdown. The second is *scapegoating violence*, in which social reconciliation and unity are restored through the execution of a designated victim. The third is the *creation of a myth* that disguises the murder of the scapegoat as a divinely sanctioned and necessary sacrifice to an offended deity and that is embodied in a *ritual* by which the mythologized sacrificial death can, in bloody or unbloody manner, be repeated when later crises threaten the group.

First, Girard points out that the world's great literature, especially the tragedies of the ancient Greeks and Shakespeare and the novels of Dostoevsky, as well as our own experience show us that we humans do not straightforwardly desire things because we see them as good. Rather, we learn to see something as desirable because someone else has or desires that object. Desire, in other words, is mimetic or imitative. The mother persuades the baby to desire mashed carrots by pretending that she finds the orange mush delicious. The teenager covets a particular brand of sneakers because the most popular boy in the class wears them. The same dynamic drives adults "to keep up with the Joneses" even when they neither need nor want the bigger car or the more exotic vacation.

---

[25] Two of the most original and fruitful extensive uses of Girardian theory to deal with the widespread and dangerous misunderstanding of the crucifixion of Jesus as salvific are the following: James Alison, *Knowing Jesus* (1933; reprint, London: SPCK, 1998), and Heim, *Saved from Sacrifice*.

[26] For a more detailed summary of Girard's thought, see Kirwan, *Discovering Girard*, or Alison, *The Joy of Being Wrong*, chap. 1, "René Girard's Mimetic Theory."

[27] I will be particularly dependent in this section on the work of Heim, *Saved from Sacrifice*; see esp. chap. 4, "The Paradox of the Passion: Saved by What Shouldn't Happen," on this subject.

International conflicts arise when one nation covets the assets—territory, resources, labor, markets, power—of another. But in many cases, especially when only one can have the coveted object, whether in the schoolyard, in the board room, or on the battlefield, conflict ensues. Victory only incites retaliation against the winner, which keeps the cycle of violence going.

Imitative or mimetic desire, leading to acquisitive rivalry, leading to competition and eventually to conflict in a society, tends inevitably toward the war of all against all as everyone struggles to be at the top of some mimetic pileup. As violence escalates, social chaos threatens the survival of the group—small groups like a family struggling over an inheritance or big ones like Iraq and the United States struggling over oil in the Middle East. Enter the second dynamic in Girard's theory, the remedy for contagious, escalating violence, namely, scapegoating. Something must be done to arrest mutual destructiveness and channel the violent energy of all into a common and unifying effort. The age-old remedy for social chaos, for the disunity of "all against all," is the unification of "all against one," against the beautiful older sister who has always pretended to be more devoted to their rich father than the other siblings or against Saddam Hussein who is surely hiding weapons of mass destruction that he fully intends to use. Nothing unites like a common enemy. The scapegoat is simply the designated enemy.

It is vitally important to realize that the structurally and dynamically simple scapegoat mechanism really does work. In a group convulsed by mimetically inspired social chaos, someone, by the mere fact of being somehow different from the majority, is identified as responsible in some way for the social disarray. Almost any kind of difference will do to constitute the scapegoat: skin color, sexual orientation, gender, a speech impediment or foreign accent, size, poor grooming, coming from the wrong part of town, or even just being "new" in the schoolyard. The point is that someone must be responsible for the trouble in the group, and it cannot be anyone like "us" because that would suggest that "we" might be the source of our problem, that "we have met the enemy, and it is us."[28] We have only to look at the wars we are currently waging, at

---

[28] After defeating the British fleet in the Battle of Lake Erie on September 10, 1813, Oliver Perry, commander of the American fleet, dispatched his famous message to Major General William Henry Harrison: "We have met the enemy, and they are ours." In 1970 cartoonist Walt Kelly famously paraphrased the statement as "We have met the enemy, and he is us" in an Earth Day poster that featured characters from his long-running strip *Pogo* to lament the sad state of the environment.

the attempts to deal with the current experience of economic crisis in our country, or at the moral crisis in the Catholic Church to recognize the recourse to this scapegoating dynamic.

The antagonism toward the scapegoat spreads by contagion and turns the crowd into a mob, a single collectivity like the gang of bullies on a playground or a Ku Klux Klan posse descending on the home of a black family or the country gearing up for preemptive war, moved by motives for which no one feels personally responsible at the time, although by "the next morning"—literal or figurative—some individuals might begin to wonder how they ever could have participated in "what happened [not 'what we did'] last night." But the peace that miraculously descends on the group now that the mission is accomplished, the victim gone, "proves" that the destruction of the scapegoat was something that "needed to happen." Things are back to normal. The scapegoat principle is vindicated: "it is expedient that one person die to keep the whole group from perishing" (see John 11:50).

The third dynamic in the scapegoat process is the mythic and ritual appropriation by which the murder of the scapegoat is transformed into religious sacrifice. In classical ancient society, the reunited community disguises the violence and injustice of the victimization by creating a myth or sacred story that retells the event not as the lynching it was but as an expiatory sacrifice offered to placate an offended deity whose punishment of the community in the form of war, disease, famine, etc., is now lifted. They then create a ritual or sacred drama that allows the sacrifice to be reenacted, in bloody or unbloody form, whenever social chaos, infertility, crop failure, plague, war, or some other catastrophe makes renewal necessary. In modern societies, the "gods" are different, e.g., patriotism or "the American way of life," and the myths and rituals are often secular, e.g., toppled statues, flags and yellow ribbons flying. But the process and its purposes are the same: reunification of fractured social solidarity through the "all against one" dynamic.

The function of the sacrificial myth is to render the scapegoat's unjust victimization invisible either through vilification of the scapegoat as one who deserved to die because he or she had imperiled the community, or through posthumous exaltation of the victim as the selfless savior of the people who willingly offered his or her life for the community. In some cases the myth begins as vilification and is later transmuted into divinization. Jesus enraged his opponents by pointing out to them how often they had killed the prophets God sent to them who, like Jesus himself, destabilized the community by the proclamation that God was not pleased with their behavior. Later the vilified and murdered prophet was honored as a voice that had been crying in the wilderness even as the descendants of the murderers claimed that *they* would never have done what their ancestors did. Jesus, of course, was warning them that they were already plotting to do to him precisely the same thing their forebears had done to the prophets before him (see Matt 23:29-39 and Luke 11:47-51), namely, to scapegoat him "for the sake of the people."

Scapegoating, however, is always a temporary fix. It has to be renewed, actually or ritually, again and again because the cure is identical with the disease. Supposedly "good" violence is used against "bad" violence, begetting first renewed unity and then, inevitably, more violence.

V. Jesus' Execution as Scapegoating Violence

No great stretch of imagination is necessary to see how this Girardian analysis applies to the Passion and death of Jesus. The crucifixion was a classic case of scapegoating, and Jesus is the paradigmatic scapegoat who enters freely into the dynamic in order to subvert it at its root and definitively conquer the Ruler of this world on his own turf. Satan is condemned, John says, by the judgment he inspires against Jesus, the Scapegoat who will expose once and for all the evil and futility of this strategy for self-salvation and will offer humanity an alternative.

The religious and political chaos threatening Jerusalem at Passover the year of Jesus' death was precisely the kind of social situation for which the scapegoat mechanism is a solution. And Jesus was "different" enough in the eyes of his contemporaries to make him a natural scapegoat. In John's gospel he was regarded as a Galilean (see 7:40-52), a native of the hotbed of social and political resistance to Roman occupation, and a leader of the *am ha'eretz*, "those common people" despised by the religious purebloods of Jerusalem. It was even suggested that he might be a hated Samaritan (see 8:48). He was quite possibly illegitimate.[29] His dealing with evil spirits looked a lot like demon possession (John 8:48; Matt 10:25; 12:24; Mark 3:22; Luke 11:15-19). He was in his thirties and not married, which could have several unsavory explanations. His teaching and actions challenged the law and especially its established interpreters and enforcers. Someone had heard him say something threatening

---

[29] In John there is both a recognition that Jesus is the son of Joseph and Mary (6:42) and a veiled insinuation of illegitimacy in his interlocutors' claim that *they* are not (like Jesus?) children of fornication.

about the temple, although no one could remember exactly what, and his claim to be to the Son of God was both a challenge to the emperor, who claimed that title, and certainly blasphemous to pious Jewish ears. Who needed a trial? (See Matt 26:63-65 in relation to John 7:46-53.) Obviously, the riot simmering in the streets was due to this "odd man out," this messianic pretender, who must be eliminated.

Pilate knew that Jesus was innocent and in John's gospel announces it three times (18:38; 19:4, 6). So did Caiaphas who had baldly declared to his colleagues that if Jesus was allowed to go on, the whole world would follow him, and the Romans would wipe out "our place [i.e., the temple] and our nation" (see 11:48). The scapegoat principle was clearly enunciated by Caiaphas: "It is expedient that one man die rather than that the whole nation perish" (see 11:50 and 18:14). The real guilt or innocence of that one man, which the Pharisee Nicodemus challenged his colleagues to establish by the just procedures demanded by the law (see 7:50-53), was intrinsically irrelevant. What was important was the mob catharsis that would pacify the people and avert the chaos that would precipitate Roman retaliation.

Pilate and the Jewish hierarchy play off each other in the scenes in John 18–19. They whip the Passover crowd into a mindless mob screaming for the death of someone against whom most have not even heard the charges and for the release of Barabbas, already convicted of the very crimes for which Jesus will be killed (see 18:39-40). Pilate offers them the scapegoat, dressed as a fool, so brutalized that he in no way resembles their respectable religious selves (see John 19:5). Civil and religious resolution of impending chaos clearly lay in the unification of all against one. Nothing short of death would do: "Crucify him! Crucify him!" (John 19:6, 15).

A few hours later, after the lynching on Golgotha, calm descends over the land. In all three Synoptic Gospels one of the executioners acknowledges that their victim was innocent, a Son of God (Matt 27:54; Mark 15:39; Luke 23:47). Luke says the crowd dispersed beating their breasts (23:48). In John, Pilate is relieved to get Jesus' body out of sight before people come to their senses and realize what they have done (see John 19:38). The pious go "off to church," that is, home for the solemn celebration of the Sabbath, which, this year, was Passover, while the Roman soldiers wash their hands of another gruesome tour of duty, just following orders. The important thing for everyone is to relish the restored order, the religious and social calm, the closure that the scapegoating sacrifice has accomplished, and to try not to think too much about the details.

Jesus, in other words, was not sacrificed by or to God, nor did he will his own death. He was murdered as a scapegoat by the collusion between the Jerusalem hierarchy manipulating a hysterical mob and the Roman power structure represented by a self-serving but terrified tyrant for their respective religious and political purposes. There was, in other words, nothing good about Jesus' violent victimization. Therefore, to understand it theologically as that by which God in Jesus takes away the sin of the world, it is crucial to identify it properly as the scapegoating murder that it was. As James Alison forcefully put it:

> God gives his Son, out of love for the world, which sacrifices him. . . . [T]he self-giving is prior, anterior to the sacrifice, and the sacrifice is incidental, accidental, to the self-giving. So Jesus did not give himself so as to be a victim, he gave himself, in the full awareness that he was to be a victim, but did not want this at all. . . . This is why John stresses particularly Jesus' freedom with relation to his "hour."[30]

The religious mythologizing and ritualization of the crucifixion in Christian history, presenting it as a sacrifice demanded and willed by God, is part of the self-delusion of those—namely, humanity, including ourselves as well as our forebears—who are responsible for that murder. As Jesus warned his disciples on the eve of his Passion, they would later experience what he was about to undergo, and it would be made invisible by the same religious rhetoric and ritual invoked in Jesus' death: "an hour is coming when those who kill you will think that by doing so *they are offering worship to God*" (John 16:2). This religious justification of scapegoating murder is of the essence of the scapegoating dynamic. The scapegoat nature of Jesus' execution reveals it as the incarnation of the sin of the world, the refusal to believe that God is all-sufficient salvific love. The only alternative to the acceptance of God's love is to seek our own salvation by violent resistance to whatever is threatening or oppressing us. The only alternative to love is violence. Jesus had to enter into that dynamic in order to undo it.

VI. Interpreting Jesus as Scapegoat: The Lamb of God

The conundrum for Christian theology and spirituality is how the salvific power of God operates through the intrinsically evil action of

---

[30] Alison, *Knowing Jesus*, 49.

the scapegoating murder of Jesus. The Old Testament category of the "lamb,"[31] used in John to designate Jesus as the One who "takes away the sin of the world," is, I believe, a Johannine hermeneutical sword for cutting through this Gordian knot.

Johannine scholars generally recognize three Old Testament passages as possible background for this uniquely Johannine title:[32] the "sacrifice of Isaac" in Genesis 22:1-20, in which God provides the lamb (πρόβατον) for the holocaust; the paschal lamb (πρόβατον), whose blood saves the Hebrews in Egypt and whose flesh becomes their Passover communion meal (Exod 12:1-14); the Suffering Servant in Isaiah 53:7-8, who is compared to a silent lamb (πρόβατον and ἀμνός) led to slaughter.[33] Most scholars opt for one of the three as dominant with one or both of the others as possible references.[34] The fact, however, that there is explicit

---

[31] Jesus is associated, perhaps, with the paschal lamb in 1 Cor 5:7, which refers to Christ as τὸ πάσχα ἡμῶν (our Passover [lamb or meal or feast understood]) and by comparison in 1 Pet 1:19, which says that we were ransomed τιμίῳ αἵματι ὡς ἀμνοῦ ἀμώμου καὶ ἀσπίλου Χριστοῦ (with the precious blood of Christ, like that of a lamb without defect or blemish), which is a clear evocation of the paschal lamb. But there is no explicit reference in the NT to the "lamb of God," or to Jesus as "lamb of God," outside the Fourth Gospel. But since both of these NT references are actually a reference to an OT type, our search for the precise significance of the "Lamb of God" designation is properly focused on the OT.

[32] C. K. Barrett, *The Gospel according to St. John: An Introduction with Commentary and Notes on the Greek Text*, 2nd ed. (Philadelphia: Westminster, 1978), 176–77, gives most of the relevant exegetical data. For a more developed interpretation of the symbol of the "Lamb of God," see C. Koester, *Symbolism in the Fourth Gospel: Meaning, Mystery, Community*, 2nd ed. (Minneapolis: Fortress Press, 2003), 216–24.

[33] The Songs of the Suffering Servant are poems describing the scapegoat death of an innocent victim. The four songs or poems are found in Isa 42:1-4; 49:1-6; 50:4-9; and 52:13–53:12. The Servant, like other "suffering just ones" in the OT, such as Jonah, Susannah, and the Wisdom Hero, suffers unjustly and, in the case of the Servant, is killed but ultimately vindicated by God, and his suffering plays some mysterious role in the salvation of his people, Israel. The theory of the scapegoat helps illuminate the causality of the redemptive power of unjust suffering.

[34] Most commentators see some reference to the paschal lamb (e.g., Barrett, Brown, Earl, F. J. Moloney, et al.) because of the clear evocations of the paschal lamb in the Johannine passion narrative, though all point out that the paschal lamb was not an expiatory sacrifice but the food of a communion meal, which I will try to show is precisely the point. The Suffering Servant is probably the most widely accepted OT type because there is a direct citation from one of the Servant Songs (Isa 53:1) in John 12:38. There is little acceptance of the Isaac typology. Leon Morris, *The Gospel according to John: The English Text with Introduction, Exposition and Notes* (Grand Rapids, MI: William B. Eerdmans, 1971), 143–48, gives a concise summary of major positions, indicating that for each candidate text there are both reasons for and reasons against

textual reference in John to all three Old Testament types suggests to me that all three, in interaction, are necessary to make sense fully of the Johannine use of the lamb typology.

The most universally accepted reference is to the Suffering Servant in Isaiah 52:13–53:12. The Servant is described in Isaiah 52:13 as ὁ παῖς μου καὶ ὑψωθήσεται καὶ δοξασθήσεται σφόδρα (my servant [or son] who is raised [lifted] high or highly exalted and glorified). This is clearly the background for the consistent and uniquely Johannine description of the death of Jesus, the servant and son, not as a *kenosis* or abasement, but as a "lifting up" on the cross, which is both an exaltation and a Glorification.[35] In the continuation of this Servant Song, in 53:1, we have the text about the Servant that is applied verbatim to Jesus in the summary of the Book of Signs in John 12:38, recognizing and lamenting his final rejection by his own: "This was to fulfill the word spoken by the prophet Isaiah: 'Lord, who has believed our message, and to whom has the arm of the Lord been revealed?'" Besides the pervasive allusions in the Johannine passion account to the images in the Servant Songs, for example, Jesus' marred appearance (19:4-6), his placement among the evildoers (18:30), his being pierced for our offenses (19:37), and the grave assigned to him among the rich (19:39-41),[36] this is the one Old Testament text (Isa 53:7) in which both Greek terms for "lamb," πρόβατον and ἀμνός, occur in the LXX.[37] The comparison of the Servant to the lamb silent before its shearers finds echo in Jesus' silence before Pilate, who condemns him to death (see 19:9-10).

The reference to the Passover Lamb is quite clear in the Johannine passion account. John's chronology of the Passion departs from that of

---

accepting it as typological. He concludes: "The lamb figure may well be intended to be composite, evoking memories of several, perhaps all, of the suggestions we have canvassed. All that the ancient sacrifices foreshadowed was perfectly fulfilled in the sacrifice of Christ" (147–48).

[35] Jesus' death is referred to as "exaltation" or "lifting up" in 3:14; 8:28; 12:32 and as "glorification" in 7:39; 11:4; 12:16, 23; 13:31-32.

[36] The LXX, which was probably the OT text used by the Fourth Evangelist, gives "rich" where the Hebrew has "evildoers." John seems to have picked up the LXX nuance by having Jesus buried by the rich man, Joseph of Arimathea, with a large quantity of expensive spices provided by Nicodemus and in a "new tomb" (19:39-41). In other words, Jesus is accorded a royal burial.

[37] Some scholars consider this reference weak because the "lamb" is not equated with the Servant but is used as a metaphor or comparison. I find this unconvincing since, obviously, a person cannot be literally a lamb.

the Synoptics so that Jesus dies not on Passover but on the preparation day, at the very hour when the paschal lambs were being slain in the temple in Jerusalem (19:14). The wine he is offered to quench his thirst is raised to his lips on a branch of hyssop (19:29) whose symbolic significance is emphasized by the fact that a literal hyssop branch would not be solid enough to bear the weight of a soaked sponge. But hyssop was the instrument with which the blood of the paschal lamb was applied to the doorposts of the Hebrews in Egypt to protect them from the angel of death (see Exod 12:22) as they prepared, by eating for the first time what would later be the Passover meal, to leave the land of slavery. When the legs of the two crucified with Jesus are broken to hasten their deaths, Jesus' legs are not broken (19:33), to fulfill, we are told explicitly, the text of Exodus 12:46, which specifies that no bone of the passover lamb is to be broken.[38]

Finally, the account of the binding of Isaac in Genesis 22 is invoked by a few scholars but regarded by most as the weakest background and by a few as irrelevant.[39] There is only one fairly explicit allusion in the passion account to this Old Testament passage, namely, that Jesus went out to Golgotha "carrying the cross himself" (19:17), as Isaac had borne to Mount Moriah the wood for Abraham's sacrifice. Géza Vermès, however, in reference to John 1:29, the Lamb of God text, writes, "For the Palestinian Jews, all lamb sacrifice, and especially the Passover lamb and the Tamid offering, was a memorial of the Akedah [i.e., the binding of Isaac] with its effects of deliverance, forgiveness of sin and messianic salvation."[40] I will argue that the sacrifice of Isaac is crucial for understanding the salvific character of the death of Jesus and especially the role of God as Jesus' Father in that death.

Each of the three Old Testament references that John clearly evokes contributes something important to an interpretation of Jesus' death not

---

[38] Some scholars, despite these clear references in John to Jesus as the Paschal Lamb, reject this typology because the paschal lamb was not an expiatory but a communion sacrifice. In my opinion, this strengthens the argument I am making. The ritual that will become central to Christian celebration of the paschal mystery is not an "unbloody reenactment of a bloody expiatory sacrifice" but a communion sacrifice in which the sharing of the meal is central. As with the paschal lamb, the death of Jesus precedes and, as it were, supplies the food, but it is not Jesus as dead but precisely as living who is the sustenance of the community.

[39] See n. 34 above.

[40] Geza Vermes, *Scripture and Tradition in Judaism: Haggadic Studies* (Leiden: Brill, 1973), 225.

as God's sacrifice of Jesus but as Jesus' free use of our scapegoating sacrificial mechanism to take away of the sin of the world. I want to attend specifically to three problematic aspects of Jesus' death that the Lamb symbolism can illuminate: God's role in Jesus' death, the role of suffering in the salvific work of Jesus, the commission of the ecclesial community to continue Jesus' saving work.

A. *God's Role in Jesus' Death*

The *role of God in the death of Jesus* is perhaps the most consistently and dangerously misinterpreted aspect of the Passion in Christian tradition. Many people raise the deeply disturbing question of why God required the death of Jesus to save the world, "the death of a son to save a slave," as the paschal proclamation poetically puts it. In John's gospel, God does not send Jesus into the world to be sacrificed, to be killed. As we have already seen, the motive of the Incarnation in John is not expiation, the repair of an original creation gone wrong through original sin, but the *very same love* that motivated God's creation of all things "in the beginning." God's gift of Jesus to the world, and Jesus' self-giving to us, precede the murder, which is read theologically, after the fact, as his willing sacrifice of himself. But the killing of Jesus was wholly the work of his persecutors. From God's point of view, "in the beginning was the Word" in whom, through whom, and for whom all things were created. It was that eternal Word that God gave to humanity and who became flesh in the Incarnation, grace upon grace (see 1:16-17), fulfilling—not replacing or repairing—creation.

John says that God so loved the world that God *gave* God's only Son "so that everyone who believes in him . . . might have eternal life" (John 3:16). Jesus identifies himself to the Samaritan woman in these same terms: "If you knew the *gift of God*, [namely,] . . . the one who is speaking to you" (John 4:10). Jesus both incarnates God's self-gift and espouses its divine motive, God's self-bestowing love, as his own motive for coming into the world and, eventually, entering into his Passion, which was not God's plan but the way humans responded to the gift. Speaking of himself, Jesus says, "No one has greater love than this, to lay down one's life for one's friends" (John 15:13). Note, Jesus in John is not sentenced to death by God. He lays down his own life, not for his enemies but precisely for his friends, because he himself loves them with the very love of God.

Jesus lays down his life in complete freedom. "No one takes my life from me," he says. "I lay it down of my own accord" (see John 10:17-18). Not only is Jesus not overpowered by those who kill him, but John is emphatic that there is no tension between God's will to give the Son to us and Jesus' desire to give himself even unto the laying down of his life for us. The gift of eternal life originates in the creative love of God and is expressed in the completely free salvific love of Jesus. God, not Moses, Jesus says, gives the true bread from heaven that gives life to the world. That bread, which comes from God, is Jesus: "I am the living bread that came down from heaven. Whoever eats of this bread will live forever; and the bread that I will give for the life of the world is my flesh" (John 6:51). To give his flesh is a Semitic way of saying to lay down his life. So Jesus' death is not a sentence God lays on Jesus but Jesus' free participation in the Father's gift to the world. The horrendous human response to that gift is what kills Jesus.

Unlike the Synoptic Jesus, the Johannine Jesus actively rejects the thought of praying that he might be spared the cup of suffering (see John 12:27). His whole life, he says, has been a preparation for this hour. By his freely accepted death, he will glorify the Father; by allowing that very death, the Father will glorify Jesus. Jesus' death, in other words, is the locus of the mutual glorification of Father and Son. It is the apex of revelation. As Jesus reveals God's love for the world in his death, so God, in that same death, reveals Jesus' true identity as the very incarnation of the self-giving God. Therefore, there is no agony in the garden in John. Indeed, except for Simon Peter's misguided outburst of violence, which serves only to emphasize by contrast that Jesus is freely undertaking this work (see John 18:11), there is no violence in the scene.[41] Jesus' would-be captors, Roman and Jewish,[42] are twice leveled to the ground by his majestic "I am" in response to their statement of whom they seek. With sovereign calm Jesus secures the release of his disciples, rejects Simon Peter's defense of him by the sword, and then freely hands himself over

---

[41] See the very interesting article on this subject by Eben Scheffler, "Jesus' Non-Violence at His Arrest: The Synoptics and John's Gospel Compared," in *The Death of Jesus in the Fourth Gospel*, 739–49.

[42] The universalization of responsibility for the Passion is often missed because of the Johannine symbolic use of "the Jews" to denote Jesus' adversaries, the Jewish authorities (while the Jews in general are not his enemies but his people), analogously to the way "the world" is used to denote the forces of evil at work in the world (which is also the good creation God so loved). Both terms, therefore, are ambiguous and necessitate careful interpretation in each context in which they are used.

to those whose saber-rattling approach is revealed to be as unnecessary as it is impotent. In other words, Jesus is completely one with God, and entirely free in undertaking the Passion (see John 18:3-12). As theologian James Alison puts it, Jesus freely moves into the place, takes up the role, of the scapegoat in order to definitively destroy from within this primary and ultimate weapon of the Ruler of this world.[43]

The story of Abraham and Isaac (Gen 22:1-18) helps illuminate this aspect of Jesus' Passion. Abraham assures Isaac that "God will provide" the sacrificial lamb. As the story proceeds, it becomes clear that the true "lamb," the sacrifice God desires, is not Isaac but Abraham's holocaust of the heart. But that interior holocaust, that complete entrusting of everything he holds dear to God, is not to be signified by the literal murder of Isaac. God does not require the death of Isaac any more than he wanted Micah to sacrifice the fruit of his loins for the sin of his soul (see Mic 6:6-7). God does not want or need, is never pleased or glorified by, the destruction of what God has created. The only holocaust worthy of God is that which mirrors God's own "holocaust" in giving to us, in Jesus, God's very self.

Abraham, therefore, is and is not a God-figure, and both the positive and the negative dimensions are important for our understanding of God's role in Jesus' death as it appears in John. Like Abraham, who so loves God as to give his only son, God so loves the world as to give God's only Son. But, unlike Abraham, God does not give by destroying. It is those to whom God offers his Son as gift who reject the gift and kill the Son. God, in ironic contrast, rejects Abraham's offer to kill the son and gives back to him the gift, the son of promise, which Abraham thought God was reclaiming. The revelation is not that of a violent God taking back his gift by demanding murder but that of the holocaust of God's own heart, the unstinting love of God for humanity, that does not withhold even God's beloved Son from us. Even more amazing, God does not withdraw the rejected Gift but gives the slain Jesus back to us in Resurrection as God returned to Abraham the son he thought he had lost.

Likewise, Isaac is and is not a Christ-figure. Like Isaac, Jesus is the beloved Son bound for death. But, unlike Isaac, Jesus is not a passive victim bound by a distraught father, and he is not rescued from death by God. Jesus is not a victim of God any more than was Isaac. As Isaac was the victim not of God's violent demands but of Abraham's misunderstanding of God's will, so Jesus is the victim not of God's wrath

---

[43] See esp., Alison, *Knowing Jesus*, chap. 3. For a much fuller explanation, see his *The Joy of Being Wrong*, esp. part 2. See also Heim, *Saved from Sacrifice*, chap. 5.

but of human scapegoating, our misguided and futile effort to control reality through violence. The mysterious interaction among Abraham, Isaac, and God illuminates once and for all the invalidity of the disguise of human sacrifice as religious worship. There is no violence in God's repertoire. God's role in Jesus' death is to accompany Jesus in his self-giving and to glorify him as the revelation of God's love by finally raising him to life and giving him back to those who killed him. God takes no part in the murder of Jesus. And God's love cannot be neutralized nor abrogated by our violence. Murder is our work from which *this* murder will finally free us.

B. *The Role of Jesus' Suffering in Salvation*

The second question concerning Jesus' identity and mission as the Lamb of God, namely, why Jesus had to die as he did to take away the sin of the world, is illuminated by the figure of the Suffering Servant in Isaiah 53, the lamb led silently to slaughter. The Isaian passage makes it very clear that it is not God's will but human malice that victimized the Servant. God responds to this malice by exalting and glorifying the Servant, making him a remedy for that malice itself:

> He was *oppressed, and he was afflicted,* yet he did not open his mouth; like a lamb that is led to the slaughter, and like a sheep that before its shearers is silent, so he did not open his mouth. By a *perversion of justice* he was taken away. . . . He had done no wrong . . . spoken no falsehood . . . [but] if he *gives his life as an offering for sin* he shall see his descendants in a long life, and the *will of the Lord shall be accomplished through him.* (Isa 53:7-9, 10)

As in all scapegoating violence, the victim is *oppressed and afflicted.* Although the slaying of the victim is always disguised by justifying rhetoric such as penal justice, necessity for the common good, or God's will, all scapegoating is, in fact, a *perversion of justice.* The scapegoat, as we will see, is always innocent of that for which he or she is scapegoated, but in this case the Scapegoat *freely offers himself for the sin of his persecutors.* With the power and generosity that advocates of nonviolence have learned, he accepts suffering by refusing to inflict it.[44] He will not have

---

[44] An excellent analytical study of the spirituality of nonviolence across religious traditions is Terrence J. Rynne, *Gandhi and Jesus: The Saving Power of Nonviolence* (Maryknoll, NY: Orbis, 2008), see esp. chap. 5.

recourse to violence to save himself; however, God is not impotent before human evil. Through this death, God's will, not that of the murderers, will be accomplished. God does not share their murderous design but is able to make God's salvific design emerge through and despite it.

How, then, does Jesus' death "take away the sin of the world," humanity's refusal of divine love revealed in God's gift of the only Son? Theologian S. Mark Heim in his remarkable book, *Saved from Sacrifice*, says that two features of Jesus' death make it possible for him to confront and defeat, once and for all, the sacrificial dynamic, the scapegoating mechanism of reconciliation through violence by the collective murder of an innocent victim. There was no other way than through suffering, and that is the answer to the question of why Jesus had to suffer. Jesus had to be simultaneously a victim *like all other scapegoats* and utterly *unique among them* so that by entering into and taking on the role of the scapegoat, he could render it forever impotent by exposing once and for all its satanic mechanism.

First, Jesus was *one more victim like all the others* in the long line stretching back to Abel, the innocent victim of Cain's mimetic rivalry. If Jesus were not like other scapegoated victims, framed and lynched for crimes of which he was innocent, his death would not be relevant to theirs. And although he freely accepted what was done to him, as do many of the bravest and noblest of humanity's victims who lay down their lives for others, it could have been prevented only by a miracle, something that is not accessible to other victims. And this is why so many find consolation in Jesus' suffering. They do not rejoice in his suffering any more than they do in their own. Nor are they seeking suffering in order to imitate him. But as they are helpless, doomed, unable to escape, they know that he experienced everything they are experiencing and therefore that his Resurrection offers real hope for theirs.

But, at the same time, Jesus was *not like other victims* in two important respects. First, Jesus was an absolutely, rather than a relatively, innocent victim. All scapegoated victims are, like all of us, guilty of something, even of many things. But scapegoats are innocent of that for which they are persecuted, namely, being the sole and real cause of the social chaos in the community, which the scapegoating process intends to bring to closure through the death of this one person.

The accusation against the scapegoat is a double disguise. It hides the innocence of the victim (by imputing to him or her such enormous guilt that it has brought ultimate threat upon the community, which only the scapegoat's death can eradicate), and it hides the guilt of the persecutors (who think that, because they are not guilty of the sin of which the victim is accused, they are therefore innocent and their murder of the victim gives glory to God, whose wrath can be pacified only by such vengeance). The perception of absolute moral difference between the guilty victim and the innocent executioners (like the woman taken in adultery and the Pharisees prepared to stone her in John 8[45]) establishes that the victim deserves to die and that the murderers are licensed, indeed obliged, to kill in the service of "justice." The "rightness" of this transaction, this "sacrifice" to the offended justice of God, reestablishes social and moral order. The execution of the victim brings "closure," which reunites the fractured community.

But, alone among humans, Jesus was actually not guilty of anything. He was the absolutely innocent victim. This difference between the person justly accused of a finite offense for which he or she might actually be justly punished and the innocent victim who is being scapegoated was clearly expressed in Luke by the "good thief" on the cross to his partner in crime: "We indeed have been condemned justly, for we are getting what we deserve for our deeds, but this man has done *nothing* wrong" (Luke 23:41). Jesus as scapegoat is unique in his total innocence, and, as such, he strips away the rationalization and reveals the innocence of all scapegoats and the guilt of all those who sacrifice them. The crucifixion, in the words of the Girardian social critic Gil Bailie, unveils the violence once and for all.[46] Jesus, by freely taking on the role of the scapegoat, exposes the inner mechanism of the scapegoating process, which can only function as long as its true nature is hidden from those who are carrying it out, as long as they "know not what they do" (see Luke 23:34). Once it becomes clear to us that we are murdering the powerless and the innocent in order to justify ourselves and thus unify the society fractured by mimetic rivalry and conflict, it becomes more and more difficult to maintain that there is some real difference between the "good violence" of the executioners and the "bad violence" they are supposedly expunging. What is the difference, really, between the killer being hanged and the executioner who opens the trapdoor beneath him?

---

[45] This is the point of the story of the Woman Taken in Adultery (John 8:3-11). When Jesus forces the stoners to recognize that they are no more innocent than she (whether their sins were the same as hers or not), they realize that she is no more guilty than they. They are not innocent enough to execute her. Jesus does not say the woman is sinless. He just points out that no one is, and thereby Jesus stops the scapegoating process. He reveals the intended execution for what it truly is: murder.

[46] This is the thesis of Bailie's very important work, *Violence Unveiled: Humanity at the Crossroads* (New York: Crossroad, 1995).

Second, Jesus is unique as victim because he does not remain in the grip of death. He truly died. But unlike any other victim in human history, he rose from the dead. In the Resurrection, God gave back to us the Gift we had rejected. Jesus returned with forgiveness on his lips to his disciples who had been complicit in his unjust death by their betrayal, denial, and abandonment.

"Peace be to you," he greets them, and they "rejoiced at seeing the Lord" (John 20:19-20). He comes into their fear, their shame, their infidelity, their cowardice not to accuse or retaliate, not to extract a confession or demand reparation, not to do to them what they have done to him. He sets no conditions for their rehabilitation.[47] Vengeance has no role in reconciliation. The risen Jesus comes only to forgive and, by forgiving, to give his disciples, as he had promised at the Last Supper (see John 14:24), the peace the world by its mechanisms of violence cannot give or take away. This is a qualitatively different peace, the peace that takes away, once and for all, the "sin of the world." It enables his disciples to accept the utterly free and unconditional love of God, which they could never deserve or earn. This is the peace that finally defeats the Ruler of this world, that reveals as false the primeval lie that humanity must seize divinity in order to be immune to death. The truth that defeats that lie is that God is infinite self-bestowing love, love that is stronger and deeper than any refusal of it, love that even the murder of the Gift cannot defeat. To believe, to finally accept this, is to know the only true God and Jesus Christ whom God has sent, which is to have eternal life (see John 17:3). The risen Jesus, returned to his own in the full integrity of his glorified humanity, is forgiveness incarnate, the very embodiment of reconciliation that is radical and permanent, of union with God, which is eternal life.

VII. Conclusion: The Banquet of the Lamb and the Forgiveness of Sins (John 20:21-23)

We turn now to the third aspect of Jesus' identity and mission as the Lamb of God, namely, his commitment to his followers of his own salvific mission. Immediately after reconciling his disciples, Jesus says again, "Peace be with you." His divine peace now becomes the solid foundation for the challenging mission he commits to them, namely, to

---

[47] For an excellent extended treatment of this point, see Alison, *Knowing Jesus*, chap. 1, "The Resurrection."

make effective in the world his overcoming of "the sin of the world" by mediating into the life of believers the forgiveness they have just received from him. He explicitly draws them into his own mission: "As the Father has sent me, so I send you." And, as the Father had poured forth the fullness of the Spirit on Jesus to identify and empower him as the Lamb of God to take away the sin of the world, so Jesus now breathes[48] into his disciples that same Holy Spirit to re-create them as the New Israel, the community of reconciliation, which replaces scapegoating violence with forgiveness.

Here, the third Old Testament reference, namely, to the Passover Lamb, is especially revelatory. The death and Resurrection of Jesus will remain salvifically effective in his community in the eucharistic celebration whose prefiguration they saw in Israel's Passover meal.[49] On the night before God rescued the Hebrews from slavery in Egypt, each Hebrew household was to take an unblemished lamb, slaughter it, sprinkle its blood on the doorposts of their homes, and share its flesh in a communion meal. Thus were they saved from death through the blood of the lamb and united as one liberated community through the sharing in its flesh (see Exod 12:1-14).

The symbolism of the paschal lamb in the account of Jesus' death must be read in light of John 6:26-66, the Bread of Life discourse, which functions in John as the institution narrative does in the Synoptics, that is, as a catechesis of Jesus' saving work on Calvary of giving his flesh (that is, his human life) for the life of the world. It takes place after the multiplication of the loaves for the crowd at Passover time. The Passover meal, as we have just seen, was not an expiatory ritual but a communion meal.

---

[48] The verb "breathe" in this text (ἐμφυσάω) is a *hapax legomenon* in the NT and occurs substantively only twice in the LXX. In Gen 2:7 God, at the first creation, breathes life into the earth-creature, and it becomes the first living human being. In Ezek 37:9-10 God commands the prophet to breathe upon the dry bones of the decimated house of Israel, "that they may live," i.e., that the people Israel might be re-created. So, the scene of Jesus commissioning his disciples would appear to be a "new creation" of the new people, the Church, who will be the community of salvation in the post-paschal time. I have developed this thesis at greater length in chap. 4 of this book.

[49] Alison, *Knowing Jesus*, 85–86, says succinctly, "The principle [*sic*] way by which all this is kept alive in our midst is: the eucharist. . . . The real presence of Jesus in the eucharist is the real presence of the crucified and risen Lord, giving himself, founding the new Israel, making possible the conversion of those who participate. It is the real presence of the grace which justifies. In all the other celebrations which we call sacraments, one or other dimension of this presence of the crucified and risen Lord is emphasized. In the eucharist however, the whole package is present, if only we have open eyes and hearts to perceive it, and to receive him!"

The point was not the killing of the lamb but the sharing in the meal. In John 6 Jesus says his flesh and blood, that is, his living self, would become the food and drink of the community. But it is as symbolizing bread that he gives himself, not as meat as some of his shocked hearers (then and now!) misunderstood. He says, "I am the *living bread* that came down from heaven. Whoever eats of this *bread* will live forever; and the *bread* that I will give for the life of the world is my flesh" (John 6:51).

"Flesh" here, as commonly in Semitic anthropology, refers not to a part of a dead organism but to Jesus himself as living mortal. Because he is mortal, Jesus can be killed and thereby become, through his Resurrection, the spiritual or living food that gives life to the world. As in the typology of the binding of Isaac and the Suffering Servant, the paschal lamb is and is not identical to Jesus. Like the paschal lamb, Jesus must be slain to become food for the community, but unlike the paschal lamb, it is not as dead and bloodless, as physical flesh or meat, that Jesus becomes their food. And the sacrifice does not need to be repeated year after year because the "lamb" that is Jesus is not dead or consumed as ordinary food. It is as "living bread" that Jesus gives himself, his flesh-and-blood self, in real symbol to his disciples.

The symbolism of the lamb draws the believer through and beyond the intended bloody sacrifice of Abraham and the literal murder of the Suffering Servant into a communion meal in which all partake of the Risen One who dies no more. The Eucharist is not an unbloody reproduction, like the pagan scapegoat rituals, of a bloody sacrifice carried out in the past but a sharing in the actual life of Jesus by a community that has repudiated all sacrifice, all trafficking in blood, all sacralized violence. We eat the bread and drink the cup to participate in Jesus' life, death, and Resurrection, and we live by that which we eat just as Jesus lives by the One who sent him (see John 6:57).

This brings us to the formulation of the great commission in John, which forms an *inclusio* with the original identification, in 1:29, of Jesus as the Lamb of God who takes away the sin of the world. It is important to start with an explicit recognition that Jesus, in this resurrection scene (20:19-23), addresses his *disciples* (20:17-18)—not, as some interpreters suggest, the Twelve, the apostles, or some specialized group representing later Church officials. "Disciple" in John is an inclusive term.[50] The com-

---

[50] I have dealt with this issue at some length in two chapters available in Sandra M. Schneiders, *Written That You May Believe: Encountering Jesus in the Fourth Gospel*, 2nd rev. ed. (New York: Crossroad, 2003), chap. 8, "Inclusive Discipleship in John (4:1-42)," 126–48, and chap. 15, "Because of the Woman's Testimony," 233–54.

munity of the Fourth Gospel clearly includes Jews, Samaritans, and Gentiles, women and men, known members of the Twelve and many who are not in that group, married and single people, itinerants and householders. In other words, the great commission of the risen Jesus, in John, is given to the whole Church, who will be, henceforth, his real presence in the world. Jesus says to them: "As the Father has sent me, so I send you. Receive the Holy Spirit. Whose sins [plural] you shall forgive they are forgiven to them." The second member of verse 23 is usually translated, erroneously I will argue, "If you retain the sins of anyone they are retained." We begin with a structured display of this problematic verse so that the subsequent argument will be clear.

	ἄν τινων	ἀφῆτε	τὰς ἁμαρτίας	ἀφέωνται	αὐτοῖς
20:23a	Of whomever	you forgive	the sins	they are forgiven	to them
	(poss. gen. pl.)	(subj. aor. act.)		(ind. perf. pass.)	
	ἄν τινων	κρατῆτε		κεκράτηνται	
20:23b	Whomever	you hold fast		are held fast	
	(obj. gen. pl.)	(subj. pres. act.)		(ind. perf. pass.)	

Although there is not space here to mount the argument in complete detail,[51] I am convinced that the "traditional" translation of 20:23b is untenable. A more adequate reading would be the following: "Of whomever [*possessive* genitive plural] you forgive the sins, they [the sins] are forgiven to them; whomever [*objective* genitive plural] you hold fast [or embrace], they are held fast." In other words, the sins in the first member are "possessed" by the forgiven. It is the persons, not sins, in the second member who are the "object grasped or held fast."

My reasons, besides a suspicion of the influence of ecclesiastical apologetics on the traditional translation, are theological in general, the theology of John in particular, the basic hermeneutical principles governing the relation of John to the Synoptics, Johannine style characteristics in relation to ellipsis and parallelism, and the grammar and vocabulary of the text in question.

The definition of this verse, John 20:23, as the institution of the Catholic sacrament of penance (confession) including a power possessed by the sacramental minister to retain sins within the penitent dates back only

---

[51] I have given the complete argument in chap. 5 above, pages 143–48.

to the Council of Trent in the sixteenth century[52] and is plainly in the service of protecting the Roman rite of individual confession from the challenge of the Reformers. The early Church, even during the controversies over the possibility of forgiveness of sins committed after baptism, never invoked this verse in defense of sacerdotal power to forgive or retain sins, and the sacrament itself was not only not instituted by Jesus but also did not exist as an individual ritual until it was developed during the fifth to the seventh centuries in the Celtic (Irish, Scottish, Welsh) churches in the context of monastic asceticism. The private, frequent, individual form of the sacrament was not accepted by the Roman Church, which considered the sacrament by nature public and communal and available only once after baptism and only for heinous crimes such as murder, apostasy, and public adultery. Not until much later, even in the Celtic Church, was the administration of the sacrament limited to the ordained. In other words, it is completely anachronistic, if not theologically suspect, to interpret John 20:23 in terms of the Catholic sacrament of individual confession that did not develop until long after the writing of the Fourth Gospel. The apologetic agenda argues against the traditional translation.

Theologically, and particularly in the context of John's gospel, it is hardly conceivable that Jesus, sent to take away the sin of the world, commissioned his disciples to perpetuate sin by the refusal of forgiveness or that the retention of sins in some people could reflect the universal reconciliation effected by Jesus.

---

[52] For an excellent history and theology of the sacrament of penance in the Catholic Church, see Kenan B. Osborne, *Reconciliation and Justification: The Sacrament and Its Theology* (1990; reprint, Eugene, OR: Wipf and Stock, 2001). See esp. chap. 8 on the Tridentine developments of the theology and practice of the sacrament. On 161–85 Osborne discusses each of the Tridentine canons on the sacrament of penance. Of concern for our purposes, he maintains (as does Raymond Brown in his commentary on John 20:23 [*The Gospel according to John*, 2:1044–45]) that Canon 3, which defines John 20:22-23 as the institution of the sacrament of penance, cannot be accepted at face value today. Osborne argues this on the basis of proper hermeneutical principles for the interpretation of doctrinal texts within their proper historical contexts and concludes: "with these words of the New Testament there is no 'proof' of an immediate and direct institution of the sacrament of penance by Jesus himself. John 20:22-24 [*sic*], neither textually nor contextually, allows such an interpretation. The focus of this canon, therefore, cannot be centered on some 'historical fact' regarding the institution of the sacrament of penance" (167). He then goes on to suggest what the canon can reasonably be held to affirm and deny in the context of the Reformation's challenge to the Catholic sacramental system.

Attempting to interpret this text as a Johannine version of Matthew 16:19 and/or 18:18 by supplying words, in this case both the direct and the indirect objects in 23b, that are supposedly missing in the Johannine text and mistranslating the verb κρατέω (hold fast) to make it equivalent to δέω (bind) is a move that should meet with general objection among Johannine scholars. In general, John cannot be legitimately read through Synoptic eyes unless there are actual literary contacts (and even then with extreme caution), which, in this case, are nonexistent. Both of the Matthean texts use δέω (bind) and λύω (loose) where John uses, in reverse order, ἀφίημι (forgive) and κρατέω (hold fast or embrace). Even more serious, there are no theological contacts between Matthew's clearly juridical text on interpretation of law (binding and loosing in relation to legal obligations) and John's theological concern with spiritual reconciliation reflected in the words "forgive" and "hold fast" or "embrace."

Furthermore, whereas in both Matthean texts the subjunctive member ("whatever you bind . . . loose") is an active aorist, indicating a punctual act, followed in the indicative member by a passive perfect ("is bound . . . is loosed"), indicating the resulting, ongoing condition, in John there is a significant variation in the tenses. As in the Matthean texts, in the subjunctive member relating to forgiveness ("of whomever you forgive the sins . . .") the verb is an active aorist indicating a punctual act (probably baptism) followed by a passive perfect (they are forgiven to them), indicating the resultant ongoing condition (membership in the community of reconciliation). Unlike Matthew's text, however, John's verse on "holding fast" has an active *present* in the subjunctive member, indicating, as is very common in John, an ongoing active behavior. This is followed by a passive perfect, indicating the ongoing condition of the one(s) who is the object of that action. The meaning would seem to be, "Those whom[53] you are holding [embracing, including in the ongoing life of the community] are indeed held fast in the communion of reconciliation."

Much more appropriate parallels to John 20:23 are found in the Fourth Gospel itself. The Evangelist makes frequent use of explicit and complete synthetic or explicative parallel constructions, for instance, in 6:37, 39; 10:27-29; 17:12; 18:19, in regard to this subject matter. I would argue that there is a clear pattern in which Jesus, receiving disciples from his Father

---

[53] Brown, *The Gospel according to John*, 2:1024, says that "It is not absolutely clear whether the object held is the men who committed the sins (OS[sin]) or their sins." He thinks the latter is "more likely by reason of parallelism" but that parallelism is what I am questioning.

and guarding them in communion with himself and the Father, is the model for the action of the disciples. My hypothesis is that this pattern is formalized and made explicit in the paschal commission to receive, through baptism for the forgiveness of sins, those whom Jesus gives to the community and to hold them fast in that communion unto the "raising up on the last day" when believers will participate fully in the Resurrection of Jesus.

Among the grammatical and syntactical problems with the traditional translation I would single out the translation of κρατέω. This verb normally takes an object, which can be either an accusative (but there is none in this verse) or, as in this case I would submit, an objective genitive, τινων. The verb means "to clasp" or "take hold of," as of a hand (objective genitive in Matt 9:25); hold fast, as to a confession of faith (objective genitive in Heb 4:14); hold firmly, as to hope (objective genitive in Heb 6:18); to embrace or clasp, as feet (accusative in Matt 28:9). No one to my knowledge has found any other text in ancient Greek, secular or biblical, in which κρατέω means retaining something interior to someone else.

If we read the text as we have it, using a normal meaning for κρατέω and standard grammar and syntax, and as John normally uses parallels, both in content as well as form, we get a theologically rich and coherent meaning for John 20:23, namely, that the disciples are commissioned by the risen Jesus to make effective throughout time his once for all salvific liberation of humanity from the sin of the world, that is, from humanity's refusal of God's totally gratuitous self-bestowing love. Just as Jesus received his disciples from the Father and holds them fast in communion with himself despite their weakness and infidelity, so his Church will draw into one through baptism those whom Jesus commits to it and will maintain them in communion through ongoing mutual forgiveness of sins. In that community, feeding on the Lamb who has taken away the sin of the world and freed from all need for sacred violence, whether physical or spiritual, they will live and offer to the world the peace that the world cannot give.

Appendix

Figure 1

NARRATIVE STRUCTURE OF JOHN 20

JERUSALEM	
GARDEN OF THE TOMB (scene of the New Creation)	**WHERE THE DISCIPLES WERE GATHERED** (scene of the New Covenant)
vv. 1-10 vv. 11-18 Simon Peter Mary & Magdalene the Beloved Disciple	vv. 19-23 vv. 24-29 The Disciples Thomas the Twin

THE CHURCH
vv. 30-31
Believers of All Times

Figure 2

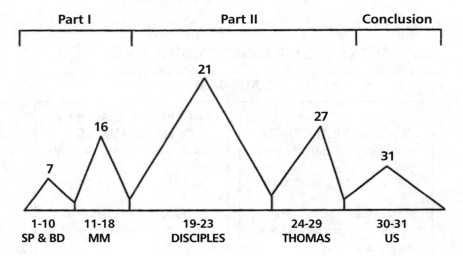

DRAMATIC STRUCTURE OF JOHN 20

Figure 3

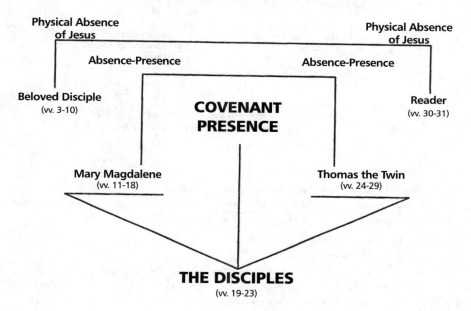

NARRATIVE SPIRITUAL STRUCTURE OF JOHN 20

Physical Absence
of Jesus

Absence-Presence

Beloved Disciple
(vv. 3-10)

**COVENANT
PRESENCE**

Physical Absence
of Jesus

Absence-Presence

Reader
(vv. 30-31)

Mary Magdalene
(vv. 11-18)

Thomas the Twin
(vv. 24-29)

THE DISCIPLES
(vv. 19-23)

Figure 4

STRUCTURE OF JOHN 20:19-23

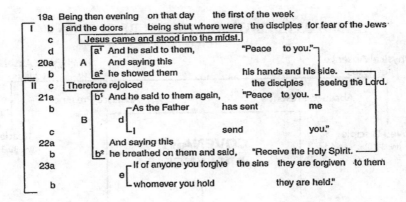

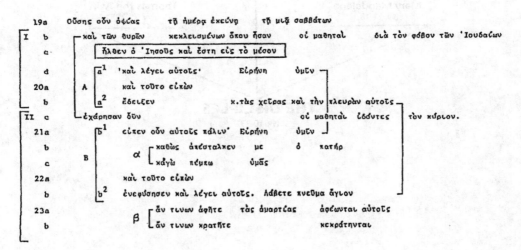

Works Cited

Alison, James. *The Joy of Being Wrong: Original Sin through Easter Eyes.* New York: Crossroad, 1998.

———. *Knowing Jesus.* 1993. Reprint, London, UK: SPCK, 1998.

Alves, M. Isidro. "Ressurreição e Fé Pascal." *Didaskalia* 29 (1989): 277–541.

Aquinas, Thomas. *Summa Theologica.* Translated by Daniel J. Sullivan. Chicago: Encyclopaedia Britannica, 1955.

Arndt, W., and F. W. Gingrich. *A Greek-English Lexicon of the New Testament and Other Early Christian Literature.* Chicago: University of Chicago, 1957.

Avemarie, Friedrich, and Hermann Lichtenberger, eds. *Auferstehung—Resurrection.* Fourth Durham-Tübingen Research Symposium on Resurrection, Transfiguration and Exaltation in Old Testament, Ancient Judaism and Early Christianity, Tübingen, September, 1999. Tübingen: J. C. B. Mohr, 2001.

Bailie, Gil. *Violence Unveiled: Humanity at the Crossroads.* 1999. Reprint, New York: Crossroad, 2004.

Barrett, C. K. *The Gospel according to St. John: An Introduction with Commentary and Notes on the Greek Text.* 2nd ed. Philadelphia: Westminster, 1978.

Beasley-Murray, G. R. "The Mission of the Logos-Son." In *The Four Gospels 1992: Festschrift Frans Neirynck,* edited by F. Van Segbroeck, C. M. Tuckett, G. Van Belle, J. Verheyden, 3:1855–68. Leuven: University Press, 1992.

Beier, Matthias. *A Violent God-Image: An Introduction to the Work of Eugen Drewermann.* New York/London: Continuum, 2004.

Bennema, Cornelis. "The Giving of the Spirit in John's Gospel—A New Proposal?" *The Evangelical Quarterly* 74, no. 3 (2002): 195–213.

Bienaimé, Germain. "L'annonce des fleuves d'eau vive en Jean 7,37-39." *Revue théologique de Louvain* 21 (1990): 281–310.

Bolen, Jean Shinoda. *Goddesses in Everywoman: A New Psychology of Women.* New York: Harper, 1984.

Borg, Marcus. *Meeting Jesus Again for the First Time: The Historical Jesus and the Heart of Contemporary Faith.* San Francisco: HarperSanFrancisco, 1994.

———. *Jesus in Contemporary Scholarship.* Valley Forge, PA: Trinity Press International, 1994.

Bracken, Joseph A. "The Body of Christ—An Intersubjective Interpretation." *Horizons* 31 (Spring 2004): 7–21.

Braun, F.–M. *Le Linceul de Turin et l'évangile de S. Jean: Étude de critique et d'exégése.* Tournai and Paris: Casterman, 1939.

Brown, Raymond E. *The Community of the Beloved Disciple.* New York/Ramsey/Toronto: Paulist Press, 1979.

———. *The Gospel according to John.* 2 vols. Anchor Bible 29A and B. Garden City, NY: Doubleday, 1966–70.

———. "The Resurrection in John 20—A Series of Diverse Reactions." *Worship* 64 (May 1990): 194–206.

———. *The Virginal Conception and Bodily Resurrection of Jesus.* New York: Paulist Press, 1973.

Bultmann, Rudolf. *The Gospel of John: A Commentary.* Translated by G. R. Beasley-Murray et al. Philadelphia: Westminster, 1971.

———. *Theology of the New Testament.* Vol. 2. Translated by Kendrick Grobel. New York: Charles Scribner's Sons, 1955.

Bynum, Carolyn Walker. "Material Continuity, Personal Survival, and the Resurrection of the Body: A Scholastic Discussion in Its Medieval and Modern Contexts." *History of Religions* 30 (August 1990): 51–85.

Byrne, Brendan J. "The Faith of the Beloved Disciple and the Community in John 20." *Journal for the Study of the New Testament* 23 (1985): 83–97.

da Capua, Raimondo. *S. Caterina da Siena: nel racconto del suo confessore il b. Raimondo da Capua.* Translated by Giuseppe Tinagli. Siena: Cantagalli, 1934.

Carson, D. A. *The Gospel according to John.* Grand Rapids, MI: Eerdmans, 1991.

———. "The Purpose of the Fourth Gospel: John 20:31 Reconsidered." *Journal of Biblical Literature* 106 (1987): 639–51.

Carter, Warren. *Pontius Pilate: Portraits of a Roman Governor*. Collegeville, MN: Liturgical Press, 2003.

Chennattu, Rekha. " 'If You Keep My Commandments': Exploring Covenant Motifs in John 13–17." Paper presented at the convention of the Catholic Biblical Association of America, August 2003.

Clifford, Richard J. "Exodus." In *The New Jerome Biblical Commentary*, edited by Raymond E. Brown, Joseph A. Fitzmyer, and Roland E. Murphy, 46–47. Englewood Cliffs, NJ: Prentice Hall, 1999.

Collins, Adela Yarbro. "Eschatology and Apocalypticism." In "Aspects of New Testament Thought," by Raymond E. Brown, Donald Senior, John R. Donahue, and Adela Yarbro Collins. In *The New Jerome Biblical Commentary*, edited by Raymond E. Brown, Joseph A. Fitzmyer, and Roland E. Murphy, 25–56. Englewood Cliffs, NJ: Prentice Hall, 1999.

Coloe, Mary. *God Dwells with Us: Temple Symbolism in the Fourth Gospel*. Collegeville, MN: Liturgical Press, 2001.

———. "Like Father, Like Son: The Role of Abraham in Tabernacles; John 8:31-59." *Pacifica* 12 (February 1999): 1–11.

———. "Raising the Johannine Temple (John 19:19-29)." *Australian Biblical Review* 48 (2000): 47–58.

Corell, Alf. *Consummatum Est: Eschatology and Church in the Gospel of St. John*. London: SPCK, 1958.

Cosgrove, Charles H. "The Place Where Jesus Is: Allusions to Baptism and the Eucharist in the Fourth Gospel." *New Testament Studies* 35 (1989): 522–39.

Coye, E. "Sent to Be Scarred: John 20:19-23." *Expository Times* 113, no. 6 (March 2002): 190–91.

Crossan, John Dominic. *Jesus: A Revolutionary Biography*. San Francisco: Harper-SanFrancisco, 1994.

Crotty, Robert. "The Two Magdalene Reports on the Risen Jesus in John 20." *Pacifica* 12 (June 1999): 156–68.

Cullmann, Oscar. "Immortality of the Soul or Resurrection of the Dead: The Witness of the New Testament." The Ingersoll Lecture, 1955. *Harvard Divinity School Bulletin* 21 (1955–56): 5–36.

Davis, Stephen T., Daniel Kendall, and Gerald O'Collins, eds. *The Resurrection: An Interdisciplinary Symposium on the Resurrection of Jesus*. Oxford: University Press, 1996.

DeConick, April D. " 'Blessed Are Those Who Have Not Seen' (John 20:29): Johannine Dramatization of an Early Christian Discourse." In *Nag Hammadi*

Library after Fifty Years, edited by John D. Turner and Anne M. McGuire, 381–98. Leiden: Brill, 1997.

Dennis, John. "The 'Lifting Up of the Son of Man' and the Dethroning of the 'Ruler of This World': Jesus' Death as the Defeat of the Devil in John 12,31-32." In *The Death of Jesus in the Fourth Gospel,* edited by G. Van Belle, 677–91. Leuven: University Press, 2007.

Denziger, Heinrich. *Enchiridion Symbolorum Definitionum et Declarationum de Rebus Fidei et Morum.* 37th ed. Freiburg: Herder, 1991.

de Dinechin, Olivier. "KAQWS: La similitude dans l'évangile selon saint Jean." *Recherches de Sciences Religieuses* 58 (1970): 195–236.

"Divino Afflante Spiritu." In *Official Catholic Teachings: Biblical Interpretation,* edited by James J. Megivern, 316–42. Wilmington, NC: McGrath, 1978.

Drewermann, Eugen. *Strukturen des Bösen. Sonderausgabe: Die jahwistische Urgeschichte in exegetischer/psychoanalytischer/philosophischer Sicht.* 3 vols. Paderborn: Schöningh, 1985–86.

Dupont, Jacques, Christopher Lash, and Georges Levesque. "Recherche sur la structure de Jean 20." *Biblica* 54 (1973): 482–98.

Durrwell, Francis X. *The Resurrection: A Biblical Study.* New York: Sheed and Ward, 1960.

Eckstein, Hans-Joachim. "Bodily Resurrection in Luke." In *Resurrection: Theological and Scientific Assessments,* edited by Ted Peters, Robert John Russell, and Michael Welker, 115–23. Grand Rapids, MI: Eerdmans, 2002.

Emerton, J. A. "Binding and Loosing—Forgiving and Retaining." *Journal of Theological Studies* 13 (1962): 325–31.

Emilsen, William W., and John T. Squires, eds. *Validating Violence—Violating Faith? Religion, Scripture and Violence.* Adelaide, SA: ATF, 2008.

Fee, Gordon D. "On the Text and Meaning of John 20,30-31." In *The Four Gospels 1992: Festschrift Frans Neirynck,* edited by F. Van Segbroeck, C. M. Tuckett, G. Van Belle, J. Verheyden, 3:2193–2205. Leuven: University Press, 1992.

Feuillet, A. "La Recherche du Christ dans la Nouvelle Alliance d'après la Christophanie de Jo. 20,11-18: Comparaison avec Cant. 3,1-4 et l'épisode des pèlerins d'Emmaüs." In *L'Homme devant Dieu: Mélanges offerts au père Henri de Lubac,* 93–112. Théologie 56. Paris: Aubier, 1963.

———. "Le temps de l'église selon saint Jean." In *Études Johanniques.* Bruges: Desclée, 1962.

Fortna, Robert T., and Tom Thatcher, eds. *Jesus in Johannine Tradition.* Louisville, KY: Westminster John Knox Press, 2001.

Fuller, Reginald H. *The Formation of the Resurrection Narratives*. New York: Macmillan, 1971.

Ghiberti, Giovanni. "Bibliografia sull'esegesi dei racconti pasquali e sul problema della risurrezione di Gesù (1957–1968)." *La Scuola Cattolica* 97 (1969 [Supplemento bibliografica 2]): 68–84.

———. "Bibliografia sulla Risurrezione di Gesù (1920–1973)." In *Resurrexit*, 643–764. Città del Vaticano: Vaticana, 1974.

Gignac, Francis T. "The Use of Verbal Variety in the Fourth Gospel." In *Transcending Boundaries: Contemporary Readings of the New Testament; Festschrift F. J. Moloney*, edited by R. M. Chennattu and M. L. Coloe, 191–200. Roma: Salesiano, 2005.

Girard, René. *The Scapegoat*. Baltimore: Johns Hopkins University Press, 1986.

———. *Violence and the Sacred*. Translated by Patrick Gregory. Baltimore: Johns Hopkins University Press, 1977.

Girard, René, Jean-Michel Oughourlian, and Guy Lefort. *Things Hidden Since the Foundation of the World*. Translated by Stephen Bann and Michael Metteer. Stanford, CA: Stanford University Press, 1987.

de Goedt, Michel. "Un schème de révélation dans le quatrième évangile." *New Testament Studies* 8 (January 1962): 142–50.

Green, Barbara. "The Wisdom of Solomon and the Solomon of Wisdom: Tradition's Transpositions and Human Transformation." *Horizons* 30 (Spring 2003): 41–66.

Hart, Thomas N. *To Know and Follow Jesus: Contemporary Christology*. New York/ Ramsey, NJ: Paulist Press, 1984.

Hatina, Thomas R. "John 20,22 in Its Eschatological Context: Promise or Fulfillment?" *Biblica* 74, no. 2 (1993): 196–219.

Heil, John Paul. "Blood and Water: The Death and Resurrection of Jesus in John 18–21." *The Catholic Biblical Quarterly* 27 (1995): 172–80.

Heim, S. Mark. *Saved from Sacrifice: A Theology of the Cross*. Grand Rapids, MI: Eerdmans, 2006.

Hellwig, Monika K. *Jesus, the Compassion of God: New Perspectives on the Tradition of Christianity*. Wilmington, DE: Michael Glazier, 1983.

John of the Cross. *The Collected Works of Saint John of the Cross*. Rev. ed. Translated by Kieran Kavanaugh and Otilio Rodriguez. Washington, DC: Institute of Carmelite Studies, 1991.

Johnson, Elizabeth A. *Consider Jesus: Waves of Renewal in Christology*. New York: Crossroad, 1990.

Jones, Larry Paul. *The Symbol of Water in the Gospel of John.* JSNT Supp. Series 145. Sheffield, UK: Sheffield Academic Press, 1997.

de Jonge, Marinus. "Signs and Works in the Fourth Gospel." In *Miscellanea Neo-testamentica* 2. Supplements to Novum Testamentum 48. Leiden: Brill, 1978.

Judge, Peter. "A Note on Jn 20,29." In *The Four Gospels 1992: Festschrift Frans Neirynck,* edited by F. Van Segbroeck, C. M. Tuckett, G. Van Belle, J. Verhey-den, 3:2183–92. Leuven: University Press, 1992.

Julian of Norwich. *Julian of Norwich: Showings.* Translated and edited by Edmund Colledge and James Walsh. New York: Paulist Press, 1978.

Käsemann, Ernst. *The Testament of Jesus: A Study of the Gospel of John in the Light of Chapter 17.* Philadelphia: Fortress Press, 1968.

Katz, Steven. "Is There a Perennial Philosophy?" *Journal of American Academy of Religion* 55 (Fall 1987): 553–66.

Kelly, Walt. "We Have Met the Enemy and He Is Us." *Pogo* Poster, Earth Day 1970.

Kendall, Daniel, and Gerald O'Collins. "The Uniqueness of the Easter Appear-ances." *The Catholic Biblical Quarterly* 54 (1992): 287–307.

Kirwan, Michael. *Discovering Girard.* Cambridge, MA: Cowley, 2005.

Knitter, Paul F. *No Other Name? A Critical Survey of Christian Attitudes toward the World Religions.* Maryknoll, NY: Orbis, 1986.

Koester, Craig R. *Symbolism in the Fourth Gospel: Meaning, Mystery, Community.* 2nd ed. Minneapolis, MN: Fortress Press, 2003.

Kremer, Jacob. *Die Osterbotschaft der vier Evangelien: Versuch einer Auslegung der Berichte über das leere Grab und die Erscheinungen des Auferstanden.* Stuttgart: Katholisches Bibelwerk, 1969.

Kysar, Robert. "'As You Sent Me': Identity and Mission in the Fourth Gospel." *Word and World* 21, no. 4 (2001): 370–76.

Lampe, Peter. "Paul's Concept of a Spiritual Body." In *Resurrection: Theological and Scientific Assessments,* edited by Ted Peters, Robert John Russell, Michael Welker, 103–14. Grand Rapids, MI: Eerdmans, 2002.

Lee, Dorothy. *Flesh and Glory: Symbol, Gender, and Theology in the Gospel of John.* New York: Crossroad, 2002.

———. "Partnership in Easter Faith: The Role of Mary Magdalene and Thomas in John 20." *Journal for the Study of the New Testament* 58 (1995): 37–49.

Lincoln, Andrew T. "'I Am the Resurrection and the Life': The Resurrection Message of the Fourth Gospel." In *Life in the Face of Death: The Resurrection*

Message of the New Testament, edited by Richard N. Longenecker. Grand Rapids, MI/Cambridge, UK: Eerdmans, 1998.

Marmion, Columba. *Christ in His Mysteries*. 7th ed. Translated by Mother M. St. Thomas. St. Louis, MO: Herder, 1940.

Matera, Frank J. "John 20:1-18." *Interpretation* 43 (1989): 402–6.

McKenzie, John L. *Dictionary of the Bible*, s.v. "Sheol."

Meier, John P. "The Absence and Presence of the Church in John's Gospel." *Mid-Stream* 41, no. 4 (2002): 27–34.

Menken, Maarten J. J. "Envoys of God's Envoy: On the Johannine Communities." *Proceedings of the Irish Biblical Association* 23 (2000): 45–60.

———. "Interpretation of the Old Testament and the Resurrection of Jesus in John's Gospel." In *Resurrection in the New Testament: Festschrift J. Lambrecht*, edited by R. Bieringer, V. Koperski, and B. Latair, 189–205. Leuven: Peeters, 2002.

———. "The Old Testament Quotation in John 19,36: Sources, Redaction, Background." In *The Four Gospels 1992: Festschrift Frans Neirynck*, edited by F. Van Segbroeck, C. M. Tuckett, G. Van Belle, J. Verheyden, 3:2101–18. Leuven: University Press, 1992.

Miles, Margaret. "The Revelatory Body: Signorelli's 'Resurrection of the Flesh' at Orvieto." *Harvard Divinity Bulletin* 22 (1992): 10–13.

Moignt, Joseph. "Immortalité de l'âme et/ou résurrection." *Lumière et Vie* 21 (1972): 65–78.

Mollat, Donatian. "La foi pascale selon le chapître 20 de l'évangile de saint Jean (Essai de théologie biblique)." In *Resurrexit: Actes du symposium internationale sur la résurrection de Jésus*, edited by E. Dhanis, 316–34. Rome: Libreria Editrice Vaticana, 1974.

Moloney, Francis J. "Excursus: Narrative Approaches to the Fourth Gospel." In Raymond E. Brown, *An Introduction to the Gospel of John*, edited by F. Moloney, 31–39. Anchor Bible Reference Library. New York: Doubleday, 2003.

———. *The Gospel of John*. Sacra Pagina 4. Collegeville, MN: Liturgical Press, 1998.

———. "The Johannine Son of Man Revisited." In *Theology and Christology in the Fourth Gospel*, 177–202. Leuven: University Press, 2005.

Morris, Leon. *The Gospel according to John: The English Text with Introduction, Exposition and Notes*. Grand Rapids, MI: Eerdmans, 1971.

Murphy-O'Connor, Jerome. "The First Letter to the Corinthians." In *The New Jerome Biblical Commentary*, edited by Raymond E. Brown, Joseph A. Fitzmyer, and Roland E. Murphy, 49:798–99. Englewood Cliffs, NJ: Prentice Hall, 1990.

Newman, Carey C. "Resurrection as Glory: Divine Presence and Christian Origins." In *The Resurrection: An Interdisciplinary Symposium on the Resurrection of Jesus*, edited by S. T. Davis, D. Kendall, G. O'Collins, 59–89. Oxford: University Press, 1997.

Nicholsburg, George W. *Resurrection, Immortality, and Eternal Life in Intertestamental Judaism*. Harvard Theological Studies 26. Cambridge, MA: Harvard University Press, 1972.

O'Collins, Gerald. *Interpreting the Resurrection: Examining the Major Problems in the Stories of Jesus' Resurrection*. Garden City, NY: Doubleday, 1984.

———. *Jesus Risen: An Historical, Fundamental and Systematic Examination of Christ's Resurrection*. New York: Paulist Press, 1987.

———. *The Easter Jesus*. Rev. ed. London: Darton, Longman and Todd, 1980.

O'Collins, Gerald, and Daniel Kendall. "Mary Magdalene as Major Witness to Jesus' Resurrection." *Theological Studies* 48, no. 4 (December 1987): 631–46.

O'Day, Gail R. *Revelation in the Fourth Gospel: Narrative Mode and Theological Claim*. Philadelphia: Fortress Press, 1986.

Okure, Teresa. "The Significance Today of Jesus' Commission to Mary Magdalene." *International Review of Mission* 81 (April 1992): 177–88.

Osborne, Kenan B. *Reconciliation and Justification: The Sacrament and Its Theology*. 1990. Reprint, Eugene, OR: Wipf and Stock, 2001.

Perkins, Pheme. " 'I Have Seen the Lord' (John 20:18): Women Witnesses to the Resurrection." *Interpretation* 46 (1992): 31–41.

———. *Resurrection: New Testament Witness and Contemporary Reflection*. Garden City, NY: Doubleday, 1984.

Popkes, Enno Edzard. "The Love of God for the World and the Handing Over ('Dahingabe') of His Son: Comments on the Tradition-Historical Background and the Theological Function of John 3, 16a in the Overall Context of Johannine Theology." In *The Death of Jesus in the Fourth Gospel*, edited by G. Van Belle, 609–23. Leuven: University Press, 2007.

Porter, Stanley E., Michael A. Hayes, and David Tombs, eds. *Resurrection* (papers from the conference on Resurrection on 21 February, 1998, in Roehampton, England). *Journal for the Study of the New Testament* Supplement Series 186. Roehampton Institute London Papers 5. Sheffield: Sheffield Academic Press, 1999.

de la Potterie, Ignace. "Genèse de la foi pascale d'après Jn 20." *New Testament Studies* 30 (1984): 26–49.

Rahner, Karl. "The Theology of the Symbol." In *Theological Investigations*. Vol. 4 of *More Recent Writings*, translated by Kevin Smyth, 221–52. Baltimore: Helicon Press, 1966.

Ricoeur, Paul. *Interpretation Theory: Discourse and the Surplus of Meaning.* Fort Worth: Texas Christian University Press, 1976.

Robinson, James Burnell. "The History of Religions and the Primordial Tradition." In *Fragments of Infinity: Essays in Religion and Philosophy; Festschrift in Honour of Professor Huston Smith,* edited by Arvind Sharma, 217–33. Dorset: Prism, 1991.

Rollins, Wayne G. Review of *A Violent God-Image,* by Matthias Beier. *Review of Biblical Literature;* http://www.bookreviews.org; April 2005.

Rynne, Terrence J. *Gandhi and Jesus.* Maryknoll, NY: Orbis, 2008.

Scheffler, Eben. "Jesus' Non-Violence at His Arrest: The Synoptics and John's Gospel Compared." In *The Death of Jesus in the Fourth Gospel,* edited by G. Van Belle, 739–49. Leuven: University Press, 2007.

Schneiders, Sandra M. "Before It's Too Late: Violence, Reconciliation, and the Church." Bellarmine Lecture delivered at Saint Louis University, St. Louis, Missouri, November 2, 2008. Printed in *Theological Digest* 54 (Spring 2010): 5–23.

———. "Death in the Community of Eternal Life." *Interpretation* 41 (January 1987): 44–56.

———. "The Face Veil: A Johannine Sign (John 20:1-10)." *Biblical Theology Bulletin* 8 (July 1983): 94–97.

———. *The Johannine Resurrection Narrative: An Exegetical and Theological Study of John 20 as a Synthesis of Johannine Spirituality.* Dissertation, Pontificia Universita Gregoriana, 1975. Reprint, Ann Arbor, MI: University Microfilms International, 1983.

———. "The Raising of the New Temple: John 20.19-23 and Johannine Ecclesiology." *New Testament Studies* 52, no. 3 (July 2006): 337–55.

———. *The Revelatory Text: Interpreting the New Testament as Sacred Scripture.* 2nd ed. San Francisco: Harper, 1991.

———. *Written That You May Believe: Encountering Jesus in the Fourth Gospel.* 2nd ed., rev. and enl. New York: Crossroad, 2003.

Sibinga, J. S. "Towards Understanding the Composition of John 20." In *The Four Gospels 1992: Festschrift Frans Neirynck,* edited by F. Van Segbroeck, C. M.

Tuckett, G. Van Belle, J. Verheyden, 3:2139–52. Leuven: University Press, 1992.

Smith, Huston. *Forgotten Truth: The Primordial Tradition*. New York: Harper and Row, 1976.

Smith, Robert Payne. *A Compendious Syriac Dictionary: Founded upon the Thesaurus Syriacus of R. Payne Smith*. Edited by Jessie Payne Smith. Oxford: Clarendon, 1903.

Smith, Wilfred Cantwell. *What Is Scripture? A Comparative Approach*. Minneapolis: Fortress Press, 1993.

Spadafora, Francesco. "Prova fisica della resurrezione de Gesù N.S." *Divus Thomas* 55 (1952): 64–66.

Suggit, John N. "Jesus the Gardener: The Atonement in the Fourth Gospel as Re-Creation." *Neotestamentica* 33 (January 1999): 161–68.

Swetnam, James. "Bestowal of the Spirit in the Fourth Gospel." *Biblica* 74 (1999): 556–76.

Teresa of Avila, *The Wisdom of Teresa of Avila: Selections from The Interior Castle*. Translated and edited by Kieran Kavanaugh and Otilio Rodriguez. New York: Paulist Press, 1979.

Van Dieman, P. "La semaine inaugurale et la semaine terminale de l'évangile de Jean: Message et structures." Dissertation, Rome, 1972.

Vermes, Geza. *Scripture and Tradition in Judaism: Haggadic Studies*. Leiden: Brill, 1973.

Vonier, Anscar. *The Glorification of Christ and the Eucharist*. Buckfast Abbey Chronicle. July 1938. Reprint, Bristol: Burleigh, 1938.

Ward, Graham. "Bodies: The Displaced Body of Jesus Christ." In *Radical Orthodoxy: A New Theology*, edited by John Milbank, Catherine Pickstock, and Graham Ward, 163–81. London/New York: Routledge, 1999.

———. "Transcorporeality: The Ontological Scandal." *Bulletin of the John Rylands University Library of Manchester* 80 (August 1998): 235–52.

Williams, James, ed. *The Girard Reader*. New York: Crossroad, 1996.

Wink, Walter. *Engaging the Powers: Discernment and Resistance in a World of Domination*. Philadelphia: Fortress Press, 1992.

———. *Naming the Powers: The Language of Power in the New Testament*. Philadelphia: Fortress Press, 1983.

———. *Unmasking the Powers: The Invisible Forces That Determine Human Existence*. Philadelphia: Fortress Press, 1986.

Wolff, Hans Walter. *Anthropology of the Old Testament*. SCM, 1974. Reprint, Mifflin-town, PA: Sigler, 1996.

Worden, T. "The Remission of Sins." *Scripture* 9 (1957): 65–79, 115–27.

Zumstein, Jean. "Lecture narratologique du cycle pascal du quatrième évangile." *Études Théologiques et Religieuses* 76 (January 2001): 1–15.

Index of Scripture References

Index of Authors